Communication and Human Values

The Language and Politics of Exclusion

Others in Discourse

edited by

Stephen Harold Riggins

SAGE Publications
International Educational and Professional Publisher
Thousand Oaks London New Delhi

For information:

SAGE Publications, Inc.
2455 Teller Road
Thousand Oaks, California 91320
E-mail: order@sagepub.com

SAGE Publications Ltd.
6 Bonhill Street
London EC2A 4PU
United Kingdom

SAGE Publications India Pvt. Ltd.
M-32 Market
Greater Kailash I
New Delhi 110 048 India

Printed in the United States of America

Library of Congress Cataloging-in-Publication Data

Main entry under title:
The language and politics of exclusion: Others in discourse / editor, Stephen Harold Riggins.
p. cm. — (Communication and human values ; v. 24)
Includes bibliographical references and index.
ISBN 0-7619-0728-9 (acid-free paper). — ISBN 0-7619-0729-7 (pbk.: acid-free paper)
1. Discourse analysis—Social aspects. 2. Discourse analysis—Political aspects. I. Riggins, Stephen Harold, 1946- II. Series: Communication and human values (Newbury Park, Calif.); v. 24.
P302.84.L36 1997
401'.41—dc21 97-4595

97 98 99 00 01 02 03 10 9 8 7 6 5 4 3 2 1

Acquiring Editor: Margaret Seawell
Editorial Assistant: Renée Piernot
Production Editor: Michèle Lingre
Production Assistant: Karen Wiley
Typesetter/Designer: Danielle Dillahunt
Cover Designer: Lesa Valdez
Print Buyer: Anna Chin

The Language and Politics of Exclusion

COMMUNICATION AND HUMAN VALUES

Contents

1

The Rhetoric of Othering

STEPHEN HAROLD RIGGINS

The chapters collected in this volume apply critical discourse analysis to texts and speech that contribute to the marginalization of minority groups. Critical discourse analysis is broadly defined in the volume as including both studies of the fine detail of language use and discussions of the political values that underlie the method. The rationale of this book is to demonstrate, especially to disciplines such as sociology, journalism, and communication studies, the usefulness of linguistic perspectives and concepts in advancing the study of prejudice and social inequality in modern multicultural societies.

This introductory chapter provides a review of the basic concepts in critical discourse analysis that are applied in the chapters that follow. The main sources are Fairclough (1995a, 1995b), Fiske (1987), O'Neill (1994), and van Dijk (1987, 1988a, 1988b, 1993). The introduction covers territory that is very familiar to specialists, who may prefer to turn directly to the case studies discussed in the chapters. However, I would like to draw attention to the analysis in this chapter of two newspaper articles that are used to illustrate the methodology. The first is a news item about interfaith marriages. It was chosen because of the number of presuppositions that readers have to infer to make sense of its implicit messages. The second article recounts the experiences of a couple of tourists kayaking on the Ganges River in India. Foreign news items and travel reports are particularly interesting sites for examining the rhetoric of Othering because writers tend to assume their readers expect "exotic" and "bizarre" features in foreign countries.

What Is Critical Discourse Analysis?

The theoretical foundations of critical discourse analysis are based on perspectives that see the relation of words and truth as highly tenuous and problematic. Any form of writing is considered to be a selection, an interpretation, and a dramatization of events. All representations of events are *polysemic*—that is, ambiguous and unstable in meaning—as well as a mix of "truth" and "fiction." Despite the desire of some writers to be utterly truthful and accurate, we are unwittingly trapped in a world of biased perceptions and "stories," all of which both exceed and shortchange "reality."

In everyday language, a *discourse* traditionally has been understood as a statement or an utterance longer than a sentence (Fiske, 1987, p. 14). But in the humanities and social sciences in recent years, the term has come to have a more elusive meaning that usually takes the work of Foucault (1972, 1984) as a starting point. Foucault seems to have emphasized the structural nature of statements, including those that are spontaneous, and the way in which all statements are *intertextual* because they are interpreted against a backdrop of other statements. The anthropologist William O'Barr, following Foucault's lead, provides a useful general definition of discourse as "a flow of ideas that are connected to one another" (O'Barr, 1994, p. 3). A more technical definition might be to say that a discourse is a systematic, internally consistent body of representations, the "language used in representing a given social practice from a particular point of view" (Fairclough, 1995b, p. 56). The practice of social work, for example, could be conceptualized in terms of at least two discourses. Social work can be seen as the provision of benevolent, professional care or as a negative and repressive form of population control (Stenson, 1993). Discourses do not faithfully reflect reality like mirrors (as journalists would have us believe). Instead, they are artifacts of language through which the very reality they purport to reflect is constructed.[1]

Discourse analysis acquires a critical dimension when the focus is on the relation of language to power and privilege. The goal of the analysis is to provide a detailed description, explanation, and critique of the textual strategies writers use to "naturalize" discourses, that is, to make discourses appear to be commonsense, apolitical statements (van Dijk, 1993). Most critical discourse analysts take an explicit political stance, identifying with those who lack the institutional levers to produce counterdiscourses, and their ultimate motivation appears to be the hope that their work will contribute to social emancipation.

To examine a text critically, it may not be essential to verify all the claims to truth that it makes (Fairclough, 1995a, p. 76). Instead, the analyst may speculate about the social impact of a text, asking the question: Which group in society is likely to benefit from the opinions expressed in this text? But with respect to the analyst's own interpretations, critical discourse analysis is inconsistent with the extreme relativism of Foucault and postmodern writers (Larrain, 1994). Implicit in critical discourse analysis is a claim to truth, although it may be modest. If a reader of a piece of research suspects that he or she is learning more about the analyst than about the content of the text, then the analysis obviously has failed. There must be a substantive consensus among those who are familiar with a piece of work (including both professionals and nonprofessionals) that there are *true elements* in it (Heller, 1990, p. 38).

In general, critical discourse analysts are more interested in dissecting texts than in theorizing about the interpretive practices of readers and listeners. Our relatively superficial interest in audiences is an obvious limitation of the methodology, but it often has been defended. If it is assumed that texts have the power to constrain readers' interpretations because words are not neutral, then it is essential to have a comprehensive understanding of the properties of texts (Fairclough, 1995b, p. 16).[2]

Self and Other

The term *Other* has only recently become part of the common terminology in sociology and has been introduced primarily through the interdisciplinarity of scholars who identify with postmodernism and cultural studies (Reader, 1995). However, in philosophy the term has an ancient history. The term *Other* as a category of speculative thought can be traced at least as far back in time as Plato, who used it to represent the relationship between an observer (the Self) and an observed (the Other) (Helicon, 1994, p. 391; Morfaux, 1980, p. 32).

In the modern social sciences, the "external Other" or the "social Other" is commonly used, in a more restricted sense than that of Plato, to refer to all people the Self perceives as mildly or radically different.

The "internal Other" refers to the subconscious, a phase of the Self, or the experience of self-estrangement (e.g., Bakhtin, 1981). Throughout this volume, the terms *Other* and *Others* are understood as referring to the external Other.

Self and external Other may be understood as unique individuals (I and You) or as collectivities that are thought to share similar characteristics (We and They). In his study of Afro-Caribbean identities, Hall (1994) suggests that self-identity be conceptualized "as a 'production' which is never complete, always in process, and always constituted within, not outside representation" (p. 392). For a person to develop a self-identity, he or she must generate *discourses of* both *difference and similarity* and must reject and embrace specific identities. The external Other should thus be considered as a range of positions within a system of difference.

Some scholars prefer the singular form, the Other, to represent the similar treatment members of such categories are likely to receive from outsiders. However, several authors prefer the plural form, Others, because it conveys the notion that the Self in its discourses of identity is continually negotiating several identities simultaneously. It might also be argued that the singular form tends to reproduce, however critically, the stereotypical homogenization of other cultures and peoples that it seeks to overthrow. Most contributors to this volume write about ethnic groups as Others, but the concept is broader than this. Others may also be women for men, the rich for the poor, Californians and New Yorkers for midwestern Americans, the young for the old, conservatives for Marxists, tourists for natives, and so on.

Past generations of sociologists defined *deviant* and *outsider* in ways that approximate the present use of the term Other. For example, structural functionalists observed that the members of a group would not be inclined to reflect about the values that unite them if deviants within their midst did not pose intellectual and political challenges (Erikson, 1966). Whether singular or plural, *Other* would appear to be a more suitable term than would *deviant* because of its vagueness. The word *Other* is an elliptic pronoun or a deictic category that can refer to practically anything, depending on the context or situation. By contrast, sociologists may claim to define deviance as a value-free term, but objectivity is undermined by the limited range of behavior that is defined as abnormal by the public. Another advantage of the term Other is that it can be used to underline the theoretical commonality of academic specialties (cultural studies, sociology, philosophy, and anthropology) that have, unfortunately, come to be distinct.

Outsiders do tend to perceive Others as a homogeneous category, except perhaps for those few individuals who are known personally. This is why the German sociologist Georg Simmel used the term "the stranger" (singular) to represent diasporic ethnicity and "the Jew" (singular) is a standard term in antisemitism (Simmel, 1971; Wodak, this volume). By contrast, the Self tends to make finer distinctions among its own members, who are perceived as constituting numerous subgroups. For instance, "English" Canadians may be quite sensitive to differences in ethnic origins (Welsh, Scottish, Irish, English, etc.) among themselves, but they may ignore the ethnic uniqueness of First Nations People in Canada, referring to all of them as "Natives" or "Indians." On the other hand, First Nations People may be equally sensitive to their ethnic origins (Mohawk, Cree, Ojibwa, etc.) while not bothering to distinguish among immigrants from the British Isles, referring to all of them as "English" Canadians.

In his study of the Spanish conquest of Mexico, Todorov (1982, p. 185) identifies three dimensions of the relationship between Self and Other: (a) *value judgments* (e.g., the Other may be deemed good or bad, equal or inferior to the Self), (b) *social distance* (the physical and psychological distance the Self maintains from the Other), and (c) *knowledge* (the extent to which the history and culture of the Other is known by the Self). Positive value judgments, low social distance, and a sophisticated knowledge of the Other are generally associated. However, there are many exceptions, especially when Self and Other are in competition for scarce resources. Historically, it is without question that difference has been more often feared than appreciated. The exception to this general pattern is the phenomenon of *exoticism.* The Other—once again misunderstood—is considered to be superior or perhaps strange but beautiful (Lutz & Collins, 1993).[3]

The public that so fervently distinguishes between Self and Other rarely realizes the illusory nature of the opposition. "The Other is the indispensable mediator between myself and me," Sartre (1965) writes. "I need the Other in order to realize fully all the structures of my being" (pp. 189-190). Others may be practically invisible if they conform outwardly and rebel inwardly. Others can assimilate in whole or in part. Others may be devalued but at the same time eroticized and envied. Others may suppress their differences and accept a devalued status—

"colonize themselves," so to speak. Self and Other actually are so intertwined that to stop talking about "them," one must stop talking about "us."

Discourses of Otherness are articulated by both dominant majorities and subordinate minorities. Others are not just groups that are devalued, marginalized, or silenced by dominant majorities. One may thus speak of the "Others of a minority" (e.g., Ahmed, 1992; Basso, 1979; hooks, 1995, pp. 31-50; Saldívar, 1991) as well as the "Others of the majority" (e.g., Arteaga, 1994; Blundell, 1994; Diamond, 1993; Essed, 1991; Gladney, 1994; Goodman & Miyazawa, 1995; Lutz & Collins, 1993; Shohat & Stam, 1994; Watt, 1991). However, for understandable political reasons, most research concentrates on the discourses of Othering constructed by majority populations.[4]

The discourses of identity articulated by majority populations are likely to be univocal and monologic because it is relatively easy for dominant groups to express and confirm their shared identity publicly (Riggins, 1983; 1992, pp. 276-288). By comparison, the discourses of identity articulated by members of subordinate minorities tend to be contradictory, complex, and ironic. Humor and satire are effective tools of minority discourse (Rosaldo, 1990). Typical examples can be found in Rodriguez's (1992) autobiographical book, *Days of Obligation: An Argument With My Mexican Father.* Self and Other in this case are the residents of California and Mexico, and it is characteristic of minority discourse that it often is not clear who is Self and who is Other.[5] Dialectically juxtaposing the two identities, Rodriguez achieves the critical distance to parody the pretensions and distortions of both groups:

> America has long imagined itself as clean, crew-cut, ingenuous. We are an odorless, colorless, accentless, orderly people, put upon and vulnerable to the foreign. Aliens are carriers of chaos. Mexicans are obviously carriers of chaos—their backs are broken with bundles of it: gray air, brown water, papacy, leprosy, crime, diarrhea, white powders, and a language full of newts and cicadas.
>
> Mexico does not say it publicly, but Mexico perceives America as sterile, as sterilizing, as barren as the nose of a missile. "Don't drink the water in Los Angeles," goes the joke, "it will clean you out like a scalpel." Because Americans are barren by choice, Americans are perceived by Mexico as having relinquished gravity. Within the porticos of the great churches of Mexico are signs reminding visitors to behave with dignity. The signs are in English. (p. 91)

In *Days of Obligation,* as well as in the chapter by Rimstead in this volume, it can be seen that minority authors rarely are able to exclude all traces of the majority's discourse of Otherness.[6] Intermingled with the celebratory and defiant discourses of the minority Self may be lingering elements of shame and self-hatred, a result of exposure to the dominant culture's educational institutions (JanMohamed & Lloyd, 1990, p. 8) and to psychological masochism (Fiske, 1987, pp. 179-197). Minority authors are likely to have a broader notion of the political, seeing the political dimensions of everyday encounters, and to have a different relationship to a community. They may either wish to represent a community or realize that their statements will be interpreted as such by outsiders (Ang, 1993).

The use of the term Other as a philosophical and sociological category generally has been confined to academia. However, in recent years, political conflicts occasionally have arisen in which the term has been used by the public. For example, in the 1995 Quebec referendum on independence from Canada, some francophone Quebeckers referred to immigrants who were not native speakers of either French or English as "the Others" (*les autres*) and to themselves as "the people" (*le peuple*).

Denigration in an Age of Civility and Official Tolerance

When Otherness is feared, the *lexical strategies* one expects to find are those that are evidence of hierarchy, subordination, and dominance (O'Barr, 1994). But today the public expression of racism, ethnicism, and intolerance is more complex than it was in the past because it tends to occur in situations where tolerance of diversity is a socially recognized norm, frequently one that is legally sanctioned. Indeed, several studies have shown a general decline in prejudice over the past 50 years (e.g., Essed, this volume; Fleras & Elliott, 1992, pp. 111-126; Wieviorka, 1994, p. 176; Wilson & Gutiérrez, 1995). Multiculturalism not only is state policy in many countries but is also used by major corporations to market goods (Hoechsmann, this volume). Consequently, the lexical terms that are likely to be preferred in public today are those that *mitigate and disguise* a speaker's or writer's tendency to discriminate. The opinions prejudiced persons express outside their circle of family members and friends will appear to be more temperate, less severe and cruel, than the opinions that they actually hold. Speakers may refer to "economic" refugees when they mean "false" refugees; to "foreigners," "immigrants," or "those people" instead of actually naming a specific group; to population "transfer" rather than "expulsion"; to "ethnic cleansing" rather than "genocide"; and so on.

The preferred terms are those that can save face if speakers or writers unexpectedly discover that their statements are not appreciated by an audience. For example, in the campaign for the Republican nomination for American president in 1996, Steve Forbes referred to his wealth by saying "I have been blessed," a term from Christian discourse, rather than saying "I am rich" (Forbes, 1996). Mitigating terms may refer to events, the context in which events occur, the identity and character of participants, or responsibility for events (Helleiner & Szuchewycz, this volume). Among the expressions of prejudice that have been voiced frequently in recent years is the "victim-victimizer reversal" (Wodak, this volume). Members of a dominant majority, historically part of a class of victimizers, claim they are being victimized by attempts to achieve social justice.

To name one's Self is a fundamental human right that frequently is denied to Others. Prejudiced people may use the names outsiders have given Others or the terms that, in the eyes of Others, have come to be seen as old-fashioned: homosexual rather than gay, tinkers and itinerants rather than Travelling people, Oriental rather than East Asian, girl rather than woman, and so on. The mode of identifying individuals also is a significant issue. Members of a "we" group may be identified by personal names more often than Others, who are identified anonymously according to occupation, age, or some other social status.

Expressions that are the most revealing of the boundaries separating Self and Other are *inclusive and exclusive pronouns and possessives* such as *we and they, us and them,* and *ours and theirs.* Carbó's chapter in this volume, a study of political speeches about Mexico's indigenous population, shows that an elite speaker's claim to believe in inclusiveness may be undermined by contradictions between words and syntax. A close reading of most political speeches should reveal that the identity of "we" fluctuates depending on the particular rhetorical point the speaker or writer is trying to make. The term *we* may refer in one sentence to the whole Mexican population, both aboriginal and European, whereas in another sentence the aboriginal population may be implicitly excluded. Contradictions also occur within phrases and sentences. In the phrase "our indigenous co-citizens," the possessive "our" implies inclusiveness contrary to the Otherness implied by "co-citizens."

Conklin (this volume) argues that the language of the law, including court decisions related to progressive humanitarian goals, is so far removed from the everyday language and interpretive categories of ordinary people that it is symbolically violent. In modern states, victims are not able to articulate their own suffering in court. Their pain and humiliation is transformed by lawyers into idealized constructs (intellectual, abstract, and apparently impartial) to make them valid according to the "chains of magical terms" that lawyers and judges alone can understand. The victims' voices are assimilated into legal discourse as reported speech. The victims are thus reduced to being Others in the interpretations constructed by lawyers and judges. The inability of victims to control or understand their own trials, and their refusal sometimes to accept the authority of the courts unless forced to do so, produces feelings of self-estrangement not unlike the external perspective Others take toward the Self.

The repetitious nature of *stereotypes* should not be mistaken for a sign that they are correct depictions of reality. Stereotypes in general, whatever group they are applied to, are repetitious and contradictory. For instance, Jews have been accused of being Communists and capitalists, too modern and too traditional, and the colonizers of Africa thought the native population was simple-minded and cunning. The chapter in this volume by Karim illustrates this idea in that it documents how stable and inconsistent Christian stereotypes of Muslims have been in Europe and North America. The same old story has been repeated for more than a millennium.

Stereotypes are fantasies, "a substitute and a shadow" of the Other (Bhabha, 1994, p. 82). They are one of the major discursive strategies that ensure that differences between people are recognized. Through stereotypes, the Self expresses *ambivalence* toward Others, expressing not just derision but derision and desire. For some scholars, this is an insignificant although interesting phenomenon; for others, it is a key issue in theorizing. JanMohamed (1985) believes that the perception of difference is influenced by economic and political motives. Because the function of Othering is exploitation, the political and economic consequences of prejudice should be the focus of research. The rhetoric of Othering dehumanizes and diminishes groups, making it easier for victimizers to seize land, exploit labor, and exert control while minimizing the complicating emotions of guilt and shame (see also Miles,

1994; Shapiro, 1988, pp. 89-123). The Self/Other relation is a "Manichean struggle," a dualistic struggle in which good and evil, colonizer and colonized, are in sharp opposition. The ambivalence the Self may feel about the Other is little more than "subconscious imperialistic duplicity" (JanMohamed, 1985, p. 80).

By contrast, Bhabha (1994, pp. 66-84) concentrates on the modes of representation of Otherness and stresses its unconscious dimensions. The "inferiority" and "evil" of the Other, which is so obvious that it does not need to be proved, cannot be proved conclusively through discourse, which, after all, is nothing but talk. Human qualities that are in some ways appealing are recognized in Others. At the same time, those qualities are disavowed but desired by the Self. The result of such logical inconsistencies in the psychic representation of the Other is a need for images that are repetitive, excessive, and rigid. For a particular stereotype to "make sense" to those who apply it, a whole chain of reinforcing ideas must accompany it. "The stereotype is a complex, ambivalent, contradictory mode of representation, as anxious as it is assertive" (p. 70). For both JanMohamed and Bhabha, stereotypes are an apparatus of power, but for the latter they rest on the most insecure intellectual foundations.

To claim that discourses of Othering are myth-making enterprises more revealing of the observer than the observed is not to say that empathetic cross-cultural communication or a mutually modifying relationship are impossible ideals. The Self actually may look for the affinities it shares with its supposed antithesis without this degenerating into stereotyping and exoticism. For instance, in his study of the influence of classic Asian poets on contemporary American poetry, Qian (1995) contends, "In this model, China and Japan are seen not as foils to the West, but as crystallizing examples of the Modernists' realizing Self" (p. 2). Probably much the same could be said for contemporary environmentalists who look to Native American and African hunters and gatherers as inspiring sources of a modern relationship with nature (Dei, this volume; Riggins, 1992, pp. 102-126).

Textual Strategies: Presence and Absence

Unlike content analysis, critical discourse analysis places a lot of emphasis on the implied messages that underlie communication. It is assumed that the ideological molding of readers takes place not just through explicit information but also through the implied propositions that are brought to bear in trying to make sense out of statements. Whatever is endowed with such self-evident truth that it does not need to be said aloud obviously must be correct. Fairclough (1995b, pp. 106-109) differentiates among four degrees of presence and absence in texts. *Foregrounded information* refers to those ideas that are present and emphasized. *Backgrounded information* refers to ideas that are explicitly stated but de-emphasized. *Presupposed information* is present at the level of implied or suggested meaning. Finally, one needs to consider *absent information,* ideas and perspectives that are relevant to a topic but neither stated nor implied in a text. Analysis should be sensitive to all of these levels.

The people who experience an event—those who see—may not be those who are allowed to speak through the media. When one *voice* speaks for another, it is inevitable that the opinions of those who are underrepresented, appropriated, or silenced will be inaccurate to some extent. Even direct quotations can be distorted through recontextualization. Changes in voice often are sudden and difficult to detect. Even a few remarks by a single speaker probably contain traces of different voices.

Most analysts (Fiske is an exception) believe that texts are characterized by a *hierarchy of meaning.* The voice identified with a dominant group appears to embody the truth, whereas the voice of the subordinated appears to provide simply a partial explanation of events. Subordinated voices may be framed in a manner that detracts from their critical dimensions—through "inoculation" (Barthes, 1972, pp. 150-151), for example. An analogy is made with the process of immunization against disease in which a patient is inoculated with a weakened form of an infectious agent to prevent sickness. A small amount of contradictory information, a counterdiscourse, may be sufficient to convey a sense of objectivity to readers and listeners, especially to those who are somewhat inattentive. Moreover, a voice may be "manipulated" long before it is recorded in the mass media. van Dijk (this volume) argues that the intolerance of the working class actually is a reflection of subtly biased racism and ethnicism expressed publicly by political and economic elites and diffused through the mass media. The apparent popular opinion is then given by the elites as a legitimate reason for activities such as barring new immigrants and abolishing civil rights programs.

Authors or speakers may distance themselves from the claims to truth made by Others through the use of *distance markers,* quotation marks and phrases such as "according to," "alleged," and "said." Analysts should evaluate whether these conventions are applied equally to all the voices in a text. It is common in critical discourse analysis to count the number of lines of *speaking space* (direct quotations) and paraphrased contextual information that is provided each voice in a text to evaluate the degree of objectivity. But it is also essential to reflect on what informants actually say because the opinions defended by those granted the most speaking space may be undermined if statements appear to readers to be naive or uninformed or if their remarks are characterized by slang and colloquial expressions.

Not only is it easier to understand a discourse identified by name, but a name in itself suggests that it is just one point of view and that there are alternatives that might be considered. In a text in which two opposing perspectives are represented, one of which is named and the other unnamed, the latter is likely to be read as apolitical commonsense (Barthes, 1972, p. 138). For instance, there has been extensive discussion of multiculturalism for several years without the public having a term for its opposite, such as monoculturalism (Goldberg, 1994, pp. 3-6).

Let us consider the following paragraph-long news item, titled "Bishop Warns Against Marrying Muslims," to illustrate the number and complexity of commonsense presuppositions that readers are likely to read into a text to make sense of it:

> An auxiliary bishop of Rome has warned Roman Catholic women against marrying Muslim immigrants, whose numbers are increasing in Italy. "Discourage this kind of marriage, especially with the girls in your parish, because they do not know what awaits them," Bishop Clemente Riva, who does not speak for the Vatican, told a meeting of city clergy on Thursday. There are an estimated 100,000 North African Muslims in Italy, most of them male. Islam is the second biggest religion in the country after Catholicism. (Reuters News Service, 1993)

How readers react to this news item could be related in part to their perception of bias in the mass media. Those readers who believe that journalists tend to have a condescending attitude toward dominant institutions and to be religious skeptics might assume that the reporter's selective attention exaggerates the contentious issues in the bishop's speech. Thus noncontroversial remarks as well as those that were complimentary or cautiously critical of Islam are assumed to have been excluded. Using this commonsense understanding of prominent *news values,* readers might conclude that if they had been given the opportunity of listening to the bishop's speech, then they would have realized he was concerned, but not alarmed, about interfaith marriages and that there was little reason for the public to be alarmed.

The topics in the column, "World in Brief," on the day the bishop's speech was reported do underline the way in which the selective attention of journalists is directed toward novelty, negativity, and deviance. The two preceding items dealt with violence against tourists in Florida and the death of a month-old infant abandoned by its mother, who was a female soldier. In addition, almost all readers would have been exposed to news stories on television and in newspapers that present Islam and Arabs in a negative light and that seem to reduce Islam to fundamentalism (Karim, this volume; Said, 1978, 1981; Shaheen, 1984; Shohat & Stam, 1994; Turner, 1994).

The bishop's speech contains one word that betrays an acceptance of gender inequality. He refers to "girls" in the parishes of his listeners. Such a statement might be interpreted as implying an old theme in literature: mature men corrupting innocent young women. Feminists also have made *girl* a highly political term when applied to adult women. But if the bishop had been given the speaking space to put forward his position more adequately, then perhaps less emphasis would be placed on the political implications of only one word.

An alternative interpretation would be to assume that journalists go to such lengths to be objective that the report actually mitigates the troublesome content in the bishop's speech. A reader's sense of threat might be heightened by the location of the bishop's speech. A menace to the Catholic Church in Rome is likely to be perceived as more disturbing than a similar situation in a culturally more marginal location. The threat may also be legitimized to some extent in the eyes of readers by the source of the information, Reuters, one of the most respected news services in the English-speaking world. The brevity and stylistic simplicity of news items may lead readers to think that they are more free of bias than longer and more personal *genres* such as background features.

Although the bishop is identified by name, his name would not be very significant to most North American readers because they would not have heard of him. Probably the only biographical information that could be inferred from his name would be his ethnicity and gender. The fact that no ideological label is attached to the bishop's name could be an indication of fairness on the part of the journalist. On the other hand, an ideological label might make it easier for readers to evaluate, positively or negatively, the bishop's remarks. How much does the bishop actually know about Islam or about North African immigrants in Italy? Is he really an authority on Muslim-Christian marriages? As a celibate male, is he an authority on marriages of any kind? It is not possible to answer any of these questions given the information in the news item. Why does the bishop say nothing about domestic violence or gender inequality in marriages between Christian Italians? Why is he silent about marriages that cross other religious and ethnic lines? The silence is likely to suggest to some readers that serious conflicts are unique to Christian-Muslim relationships.

Given the way in which this news item is framed in religious terms, there are at least four perspectives or voices on Muslim-Christian marriages in Italy: the perspectives of Christian clerics, Muslim clerics, Christian and Muslim men who are dating or have married women of the other faith, and Christian and Muslim women who are or have been involved in such relationships. Yet, in this news item, only one category, a Christian cleric, is allowed to speak. The journalist has given the position of authority to a person who is to some degree an external observer of marital relations.

Presumably, the (auxiliary) bishop "does not speak for the Vatican." Who does he represent, if not the Vatican? If he were simply expressing his personal opinion, would a reporter be sent to cover the speech? How much emphasis should be attached to the qualifying adjective *auxiliary,* which many readers may overlook? What is the difference between an auxiliary bishop and a full-fledged bishop in the Catholic Church? Some readers may discount the distance implied by the word "auxiliary" and by the claim that Riva is not a spokesperson for the Vatican. When powerful people in organizations want to make statements that may be controversial, it is a common practice to encourage peripheral members of the organization to speak out first. If the public reacts negatively, then the organization has an easy way of distancing itself from the expressed opinion. Is this what Riva is doing?

As van Dijk (1988a, 1988b; see also Riggins, 1990) shows in his research, *vagueness* and insufficient foregrounded and backgrounded information may be important forms of covert denigration of minorities at a time when the public expression of overt intolerance is criticized. Even simple everyday actions in a news story may seem strange and troubling if a reporter does not provide sufficient interpretive information. Dire consequences can easily be read into vaguely threatening statements: Christian women who "don't know what awaits them" in "this kind of marriage."

Narrative Structure

It is common in critical discourse analysis to substitute the term *news story* for *article.* If all storytellers (including journalists who strive for objectivity) elaborate on the truth for dramatic effects, then narratology is an essential component of critical discourse analysis. A story or *narrative* can be defined as the recounting of two or more nonrandomly connected events (Prince, 1987).[7] Some of the contributors to this volume use terms derived from Labov's (1972) investigation of Black English vernacular as spoken in American inner-city areas. Labov interviewed adolescent boys about fights in which they had been involved, assuming that the emotional nature of the topic would cause speakers to become so engrossed in telling stories that they would be relatively unconcerned about monitoring their statements. Labov concluded that a fully formed personal narrative consisted of six stages: (a) *abstract* (statements summarizing why a narrator is telling a story), (b) *orientation* (information identifying the time, place, persons, and situations that are related to the story), (c) *complicating actions* (obstacles that arise and hinder the actions of the characters), (d) *evaluation* (moments when the narrator suspends the movement of the action through time and judges the worth and value of the story), (e) *resolution* (information about how problems eventually were resolved), and (f) *coda* (statements that return the listener/reader to the present time or indicate that the story is finished).

An advantage of Labov's schema is that it allows for a great deal of variety in stories. Labov realized that stories may not be complete and that the stages may appear in different sequences, repeated or embedded within each other. For a discourse to constitute a story, the only stage that is essential is the complication. The evaluation may be concentrated in one stage or scattered throughout the whole story. A speaker who believes the orientation is already known to a listener may not recount this information or summarize it very briefly. For Labov, as for critical discourse analysts in general, the most interesting stage of a story is the evaluation because it contains the most explicit political information. Analysts are interested in both the kinds of justification that are given and the number of evaluative comments that are given. Narrating some stories may be perceived as requiring more "external evaluation" than others, that is, more deliberate evaluations and justifications (Labov, 1972, p. 171). Alternatively, a storyteller may assume that actions speak for themselves.

Among the various schemata for discovering an underlying structure in narratives is that of the botanist and folklorist Vladimir Propp, whose book, *The Morphology of the Folktale,* is based on the study of fairy tales (Propp, 1928/1968). Propp certainly thought that his ideas were applicable to stories other than the 100 Russian fairy tales he examined, but he left the demonstration to others. Because Propp's work is so much less abstract than that of Labov, it makes one more sensitive to the generic conventions for ending stories. Fairy tales could be conceptualized as a subgenre of adventure stories, like the autobiographical travel account analyzed in the following section. Among the expected conventions of adventure stories is a concluding stage in which heroic status is socially recognized and rewarded.[8]

Because all of the components of a story cannot receive equal emphasis, which components are highlighted is related to the type of literary or journalistic genre that is chosen as well as an author's or a speaker's personal preference. Character may be defined clearly or ambiguously. If actions or appearance function metaphorically to imply personal qualities, then character is defined indirectly. Among the conventions of realism that writers or speakers may employ to differing degrees is that appearance and environment function as clues to the moral value of characters. An author may or may not be the narrator, the person who is presented as telling the story. An *external narrator* is an outsider to the events that are described; an *internal narrator* participates in events. Distinctions may also be made about the narrator's degree of involvement in a story, whether he or she is a mere *witness* to events or a *character-narrator,* a central character in the story. Time may be presented chronologically or through analepsis (flashbacks) and prolepsis (flashforwards). Nonchronological techniques create suspense and tension, contributing to the power of a narrator (Genette, 1988).

Historical Travel Literature

One of the features of historical travel literature is the peculiar manner in which non-Western religious beliefs are reported—an assumption of invalidity implied by attitudes ranging from praise restricted to their aesthetic values to condemnation of what is construed as their cruelty and irrationality. In sophisticated postcolonial literature, this attitude has been corrected somewhat, even completely reversed sometimes, but vestigial prejudice remains alive in the mass media. Systematic investigations of the implicit semantics and rhetorical devices of travel accounts published in newspapers demonstrate that, in spite of claims to objectivity, they still convey a rather high level of prejudice against Others. This is construed not as a deliberate conspiracy but as unconscious prejudice that is carried in the fabric of everyday commonsense discourses. Characterizing Others as odd or irrational is a powerful strategy of exclusion used by a dominant majority that sees itself as normal and rational.

Before analyzing an example of the kind of travel narratives that appear in the modern media, Mills's (1991) research on female travel writers in the era of high colonialism (circa 1860-1930) is summarized as a way of introducing some of the theoretical concerns that arise in critically studying travel literature. Mills chose for her research three popular British writers—Alexandra David-Neel, Mary Kingsley, and Nina Mazuchelli—who visited Tibet, West Africa, and India, respectively. These writers have prominent roles in their own autobiographical stories as character-narrators. Although readers of travel literature expected in the 19th century (as they do today) to find stories of adventure about the exotic and bizarre, dullness functioned as a sign of truth. Everyday life is, for most people, relatively dull. To be appreciated, an author of travel literature needs to maintain a fine balance between the bizarre and the dull. If a story becomes too bizarre, then it is dismissed as fiction; on the other hand, dullness does not provide much incentive for reading.

Letters and diaries are common genres in travel literature. They have a loose, unplanned, and spontaneous-looking structure that conveys to readers a weak sense of the author as an authority. Substantial portions of the books by the women Mills studied were written after their journeys using stylistic devices, such as "historic present tense" (Fairclough, 1995b, p. 156), that tend to disguise the time of writing. Although the authors were in an omniscient position as narrators, writing in retrospect, this was not foregrounded in their accounts when they adhered to chronological order in reporting their experiences. In comparison with their male contemporaries, the women generalized tentatively about people and places, hedging claims to truth. This made readers more aware that they were reading personal opinion and experience rather than objective fact. Discussing scientific topics, providing statistical information, or reproducing maps might have helped convey a sense of authority, but readers had less patience with women than they did with men who inserted this kind of dry information in their books. In addition, many male travel writers held formal roles with prominent institutions, the government, or churches. Their roles helped convince readers that they understood the countries about which they wrote. Women travel writers, however, tended to lack such official status.

David-Neel, Kingsley, and Mazuchelli found themselves in socially contradictory positions. With respect to gender, male Others were in a superior position; but with respect to race, Others were banished to a position of inferiority. Although the women made denigrating comments about nonwhites, they nonetheless showed greater psychological involvement in the lives of the native individuals they encountered than did male travel writers. Traveling alone in foreign countries, as they did, was to make a dramatic claim to occupy the public sphere traditionally associated with masculinity. But the women tended to depict themselves in very conventional feminine terms, de-emphasizing the extent to which they behaved like men. For all of these reasons, this is literature that to modern readers appears to be oddly inconsistent and irritating: racist in one passage but antiracist in another, feminine at one moment but feminist at another.

Kayaking the Ganges

The *Globe and Mail* article, "Kayaking the Ganges: Sacred Trip?" (1993), is a story of two tourists, husband and wife, who spend 6 weeks traveling on the Ganges River in India. The wife is the author, and the husband is the photographer. The author does not say why she and her husband decided to make this journey, although kayaking would seem to suggest "adventure tourism" as their motivation. The couple began their journey at the pilgrimage city of Haridwar and concluded it 1,500 kilometers later in another pilgrimage city, Varanasi.

Two details in the headlines suggest that this article might be read as a tongue-in-cheek satire of religion. The question mark in the first-page subheadline "Sacred Trip?" suggests satire, as does the hesitant "Viewed as Sacred" in the second-page headline. Because it is difficult to convey satire through writing unambiguously, it is a textual device that expands considerably the polysemic nature of discourse. Some readers may interpret everything an author writes literally and seriously, not even noticing satirical elements, which in this article are indeed quite subtle. Some readers may catch a few instances of satirical treatment. Still other readers may exaggerate an author's satirical intentions, imputing insincerity to all sorts of statements that were not supposed to be taken in that light.

Qualities that indicate satire include "inappropriate exaggeration" (Rabinowitz, 1987) and "known error" (Booth, 1974), a discrepancy between the opinions expressed by an author and what readers assume the author actually believes. The level of enthusiasm that some Hindus express toward the travelers might be read as examples of inappropriate exaggeration. Hindus "rush over" to talk to the tourists and "bombard" the tourists with questions, and the faces of Hindus "light up" when they discover the tourists are on a "holy journey." There are also at least two "errors" in this article: the auspicious significance that pilgrims and mourners impute to the travelers and the unbelievable age of a guru (discussed subsequently).

The first page of this article is illustrated with one photographic portrait and a map of India. The portrait is an extreme close-up shot of the face of an "ash-smeared saddhu" (a holy man) who has ill-kept hair and a beard. He stares intently, without expression, at something outside the frame of the picture. Depending on one's perspective, his mood could be read as self-absorbed, intense, or inaccessible. But it certainly would be difficult to see intimacy and friendliness in the photograph. The saddhu does not acknowledge the camera, either by smiling or by returning the gaze, despite its proximity a little below his eye level. From an analysis of hundreds of photographs in *National Geographic,* Lutz and Collins (1993, p. 199) conclude that people culturally defined as weak are likely to face the camera, whereas those culturally defined as powerful tend to look away.

On the second page, the article is illustrated with two photographs. In one, the author is sitting on the ground behind the kayak and surrounded by an indistinct, small group of Indians. Her gaze is directed toward a miniature banana leaf boat used for ceremonial purposes. The second photograph is a long-distance shot of the Ganges and plains. Consistent with the emphasis in the article on the landscape, this shot of the Ganges is the largest illustration. Scale is conveyed in the picture by a few small boats and people in the distance.

The first paragraph, which reports a fragment of an obviously longer conversation with a tourism official, may seem a bit disorienting to readers, who would not yet have any information to serve as a reference point for judging the official's wisdom: " 'Kayaking down the Ganges?' cried Gupta. . . . 'You must be potty!' " However, the disorientation may make the opening an effective hook to attract the attention of readers. At the Ministry of Tourism in New Delhi, the couple face "almost universal skepticism" about the appropriateness of making the trip. In the second paragraph, the quoted remark of another official highlights conflicts between secular and religious worldviews. With respect to even bathing for a few moments in the Ganges, he is quoted as saying, "I struggle between my faith and my knowledge of bacteriology." The third paragraph is either a flashback to the first official or the report of a second visit with the same man who concludes, "You are definitely potty."

In Labov's terms, the three opening paragraphs might be classified as an *abstract* for the first story. Because the sharing of travel stories does not require much justification (a speaker or writer can assume that people naturally want to hear or read about strange experiences), minimal justification may be given to establish that the events are in fact unusual. The author of the article thus introduces the tourist officials, who will not be traveling with her and her husband, to provide a more objective evaluation of her experiences.

In the *orientation,* the author explains where Haridwar is situated and where the action takes place, on the "ghats," steps on the banks of the Ganges. The other people on the ghats are pilgrims who are present to be "washed free of sin" by bathing in the river. The author does not question the religious interpretation of reality by the use of distance markers. Nothing is said about how the couple managed to reach Haridwar. Not even the form of transportation is mentioned, perhaps because a train, an airplane, or an automobile would conflict with her picturing of Indian society as premodern.

The *complication* that creates the first narrative is the dilemma the couple faces about how to react publicly to the religious demands pilgrims exert on them. This dilemma actually is the complicating factor in three of the stories she tells. At the outset of the journey, when the couple set their kayak in the river, they are persuaded by a man who cries "You must do *puja*!" to participate in an "act of worship to Ganga, the goddess of the river." It might be more accurate to say that in Hinduism, Ganga and the river are one entity, goddess and river, not two separate entities.[9]

The complication is *resolved* in the same way that it is in some of the subsequent stories. The couple actively participate in Hindu rituals and keep to themselves any doubts they may have about Hinduism. The decision does not seem to be a difficult one to make. Whether they cooperate out of respect for Others or because the religious rituals of Others are not important to them, not being a serious competitor to their own religious or secular worldview, could be debated. Both seem to be consistent with the content of the article.

The author's only "deep misgiving" about the *puja,* which apparently is not voiced aloud, is the fear that drinking polluted water might make them sick. During the *puja,* incense sticks are "jammed" between the rough stones of the steps. Jamming is an aggressive action not normally associated with spiritual ceremonies. The author was sprinkled with coconut milk, had paste "smeared" on her forehead, and had red string tied around her wrist. No meaning is offered for any of these symbols.

This episode ends dramatically and abruptly. The concluding phrase of the last sentence is the only *coda: " 'Ganga Ma Ki Jai!'* cried the priest—Hail Mother Ganga!—and we were on our way." The stage of *evaluation,* at least an explicit one, is not present in the first story. However, an evaluation is provided for all the stories in the article's final paragraph, which is quoted subsequently.

Following the first story are descriptive passages about the landscape. The sentences in the article that are the most elaborate stylistically tend to be those that report on the landscape and the narrator's own emotions. In general, a topic, an experience, or an emotion that is valued by a writer is likely to be written in a more elaborate style. Complex sentences focus attention on literary style and confer higher value to the experiences they report.

> We wormed our way across it [the desert through which the Ganges flows], contending with searing winds, submerged sandbanks that snared the kayak and patches of quicksand that sucked us in up to our thighs. As the days passed, I fancied us shrinking away in the midst of this solitary wasteland until we were specks almost swallowed up by space, light and silence.

The Ganges is for Hindus the most meaningful landscape imaginable rather than a "solitary wasteland." In the absence of other people, Hindu travelers might have animated the landscape by recalling the many associations it has with the history, literature, and religions of India. Not knowing this information, the author describes the landscape in her own terms, a vocabulary concentrating on her own adventurous confrontations. In that sense, she inadvertently has colonized the landscape, using an outsider's perspective, shaped perhaps by popular notions of Romanticism. Her descriptions also seem to be consistent with MacCannell's (1976) account of modern tourism: "The modern touristic version of nature treats it not as a force opposing man, something we must join forces together to fight against, but as a common source of thrills" (p. 81).

Passages in the *Globe and Mail* article describing both people and the landscape tend to be full of clichés.

> Then, as if from nowhere, people appeared: Men swathed in brown blankets, women wearing bright saris and balancing shiny brass bowls on their heads. With them was a buffalo pulling a wooden-wheeled cart.

Although the couple frequently is defined as "pilgrims" by the Hindus they meet, the status attributed to them sometimes is loftier than that of ordinary pilgrims. This is the topic of the second narrative about the events that occur near the end of a cremation. The unexpected arrival of the couple is defined as "highly auspicious." To the son of the deceased, the travelers were "sent as a blessing to comfort them in their grief." With some hesitation, the travelers accept the son's invitation to visit his home, where they "graciously submit [them]selves to the intense and constant scrutiny of [their] hosts." "Hospitality is heaped upon" them. In exchange for food, which the couple accept with guilt, they again adapt to the Other's definition of the meeting.

The we-they boundary is drawn implicitly so that "they" encompasses all Indians: "time rolled back, a culture practically untouched by Western influence." The division occasionally is reconfigured, however, to encompass the tourists and poor Indians within the same category: "The ministry officials in New Delhi may have been skeptical about our journey, but these farmers weren't."

Perhaps the most interesting story in this article is the third one, the report of meeting a 110-year-old guru and his small group of followers. Oddly, the author does not question the man's alleged age by the use of any form of distance markers. But she does provide information about his poor physical health and seems to attribute childlike qualities to him that could be seen as undermining his stature as a believable and vigorous religious leader: "[He was] a tiny, wizened man with a bent back and rheumy eyes. He tottered down to the river with us to see the kayak, then promptly asked to be taken for a spin!" The demanding behavior of the guru suggests the actions of a child. The slang term *spin* normally would be associated with vehicles that have wheels.

These three relatively elaborate stories foreground the more folkloric and colorful aspects of Indian society. They also convey rather flattering portraits of the tourists. People and nature test the couple's skills, but not in a seriously challenging manner. The generally positive and friendly encounters with religious people require little more than impression management from the tourists. The author's early awareness of the beauty of the Ganges mitigates the obstacles posed by nature.

A series of mini-narratives about disagreeable and offensive events that is two paragraphs long follows. They include the sight of partly cremated bodies floating in the river, a visit to a highly industrialized city, and a pervasive fear of bandits. These stories probably are relegated to the latter part of the article and are rather brief because they conflict with the emphasis on entertainment that is so characteristic of travel literature.[10] These stories also generate a climax for the article, although not much effort is made to heighten tension and suspense. Some people react coldly or indifferently to the travelers, distant "but accepting of [their] presence." Fishermen shout "Go away" for some unexplained reason. (Earlier, the author claimed that "everyone" they met defined them as pilgrims.) The allusions to cremation might serve to remind one of the transitoriness of life, which in Hinduism should be embraced rather than resisted. Instead, these incidents are reported as being "gruesome" but only momentarily threatening.

The author herself makes a somewhat unpretentious claim to heroic status; she and her husband are "exceptions" to the rule that no one travels along the Ganges. The more emotional *recognition* of their heroic status comes from others. In the village of Sultanpur, people were "incredulous" to hear that they had come all the way from Haridwar.

> After six weeks on the Ganges, we were frazzled and exhausted, yet we dreaded the moment when we would have to pack up our kayak and leave the river. Despite its hardships, our journey had been magical and entrancing, taking us through time, place and culture far removed from our own.

The egocentric nature of these narratives and the silence about several crucial topics make it difficult to assess the author's gender strategy.

Stories are told only from her perspective. Readers learn little about the husband's experience of the trip. Nothing is written about her occupation and background. However, this silence also would contribute to the false impression that the author, a character-narrator, is an objective observer.

The author cites the full name of only one person (the elderly guru), the family name of one tourism official, and the first name of the son of the deceased old man. Otherwise, characters are designated by occupation (priest, fisherman, holy man, farmer, bandit, ministry of tourism official), by religious status (pilgrim, mourner), and, most frequently, by highly anonymous terms (man, woman, people, Hindu). The author stresses action and location in the stories rather than character, time, and explanation of events.[11] Her stories should be classified as "singulative narratives," that is, stories that avoid repetition. The exception occurs in the final paragraph when she reflects back on the official's earlier remark that she and her husband are "potty." This gives the article a kind of circular structure indicative of the importance attached to concluding statements in the genre of background feature.

Perhaps it is not Hindus who are the Other in this case but rather anyone who is deeply committed to a religious perspective. Most religions may be "misunderstood" by people who are committed to secularism. Wroe (1995), in an article on religious journalism in the American mainstream press, argues persuasively that reporters who are religious skeptics consistently misperceive the religiosity of their own society:

> The Roman Catholic Church, although it has more adherents in America than any other single faith or denomination, is still treated as a strange foreign institution. . . . It is portrayed as both primitive and exotic, with the added whack of authoritarianism—not only misguided but forcing otherwise intelligent politicians . . . to go through agonies to conform with it. (p. 53)

In conclusion, the explicit judgments that the author makes of India and Hinduism would appear to be primarily neutral and positive, despite the occasional use of terms that have negative connotations and the satirical frame suggested in the headlines. Certainly, there are no outward criticisms of Hinduism or India. In addition, on several occasions, she allows Others to define and control situations. On the other hand, given the way in which newspapers are hurriedly read—most readers never finish articles if indeed they get further than the illustrations and headlines—the satirical frame suggested in the headlines would seem to be significant. It is in this realm of presupposed and absent information that one can find evidence of the modern rhetoric of Othering. This would include the distance the author maintains from the religion of the people she meets and her poor knowledge of that religion. But which theme is the discourse and which is the counterdiscourse, the satire and implied criticism or the positive statements that the trip was "magical and entrancing," is ambiguous to say the least.

Visitors to India encounter a mix of the premodern, the modern, and the postmodern (e.g., the multilingualism and multiculturalism of the country). That the author has chosen to ignore the latter two characteristics is typical of the exoticism and selective attention of travel writers. However, relegating Others to distant times is also a common form of subtle denigration (Fabian, 1983). Admittedly, there are features of Hinduism that would strike many Christians and secular humanists as strange, but parallels could easily have been found that would make Hinduism appear to be more familiar; water is used for purifying purposes in Christianity as it is in Hinduism, pilgrimages were once common in Christianity, a religious blessing at the outset of a journey is not unusual in most cultures, searching for signs of God's favor or for lucky omens is common everywhere, and so on.

Despite the author's participation in Hindu rituals, she relates to Hinduism solely as an external observer. She makes no effort to reach out to understand the religious sentiments of Hindus or to convey them to readers. The author was not concerned about discovering the wisdom she might have acquired from a guru; instead, she presents him indirectly as a rather ridiculous figure. By implication, a Hindu worldview is dismissed when the whole adventure of kayaking down the Ganges is reduced to a series of challenges that glorify the Self.

Coda

Critical discourse analysis should not be seen as an indictment of individual journalists, who operate within larger discourses that transcend them. Nevertheless, journalists can contribute unwittingly to the marginalization and denigration of Others. As far as the mainstream mass media are concerned, this rhetoric rarely is the result of a deliberate strategy of dominance, although this possibility cannot be excluded.

A better understanding of the ways in which discourses operate might contribute to more efficient self-monitoring on the part of journalists, who constantly are asked to write about groups to which they do not belong. It might be utopian to believe that knowledge suffices to solve the problems generated by human tribalism and aggression, but if the principles of critical discourse analysis were part of the educational curricula in journalism schools, then at least no one would have the excuse of ignorance.

Notes

1. Lemke (1995, p. 16) makes a useful distinction between *discourse* and *Discourses*. The singular term, discourse, refers to "what we are actually saying (and doing)." The plural and capitalized form, Discourses, refers to the "social habits of different people saying (and doing) the same sorts of things in the same ways time and again."

2. An excellent summary of theories about the relative power of texts and readers in determining meaning is provided in *The Postmodern Bible* (Bible and Culture Collective, 1995, pp. 20-69).

3. One of the modern authors who was the most interested in understanding the exotic was the French writer Victor Segalen. The notes that he made for an unfinished book outline a project of expanding the concept of the exotic so that it would not be limited to the colorful characteristics of tropical countries. See Todorov (1993, pp. 323-338).

4. Additional categories of Otherness in the literature include general and particular Others (Gupta, 1993), absolute and relative Others (MacCannell, 1976), ontological Others (Wynter, 1990), and the dialogic Other (Fabian, 1983, p. 85).

5. Rodriguez (1992) is also aware that within himself there are other suppressed ethnic identities: "I would no more have thought of myself as an Aztec in California than you might imagine yourself a Viking or a Bantu" (p. 3).

6. For example, West (1995) writes, "Both groups [Jews and blacks] have been hated and despised peoples who find it difficult, if not impossible, to fully overcome group insecurity and anxiety as well as truly be and love themselves as individuals and as a people" (p. 2).

7. Some narratologists have proposed a minimalist definition of narrative in which only one event is explicitly recounted and the second is implied (Toolan, 1988, p. 7). In this sense, a remark as brief as "John is angry" might qualify as a narrative if a reader or listener read into the statement a sequence of interactive events about the unjust treatment that led to John's emotional state.

8. Contemporary researchers who have been inspired by Propp include Fiske (1987), Jonnes (1990), Silverstone (1981), and Wollen (1982). Many of Propp's (1928/1968) ideas in *The Morphology of the Folktale* obviously need to be reformulated to make them suitable to travel stories. First, one would expect a greater diversity in the allocation of character roles and in the linear sequence of published travel stories than one would in orally transmitted folklore. The structure of fairy tales was constrained by the restrictions of memory, which are not a factor in print journalism, although the limitations of attention span are still binding. Second, in travel stories, character roles may be more diverse and

may overlap. Roles may be occupied by inanimate forces, such as fate, as well as by people or anthropomorphic animals. The same individual might be both hero and villain, helper and villain, and so on. Third, courtship and desire, although not altogether absent in travel stories, may play a smaller part in events than they do in fairy tales. The term *object of desire* might be substituted for the term princess because it is gender neutral and could include inanimate forces. The object of desire should be decoupled from the figure of authority, which Propp specified as the father of the princess.

9. Saraswati (1984) writes, "In the *Rig Veda,* waters, rivers in general and certain rivers mentioned by name are referred to with great reverence as divine and are deified" (p. 37).

10. Even travel literature that recounts a long series of exceptionally trying experiences can be framed as ironic and humorous. See, for example, Ward's (1990) *What the Buddha Never Taught.*

11. All that readers are told about the date of the journey is that it took place during the "pre-monsoon season" of an unspecified year. The author does not look for sights, either year or season, that would clearly date the trip for North Americans. The year could be inferred if one assumed that the trip occurred not long before the article was published.

References

Ahmed, A. (1992). *Postmodernism and Islam: Predicament and promise.* London: Routledge.

Ang, I. (1993). To be or not to be Chinese: Diaspora, culture, and postmodern ethnicity. *Southeast Asian Journal of Social Science, 21,* 1-17.

Arteaga, A. (Ed.). (1994). *An other tongue: Nation and ethnicity in the linguistic borderlands.* Durham, NC: Duke University Press.

Bakhtin, M. (1981). *The dialogic imagination.* Austin: University of Texas Press.

Barthes, R. (1972). *Mythologies.* New York: Hill & Wang.

Basso, K. (1979). *Portraits of "the whiteman": Linguistic play and cultural symbols among the western Apache.* Cambridge, England: Cambridge University Press.

Bhabha, H. (1994). *The location of culture.* London: Routledge.

Bible and Culture Collective. (1995). *The postmodern Bible.* New Haven, CT: Yale University Press.

Blundell, V. (1994). "Take home Canada": Representations of aboriginal peoples as tourist souvenirs. In S. Riggins (Ed.), *The socialness of things: Essays on the socio-semiotics of objects* (pp. 251-284). Berlin: Mouton de Gruyter.

Booth, W. (1974). *A rhetoric of irony.* Chicago: University of Chicago Press.

Diamond, N. (1993). Ethnicity and the state: The Hua Miao of southwest China. In J. Toland (Ed.), *Ethnicity and the state* (pp. 55-78). New Brunswick, NJ: Transaction Books.

Erikson, K. (1966). *Wayward Puritans: A study in the sociology of deviance.* New York: John Wiley.

Essed, P. (1991). *Understanding everyday racism: An interdisciplinary theory.* Newbury Park, CA: Sage.

Fabian, J. (1983). *Time and the Other: How anthropology makes its object.* New York: Columbia University Press.

Fairclough, N. (1995a). *Critical discourse analysis: The critical study of language.* London: Longman.

Fairclough, N. (1995b). *Media discourse.* London: Edward Arnold.

Fiske, J. (1987). *Television culture.* London: Methuen.

Fleras, A., & Elliott, J. (1992). *Multiculturalism in Canada: The challenge of diversity.* Scarborough, Ontario: Nelson.

Forbes, S. (1996, January 28). *Face the Nation* (CBS television program).

Foucault, M. (1972). *Archeology of knowledge.* London: Tavistock.

Foucault, M. (1984). The order of discourse. In M. Shapiro (Ed.), *Language and politics* (pp. 108-138). London: Basil Blackwell.

Genette, G. (1988). *Narrative discourse revisited.* Ithaca, NY: Cornell University Press.

Gladney, D. (1994). Representing nationality in China: Refiguring majority/minority identities. *Journal of Asian Studies, 53,* 92-123.

Goldberg, D. (1994). *Multiculturalism: A critical reader.* Oxford, England: Blackwell.

Goodman, D., & Miyazawa, M. (1995). *Jews in the Japanese mind: The history and uses of a cultural stereotype.* New York: Free Press.

Gupta, D. (1993). Between general and particular "Others": Some observations on fundamentalism. *Contributions to Indian Sociology, 27,* 119-137.

Hall, S. (1994). Cultural identity and diaspora. In P. Williams & L. Chrisman (Eds.), *Colonial discourse and post-colonial theory: A reader* (pp. 392-403). New York: Columbia University Press.

Heller, A. (1990). *Can modernity survive?* Berkeley: University of California Press.

hooks, b. (1995). *Killing rage: Ending racism.* New York: Henry Holt.

Helicon. (1994). *Hutchinson dictionary of ideas.* Oxford, England: Author.

JanMohamed, A. (1985). The economy of Manichean allegory: The function of racial difference in colonialist literature. *Critical Inquiry, 12,* 59-87.

JanMohamed, A., & Lloyd, D. (1990). *The nature and context of minority discourse.* New York: Oxford University Press.

Jonnes, D. (1990). *The matrix of narrative: Family systems and the semiotics of story.* Berlin: Mouton de Gruyter.

Kayaking the Ganges: Sacred trip? (1993, April 14). *Globe and Mail* (Toronto), pp. A14, A17.

Labov, W. (1972). *Language in the inner city: Studies in the Black English vernacular.* Philadelphia: University of Pennsylvania Press.

Larrain, J. (1994). The postmodern critique of ideology. *Sociological Review, 24,* 289-314.

Lemke, J. (1995). *Textual politics: Discourse and social dynamics.* London: Taylor & Francis.

Lutz, C., & Collins, J. (1993). *Reading* National Geographic. Chicago: University of Chicago Press.

MacCannell, D. (1976). *The tourist: A new theory of the leisure class.* New York: Schocken Books.

Miles, R. (1994). Explaining racism in contemporary Europe. In A. Rattansi & S. Westwood (Eds.), *Racism, modernity, and identity: On the Western front* (pp. 189-221). Cambridge, England: Polity.

Mills, S. (1991). *Discourses of difference: An analysis of women's travel writing and colonialism.* London: Routledge.

Morfaux, L.-M. (1980). *Vocabulaire de la philosophie et des sciences humaines.* Paris: Armand Colin.

O'Barr, W. (1994). *Culture and the ad: Exploring Otherness in the world of advertising.* Boulder, CO: Westview.

O'Neill, P. (1994). *Fictions of discourse: Reading narrative theory.* Toronto: University of Toronto Press.

Prince, G. (1987). *A dictionary of narratology.* Lincoln: University of Nebraska Press.

Propp, V. (1968). *The morphology of the folktale.* Austin: University of Texas Press. (Originally published in 1928)

Qian, Z. (1995). *Orientalism and modernism: The legacy of China in Pound and Williams.* Durham, NC: Duke University Press.

Rabinowitz, P. (1987). *Before reading: Narrative conventions and the politics of interpretation.* Ithaca, NY: Cornell University Press.

Reader, K. (1995). The Self and Others. In J. Forbes & M. Kelly (Eds.), *French cultural studies: An introduction* (pp. 213-231). Oxford, England: Oxford University Press.

Reuters News Service. (1993, February 27). Bishop warns against marrying Muslims. *Globe and Mail* (Toronto), p. A12.

Riggins, S. (Ed.). (1983). Native North Americans and the media: Studies in minority journalism [Special issue]. *Anthropololgica, 25*(1).

Riggins, S. (1990). News as texts and actions. *Semiotica, 78,* 359-372.

Riggins, S. (Ed.). (1992). *Ethnic minority media: An international perspective.* Newbury Park, CA: Sage.

Rodriguez, R. (1992). *Days of obligation: An argument with my Mexican father.* New York: Penguin.

Rosaldo, R. (1990). Politics, patriarchy, and laughter. In A. JanMohamed & D. Lloyd (Eds.), *The nature and context of minority discourse* (pp. 124-145). New York: Oxford University Press.

Said, E. (1978). *Orientalism.* New York: Vintage.

Said, E. (1981). *Covering Islam: How the media and the experts determine how we see the rest of the world.* New York: Pantheon.

Saldívar, J. (1991). *The dialectics of our America: Genealogy, cultural critique, and literary history.* Durham, NC: Duke University Press.

Saraswati, B. (1984). *The spectrum of the sacred: Essays on the religious traditions of India.* New Delhi, India: Concept.

Sartre, J.-P. (1965). *The philosophy of Jean-Paul Sartre* (Robert Cumming, Ed.). New York: Random House.

Shaheen, J. (1984). *The TV Arab.* Bowling Green, OH: Bowling Green State University/Popular Press.

Shapiro, M. (1988). *The politics of representation: Writing practices in biography, photography, and policy analysis.* Madison: University of Wisconsin Press.

Shohat, E., & Stam, R. (1994). *Unthinking Eurocentrism: Multiculturalism and the media.* London: Routledge & Kegan Paul.

Silverstone, R. (1981). *The message of television: Myth and narrative in contemporary culture.* London: Heinemann.

Simmel, G. (1971). The stranger. In D. Levine (Ed.), *Georg Simmel on individuality and social forms* (pp. 141-149). Chicago: University of Chicago Press.

Stenson, K. (1993). Social work discourse and the social work interview. *Economy and Society, 22,* 42-76.

Todorov, T. (1982). *The conquest of America.* New York: Harper.
Todorov, T. (1993). *On human diversity: Nationalism, racism, and exoticism in French thought.* Cambridge, MA: Harvard University Press.
Toolan, M. (1988). *Narrative: A critical linguistic introduction.* London: Routledge.
Turner, B. (1994). *Orientalism, postmodernism, and globalism.* London: Routledge.
van Dijk, T. A. (1987). *Communicating racism: Ethnic prejudice in thought and talk.* Newbury Park, CA: Sage.
van Dijk, T. A. (1988a). *News analysis: Case studies of international and national news in the press.* Hillsdale, NJ: Lawrence Erlbaum.
van Dijk, T. A. (1988b). *Racism and the press.* London: Routledge.
van Dijk, T. A. (1993). Principles of critical discourse analysis. *Discourse & Society, 4,* 249-283.
Ward, T. (1990). *What the Buddha never taught.* Toronto: Sommerville House.
Watt, W. (1991). *Muslim-Christian encounters: Perceptions and misperceptions.* London: Routledge.
West, C. (1995). Introduction. In M. Lerner & C. West (Eds.), *Jews and blacks: A dialogue on race, religion, and culture in America* (pp. 1-5). New York: Penguin.
Wieviorka, M. (1994). Racism in Europe: Unity and diversity. In A. Rattansi & S. Westwood (Eds.), *Racism, modernity, and identity: On the Western front* (pp. 173-188). Cambridge, England: Polity.
Wilson, C., & Gutiérrez, F. (1995). *Race, multiculturalism, and the media: From mass to class communication.* Thousand Oaks, CA: Sage.
Wollen, P. (1982). *Readings and writings: Semiotic counter-strategies.* London: Verso.
Wroe A. (1995). The fires of faith. *Media Studies Journal, 9*(4), 47-55.
Wynter, S. (1990). On disenchanting discourse: "Minority" literary criticism and beyond. In A. JanMohamed & D. Lloyd (Eds.), *The nature and context of minority discourse* (pp. 432-469). New York: Oxford University Press.

2

Political Discourse and Racism: Describing Others in Western Parliaments

TEUN A. VAN DIJK

Discourse plays an important role in the production and reproduction of prejudice and racism. From the socialization talk of parents, children's books, and television programs to textbooks, news reports in the press, and other forms of public discourse, white people are engaged daily in communication about ethnic minorities and race relations. In this way, they acquire the mental models, the social knowledge, the attitudes, and the ideologies that control their action, interaction, and dialogues with—or about—minorities.

In this chapter, I examine the ways in which politicians speak about race and ethnic relations, immigrants, refugees, and other minorities as well as how they contribute—through media coverage of their discourse—to the ethnic consensus in white-dominated societies. Analysis of fragments of parliamentary debates about ethnic affairs in Europe and North America shows that such talk often is premised on humanitarian values of tolerance, equality, and hospitality. At the same time, however, politicians participate in more subtle forms of elite racism when they present immigration and minority relations as essentially problematic, if not threatening, while defining refugees, immigrants, or minorities as a main cause of many societal problems.

Our analysis of political discourse is part of a larger project on discourse and racism in which earlier research was done on everyday conversations, textbooks, news reports in the press, and academic and corporate discourse. The goals of this project were to examine (a) the ways in which white people write and talk about minorities and ethnic/racial affairs, (b) the social cognition that is the base of such discourse, and (c) the social, cultural, and political functions of such discourse and cognition in the reproduction of ethnic inequality (van Dijk, 1984, 1987, 1991, 1993).

One result of these earlier projects was to discover that the various elites play a major role in these discursive reproduction processes of the system of racism (van Dijk, 1993). Popular racism exists; sometimes it may be more overt and blatant than elite racism. But many of the beliefs, prejudiced attitudes, and ideologies of popular racism are derived from interpretations of elite discourse such as media messages, textbooks, corporate discourse, and, especially, political discourse.

Against this background, I studied some parliamentary debates of the 1980s and early 1990s in the Netherlands, Germany, France, and Great Britain as well as in the U.S. House of Representatives (van Dijk, 1993; see also Reeves, 1983). In Europe, these debates often dealt with the increasing pressures of the East-West and especially South-North migration of refugees and others seeking asylum and work in the rich but increasingly barricaded fortress of the European Community. In the United States, congressional debate focused on civil rights, for instance, during the debate on the Civil Rights Bill of 1990, which would have provided minorities with more solid legal means to fight discrimination in the labor market. After being adopted by the Democratic majority in the House, this bill initially was vetoed by President Bush, who claimed that the bill favored quotas. A year later, a modified bill (also focusing on the rights of women) finally was adopted and signed into law.

Theoretical Framework

White European racism is understood in our work as a complex societal system of inequality in which immigrants and other ethnic-racial minorities (mostly from the South) systematically have less access to, or control over, society's power resources such as adequate conditions of residence, housing, employment, welfare, education, safety, knowledge, and status (Barker, 1981; Dovidio & Gaertner, 1986; Essed, 1991; Kalpaka & Räthzel, 1992; Katz & Taylor, 1988; Miles, 1989; Omi & Winant, 1986; Wieviorka, 1992; Wodak et al., 1990).

This system of inequality is reproduced in many ways. Dominant white group members may engage in everyday discrimination against dominated groups and their members while at the same time acquiring and using the beliefs that form the mental basis of such discrimination. This double system of everyday action (discrimination) and cognition (prejudices, racist ideologies) at the micro level implements and sustains the macro-level system of group inequality and the role of organizations and institutions in the reproduction of racism. Given the increasing role of culture as a substitute for race in many forms of "modern" racism, racism is understood here as also encompassing certain forms of ethnicism, Eurocentrism, and anti-Semitism, especially when criteria of origin and appearance are combined with those of culture (such as religion, language, customs, norms, and values).

Discourse plays a role at both the micro and macro levels as well as in both interaction and cognition. At the micro level, discourse as a form of interaction may be directly discriminatory, for example, when white speakers or writers derogate minorities. At the same time, discourse expresses and influences social cognitions such as ethnic prejudices, and this contributes to their acquisition, use, and reproduction in everyday life. At the macro level, genres or orders of discourse, such as those of the media and politics, may be seen as the overall manifestations of organizations or institutions in the system of ethnic-racial relations and as expressing the shared ideologies of the white dominant group.

It already was suggested that elite groups within the white dominant group play a prominent role in these processes of reproduction. Their power is defined not only by their preferential access to material social resources but also by their preferential access to, and control over, various forms of public discourse. This also is the major means in the production of public opinion and the dominant consensus on ethnic affairs. Thus politicians, journalists, columnists, professors, corporate managers, church or union officials, and many other leading elites in society play a role in a complex process in the definition of the ethnic situation. This role may effectively contribute not only to the reproduction of racism but also to the (often marginal) forces that combat racism.

Political Elites

In this complex system of double dominance by the elites, namely of class and position within the dominant white group itself and of ethnicity and race with respect to minority groups, the politicians and their sustaining bureaucracies play a central role. They are the ones who ultimately make the decisions on immigration and immigration restrictions, on discrimination and measures against it, on affirmative action policies, and on general resources for housing, welfare, and education for immigrants and minorities (Layton-Henry, 1984; Layton-Henry & Rich, 1986). When new immigrants appear at the borders, or when ethnic conflicts take place, politicians are the ones who are supposed to provide the first "official" definition of the situation. Such definitions, as well as the discourses that enact them, also have a long tradition. The same is true for the tradition of political racism (Lauren, 1988).

Obviously, politicians do not provide such definitions from scratch. For most ethnic events, they derive their information and beliefs partly from the mass media, bureaucratic reports (e.g., those produced by the ministries), reports of scholars or other experts, and talk with other elites such as party officials, corporate managers, and professionals (Lau & Sears, 1986; Reeves, 1983; Swanson & Nimmo, 1990).

Officially (i.e., according to democratic theory and norms), politicians are supposed to base their opinions on popular reactions to immigration and ethnic affairs, for instance, during election campaigns, hearings, or speeches they give for party members and others. However, their access to truly popular opinion is marginal or at best indirect; politicians talk mostly to other elites, and what they read is written by elites, even when such discourses claim to express the concerns of the population at large. Popular resentment against immigration, such as that in Western Europe, is filtered through the constructions or interpretations of popular reactions by journalists or other professionals. This means that both the media and the politicians are able to construct popular resentment as meaning what they please, for instance, as a "democratic" majority legitimation for the restriction of immigration or civil rights.

Conversely, the media and other elite institutions may in turn be influenced by political discourse and decision making (Gormley, 1975; van Dijk, 1991). In sum, political cognition and discourse essentially are a product of complex interelite influences, that is, of other elite discourses, namely those of the mass media, ministries, state agencies, scholars, and other experts. A full-fledged analysis of the political discourse on race should exhibit such multiple influences and dependencies.

Finally, these assumptions about the role of politicians and political discourse in the reproduction of racism should be examined not only in the context of a theory of racism or a theory of discourse but also within the framework of political theory. The role and influence of elites in general, and that of political elites in particular, is one element in such a theory (Domhoff, 1978; Herman & Chomsky, 1988; Mills, 1956). Analysis of parliamentary debates, however, presupposes assumptions about the role of democratic institutions; about the functions, tasks, and conceptions of parliamentary representatives; about the relations among the legislature, government, and agencies of the state; about the relations between parliament and other political and social institutions; and about the relations among parliamentarians, their constituencies, and the population at large. Obviously, these and many other structures that are among the objects of political theory cannot all be examined in this chapter, although several of these relations are mentioned briefly.

Within our discourse analytical perspective, I prefer to focus on the structures and functions of political discourse. Against this background, it is not only the power of legislation and policymaking in ethnic affairs that is a crucial element in the reproduction of systems of inequality such as racism, but also the influence of politicians on public discourse (through the media) and hence on public opinion. Along this political power dimension, we discover the double dimension of discrimination and prejudice that defines the system of racism. As a group, white politicians sustain and legitimate the dominance of the white group with which they identify, and their extraordinary legislative powers allow them to play a primary role in the reproduction of this system of dominance. They have the prerogative to legislate in matters of racism, discrimination, affirmative action, and other aspects of ethnic relations that are of crucial importance for the position of minorities. In sum, their role in ethnic affairs is not marginal, and this also is how we should understand their discourses and the functions of such text and talk in the reproduction of ethnic relations in general and in the reproduction of racism in particular.

Parliamentary Debates: General Strategies

Before I proceed to a more detailed analysis of fragments of parliamentary discourse about Others, I should summarize some general strategic properties of such institutional talk about ethnic affairs. It should first be recalled that most contributions to parliamentary debate are "for the record" and usually are read and prepared in advance. They are spontaneous only in moments of direct interaction such as interruptions, catcalls, or other reactions from their colleagues in the House or in Parliament. Especially on the topic of ethnic-racial affairs, such monitoring by prepared statements is essential, given the controversial nature and the moral and political implications of the issue; white politicians know that the choice of even one "wrong" word may lead to angry reactions from minority groups as well as from white antiracists or other liberals. Indeed, they know they may be accused of bias, xenophobia, or even racism as soon as they derogate immigrants or minorities. As elsewhere, but especially in this official role and for the record, talk of ethnic affairs is highly self-controlled.

Therefore, given the dominant norms (and laws) that prohibit discrimination and expressions of racial hatred, most parliamentary delegates will refrain from overt, blatant expressions of prejudice. This means that if they play a role in the reproduction of the negative social cognitions that underlie the dominant system of ethnic inequality, then they need to do so in the rather subtle and indirect ways that characterize what is variously referred to as "symbolic," "subtle," or "modern" racism (Dovidio & Gaertner, 1986). Systematic and explicit discourse analyses are among the more successful means of assessing this "delicate" political talk on race.

Our earlier analyses of these parliamentary debates resulted in the detection of a number of rather characteristic overall strategies, which may be summarized as follows (for details, see van Dijk, 1993).

1. *Positive self-presentation.* Parliaments are the typical sites of national rhetoric. Self-glorification, in comparison to other nations, is routine, especially in large countries such as the United States, Great Britain, Germany, and France. With respect to immigration and ethnic-racial relations, we encounter many references to "long traditions" of hospitality, tolerance, equality, democracy, and other values. These are, so to speak, the "national" correlates of what are known as face-keeping or impression management strategies in everyday interaction and dialogue.

2. *Negative Other-presentation.* Especially among conservative parties or in general when restrictions on immigration or civil rights are being defended, positive self-presentation often functions as a strategic disclaimer that introduces sequences of negative Other-presentation. Immigration, the multicultural society, or equal rights may be presented in a negative light; immigration is defined as "illegal" (if not "threatening"), refugees are defined as "economic" (and hence fake), race relations and the situation in the inner cities are seen as marred by popular white resentment (often justified by the inability of immigrants to adapt), and social resources are seen as under severe pressure because of the influx of "foreigners." The well-known numbers game is only one

of many moves that may be used in this strategy of negative Other-presentation. There is no balance between the positive and negative sides of immigration; political talk seldom focuses on the economic, social, or cultural contributions of new immigrants or resident minorities. The political definition of the ethnic situation, especially in Europe, is predominantly negative. At the extreme right, delegates may even engage in overtly racist talk about minorities.

3. *Denial of racism.* At the same time, it is necessary to make sure that such negative talk and cognitions are not perceived as biased or prejudiced, let alone racist. Closely related to the moves of positive self-presentation are the usual disclaimers in which speakers deny that they are racist or otherwise biased: "We have nothing against immigrants [or minorities], *but* . . ." Another move in such strategies of denial is the mitigation of racism in the country or the transfer of racism as "popular resentment" to the white lower class. Denial, mitigation, and transfer also are typical moves of elite racism used by politicians.

4. *Apparent sympathy.* Similarly, decisions that have negative consequences for immigrants or resident minorities often are defended by constructing them as being "for their own good." Potential immigrants are encouraged to stay where they are, for example, with the argument of helping to "build up" their own countries or to avoid coming to "our" country because they may be confronted by (popular) resentment, if not by the cold or other unpleasant surprises in the North. It is only in such strategic arguments that "our" country is presented as a disagreeable place to be—for immigrants, that is. At the same time, immigration restrictions may be supported by arguing that they are necessary for "harmony" in society. That is, it is in our common interest for "them" to stay away.

5. *Fairness.* Within the framework of positive self-presentation, discourse and decisions on ethnic affairs are premised on principles of humanism, tolerance, and equality. However, political "reality" is seen as "forcing" politicians to sometimes make "unpleasant" decisions. This dualism is routinely expressed by the well-known "firm but fair" move: Pragmatic decision making requires that we are "firm" but at the same time remain "fair." Of course, politicians will claim that such firmness has nothing to do with prejudice or racism, even when people with

another color or culture (and generally immigrants from the South) are the victims of such "fair" policies.

6. *Top-down transfer.* I already have argued that the denial of one's own racism may be accompanied by various forms of transfer. These also are characteristic of other types of elite discourse, for instance, when corporate managers blame their subordinates for prejudice or discrimination against minorities in the company, when newspaper editors blame their readers for "abusing the truth" about the minority issues on which they report, or when shop or cafe owners blame their white clients for "forcing" them to discriminate against minorities. Politicians, if admitting at all the incidents of resentment, intolerance, xenophobia, and/or racism in the country, will tend to blame the extreme right or, more often than not, "ordinary" white people. Frequently, such blame may be mitigated or distributed, justifying resentment by assigning part of the blame to minorities whose behaviors or cultures are said to irritate or harass the native population. For the political elites, racism always is *elsewhere*—if not abroad, then at least at the extreme right or among the lower class.

7. *Justification: The force of facts.* Negative decisions, or even derogation of Others, routinely are justified by referring to the "force of facts"; the international situation, agreements, financial difficulties, number of refugees, and so on are among the many "good reasons" being used in justification tactics for negative decisions. Again, the argument of popular resentment may be one of these "facts," even when it is largely constructed or exacerbated by politicians in the first place. This argument also may be used as one of the steps in the "fair but firm" argument.

These are among the major strategies of cognition and talk on ethnic affairs in parliamentary debates in Western Europe and North America. It is striking to find that, despite local differences of style and rhetoric, the overall strategic arguments and other moves are so much alike in different countries. It is as if the very topic of ethnic affairs or the sociopolitical situation of immigration or race relations invites a typical mode of perception and argumentation across national boundaries. This is not surprising when we realize that the overall goals and functions of such talk are to maintain and legitimate white group dominance. This means that immigration and residence of "different" people generally will be seen and characterized as at least problematic, if not threatening, and that the concrete implementation of equal rights implies loss of power for the dominant group, as is obvious in the continuing debates on affirmative action, multicultural education, measures against discrimination, and related issues.

Parliamentary Debates: Further Analysis

Against this background of elite racism in general, and the role of parliamentary politics in particular, we need to probe somewhat deeper into some of the mechanisms, moves, and strategies employed by parliamentarians in defining the ethnic situation. Therefore, in the remainder of this chapter, I focus on the detailed ways in which politicians speak about Others and on how such discourse may contribute to the reproduction of ethnic prejudice and hence to the system of racism.

Our examples are taken from debates in the United States, Great Britain, Germany, France, and the Netherlands that were held between the early 1980s and 1990s. To understand the many details of these debates, one would have to explain in detail the social and political situation in each of the respective countries. Space limitations, however, do not allow such a lengthy explanation of background. I provide it, ad hoc, where it is directly relevant for understanding our interpretations.

For most European debates, the most prominent background was the continued immigration of family members of resident minorities, primarily from the Mediterranean (in the case of "guest workers" from Turkey, Morocco, and other countries in North Africa), as well as of citizens from former colonies in the Caribbean (in the United Kingdom, France, and the Netherlands), from Africa (in the United Kingdom and France), and from Asia (in the United Kingdom and the Netherlands). More prominent toward the end of the 1980s was the increasing arrival of refugees in Western Europe (mostly from Eastern Europe, Africa, and Asia) and in the United States (mostly from the Caribbean [Haiti] and Central America).

The American debate I analyzed focused on job discrimination. The Civil Rights Bill of 1990 tried to guarantee that minorities (and later also women) would be in a position to oppose such discrimination legally and effectively. More concretely, this bill essentially was aimed at repairing the "holes" in the law that were due to controversial decisions by the Supreme Court that generally were seen as inconsistent with earlier civil rights legislation and practices.

Describing Others

There is an abundant literature in anthropology, sociology, and social psychology about the ways in which "we" see and describe "them." Group perception, biases in intercultural observation, and stereotyping are well-known topics in such scholarly discourse. However, much of this work focuses on psychological or cultural perceptions, beliefs, attitudes, and ideologies; on the mental strategies of categorization, differentiation, and polarization; or on the social strategies of exclusion, inferiorization, and marginalization, among others (Asad, 1973; Fabian, 1983; Hamilton, 1981; Miller, 1981; Zebrowitz, 1990).

In the scholarly approaches to the perception and treatment of Self and Others, the fundamental social practice of *discourse* generally has been ignored. "We" write and talk about "them," especially when "their" presence has become socially salient or otherwise "interesting." Theoretically, this discourse reflects underlying cognitive structures and strategies, for example, mental models, attitudes, and processes (such as categorization and polarization) and their societal functions (such as persuasion and legitimation for discrimination).

In other words, analyzing parliamentary discourse on Others contributes to our insight into the broad ideological and sociocultural system of group relations, power, and dominance. In that respect, discourse analysis may be seen as a method of social analysis. At the same time, such discourse, as part of the system of political decision making and legislation, is itself a form of action and interaction. This means that analyzing political discourse directly contributes to political theory itself, while highlighting the structures and practices of the body politic, as well as to a theory of racism, while studying the role of politicians and their discourses in the complex process of the reproduction of discourse.

In this complex framework of the study of discourse about Others, explicit and systematic analyses of text and talk may proceed in many ways. After all, discourse about Others is first of all discourse. That is, all dimensions and levels of such discourse should be characterized systematically, from graphic, phonetic, phonological, morphological, and syntactic "surface" structures and their context-dependent stylistic variations or rhetorical manipulations to the "underlying" structures of local and global meaning and speech acts and the interactional functions of dialogue and conversation, among other structures and dimensions of systematic description (van Dijk, 1985).

However, such full-scale analysis is more like a fishing expedition than a theoretically guided investigation of those discourse structures that are particularly relevant for the expression of social representations of other groups and the societal and cultural functions of this expression and representation within the system of racism. Even intuitively, we may surmise that the stylistic choice of words used to denote other groups will be more directly revealing about "underlying" attitudes and discriminatory and exclusionary functions than, for instance, phonetic articulation (pronunciation) or the degree or complexity of syntactic clause embedding. The same is true for the analysis of storytelling and argumentation about "foreigners," which also tells us how in-group members see and find ethnic events as well as which personal and socially shared opinions and attitudes are involved in the construction of mental models of "ethnic reality" or in strategies of interpretation, planning, or decision making in ethnically relevant action and interaction.

Theoretically and methodologically, we need to focus on those structures that (a) are the preferred sites of expression or articulation of crucial underlying social cognitions (e.g., models of ethnic events or attitudes about other groups) and that (b) play a primary role in communicating, in influencing other group members, and hence in reproducing such social cognitions. The latter point is as obvious as it is tricky. Overt uses of blatantly derogatory remarks are rather reliable signals of underlying prejudices while also having a clear function of persuasive reproduction of racist beliefs. However, because they are so overt and blatant, interlocutors may be less easily influenced by them, precisely because of extant norms against racism and the usual strategies of resisting persuasive messages.

Thus it may well be that more subtle and indirect expression of seemingly reasonable, humane, or tolerant beliefs or arguments are much more insidious and influential in persuasion (Dovidio & Gaertner, 1986). Obviously, this is particularly relevant in public parliamentary discourse. The same is true for structures of discourse that usually are processed more or less automatically, such as the schema of a story or that of a news report; what is mentioned or ignored in a headline or lead paragraph may easily be noticed, but the structural functions of such prominent placement in the text rarely are noticed. This is even more characteristic for sentence structures, rhetorical figures, and other local properties of text and talk.

In other words, in the analysis of the description of Others, we must focus on several discourse dimensions that either overtly or more subtly play a prominent role in the expression and communication of the social representations of Others as well as their social and especially their political conditions and functions. Once we have this theoretically guided analytical schema, we will know what to look for when analyzing parliamentary debates.

To cut short a long theoretical analysis of relevant discourse structures and strategies, we may summarize the major elements of such a schema as follows.

1. *Meaning:* generalized references to inherent "traits" or "typical" actions of minorities. These may reflect social attitudes and ideologies (stereotypes, prototypes, etc.).
2. *Meaning:* references to relevant (in-group or "universal") norms and values, for example, in argumentation. These may express the building blocks of ideological structures that organize attitudes about Others.
3. *Meaning:* references to in-group goals. These may dominate group interests and the overall orientation of ethnic ideologies.
4. *Semantic moves such as disclaimers:* These play a role in impression management and persuasion while exhibiting the underlying structures of ethnic attitudes.
5. *Storytelling about ethnic events including personal experiences with Others:* These express mental models of such events and the opinions storytellers have about them.
6. *Argumentation structures:* Arguments and the various strategies of supporting them presuppose shared sociocultural knowledge, beliefs, and attitudes about Others while expressing the model-based interpretation of the ethnic situation. Also, arguments play a functional role in the genre and context of parliamentary debates as conducted between government parties and the opposition.
7. *Lexical style of the descriptions of the properties and actions of Others:* The choice of specific words signals not only contextual functions or genres (e.g., a parliamentary debate) but also model-based opinions about Others.
8. *Rhetorical figures:* These usually function as special strategies in processes of attention manipulation, credibility enhancement, impression management, and other modes of persuasion.

Of course, this is not a complete list but merely a limited number of practical suggestions for the analysis of political text and talk. In principle, virtually any type of discourse structure may be relevant, depending on one's research questions. It is crucial to establish how underlying attitudes about minorities tend to be strategically expressed (or indeed concealed) in discourse structures or, conversely, which discourse structures typically are used to influence the mental models and the social cognitions of the audience. More specifically, we need to know which discourse structures characterize political (parliamentary) text and talk about ethnic affairs.

Talk About Others in the British House of Commons

Debates on ethnic affairs in the British parliament, like those in most other Western European parliaments, tend to focus on immigration. From the 1980s to the mid-1990s, this meant that proposals to restrict or otherwise regulate immigration were made by the Thatcher and Major administrations and routinely attacked by Labour representatives. The latter then usually took a more humanitarian point of view in which immigrants and minorities were presented in a more positive light than they were in Conservative rhetoric. Generally, however, in Conservative contributions to these debates, blatant derogation of immigrants and minorities was rare, except among some right-wing Tories. As elsewhere in Europe, substantial portions of the debate were about the many technicalities of special immigration measures and regulations. Only occasionally did these debates feature general statements about race relations in the United Kingdom or about the properties of refugees, immigrants and minorities. Let us consider some examples of this kind of talk. Quotations are taken from the weekly *Hansard,* which records the parliamentary debates in the British House of Commons.

In a debate about Kurdish refugees, the minister of state of the Home Office, Tim Renton, first reacts as follows to a moving statement by Jeremy Corbyn on the predicaments of the Kurds in Turkey:

> I want to consider the serious subject of this adjournment debate, and I will begin by explaining the general context of the government's policy towards people who claim asylum. As the [honorable] member for Islington North reminds us, the United Kingdom was one of the earliest signatories to the

> 1951 United Nations convention on refugees. We take our responsibilities very seriously, despite what is sometimes said by organizations like Amnesty International. No one who does my job can fail to be affected daily by the plight of people who are fleeing from persecution in their own country. . . .
>
> If the interests of the people genuinely fleeing from persecution are to be safeguarded, it is vital that the system designed to protect them should not be exploited by people whose main motivation is economic migration. (May 26, 1989, column 1267)

The structures and strategies of this fragment are as stereotypical as its contents. Virtually all talk on immigrants, minorities, and especially refugees opens with national rhetoric replete with various forms of positive self-presentation; policies and principles are humanitarian and "our" country has a "long tradition" of hospitality, or, as Minister of State David Waddington said in 1985, when the first Tamils came to the United Kingdom, "Our tradition of giving sanctuary to those fleeing from persecution goes back many years" (July 23, 1985, column 971). Such moves in the strategy of impression management are crucial to avoid tacit or explicit accusations of xenophobia or racism by the opposition, by relevant organizations, or by more liberal segments of the public at large. If such accusations are actually made, then they are strongly denied or attacked, as is the case here in rejecting the accusations by Amnesty International. Typically, the same rhetoric of positive self-presentation also features emotional references to the "plight" of refugees.

Whatever the sincerity or truth value of these claims may be, they are virtually always the introduction to a real or mental *but:* We should remain "realistic," we need to be "fair but firm," we need to stop illegal immigration, and we need to stop "economic" refugees. The concept of "economic refugees" was coined around 1985 when large numbers of Tamils fled from civil war in Sri Lanka and came to various European countries. It was at that time that a new conceptual and discursive categorization of refugees became imperative, not so much because most refugees suddenly began coming to Europe only to find jobs or to flee from poverty but because there simply were "too many" of them. The pitiful image of the traditional political refugees, and especially those fleeing from communism (like the Vietnamese boat people), needed to be strategically changed so that severe immigration restrictions could be enacted and legitimated among the public at large. The notion of "economic refugees" thus became the new political buzzword to denote "fake" refugees, if not simply all those profiteers who were seen as "coming here only to live from our pocket."

The press reacted accordingly. The conservative newspapers and tabloids especially further exacerbated this negative image projected by leading politicians. Fast-growing resentment among the European population at large against such "scroungers" showed that these strategies were very successful. Indeed, this manipulated voice of the people was in turn used as a "democratic" legitimation to clamp down on the "massive" immigration of refugees everywhere in Europe. The latter part of this passage from the speech of Renton should be understood in that broader framework.

Note also the more detailed structure of this fragment. Even the negative references to "exploitation" and to "people whose main motivation is economic migration" are introduced by a positive characterization of "people genuinely fleeing from persecution." The rhetorical contrast established here between "real" and "fake" refugees expresses underlying social representations in which refugees are categorized as positive and negative groups. The first category, and its concomitant attitudes, is now reserved for the traditional, pitiful political refugee who has been persecuted, whereas all others are henceforth categorized as criminals: exploiters, scroungers, liars, and so on. This rhetorical and cognitive contrast is further enhanced by an argumentative move, namely that economic immigration is not restricted so much because it hurts "our" interests; on the contrary, it is more persuasive to construct their immigration as a threat to the interests of "genuine" refugees. In sum, Renton's fragment should be heard as a defense of the interests of true refugees. Moreover, not only are true refugees welcome, but the government even purports to have a "system designed to protect them." In a passage that categorizes large segments of the refugee population as fakes, the speaker emphasizes the positive policies and points of view of his government.

To evaluate such claims, and hence to interpret their discursive implementation, we need to know that the number of "real" refugees being recognized by Western European countries is very low. According to the Foreign Office, the United Kingdom in 1991 granted asylum to only 420 refugees (whereas 1,860 received exceptional leave to stay and 2,410 were refused), much less than the number granted by most other European countries. Also, it should be emphasized that the distinction between "political" and "economic" refugees not only is vague and in many circumstances irrelevant but also is liable to the vicissitudes of a political economy of immigration. When there are many applications, the number of economic refugees increases more than proportionally. The concept is used not to make an honest separation between real and fake refugees but rather as a political and rhetorical means to restrict *all* forms of immigration of refugees.

The claim that many refugees come here for economic reasons must, of course, be supported argumentatively by "facts" that show unambiguously that the speaker is credible. There are many strategic ways in which to do this. First, there is the *numbers game,* the rhetorical manipulation of numbers of arrivals, as Renton also does in the passage that follows the one I have quoted ("In one instance they almost filled an entire charter flight of over 100 passengers"; "We are now looking at more than 1,000 Turkish cases who have arrived in the past four weeks"). The numbers of cases (not people) are persuasive by themselves while suggesting objective facts. (How many people *leave* each day, or how many are *sent back,* is not as prominently displayed in the political and media rhetoric of the numbers game.) The second strategy is to accuse criminal "middlemen" who exploit the poor refugees ("There is evidence that middlemen selling air tickets have been exploiting the economic situation in Turkey"). The proof, for Renton, that most came simply to get jobs is that 80% already went back on their "own accord" (which is not so obvious because they were refused or harassed by the British authorities):

> Many of them were, quite simply, led up the garden path, in their own towns and villages. That is not the action of people who fear imminent persecution. We are seeing a gross and transparent abuse of the asylum procedures as a means of obtaining jobs, housing and perhaps social security benefits in the United Kingdom. (May 26, 1989, Renton, column 1268)

This passage, as well as similar ones, suggests that there is only one way in which to support the point of view that refugees are economic and hence fake: their association with crime, fraud, or other violations of rules, norms, and values. At least, as this passage suggests, they were deceived. At the same time, however, it is not the alleged crimes of the middlemen (for whose existence evidence is said to exist but is not provided) that is focused on (after all, they are not immigrants); rather, it is the behavior of the refugees themselves ("not the action of people who fear . . . persecution . . . [and] gross and transparent abuse"). The natural wish to get a job and housing when one takes refuge in another country is taken here as proof of fraudulent intentions. Closely mimicking and reformulating popular racism, refugees are thus blamed for whatever they do. If they try to get work, then they will be accused of taking away jobs; if not, then they may be accused of coming only for social security benefits, which is the real proof of their being fraudulent and scroungers.

Of course, such rhetoric is hardly new. It has become prominent especially since the arrival of Tamils in 1985, which was recalled in a debate on asylum seekers in 1987. One Conservative member of Parliament (MP) rhetorically addresses his "right honorable friend," Home Secretary Douglas Hurd, as follows:

> Is he not further aware that all Western democracies are having to find other ways to contain the flow of people from Third World countries who arrive for bogus reasons? Is he not also aware that there is a substantial increase in the forgery, alteration, and counterfeiting of passports and other travel documents? (March 3, 1987, John Wheeler, column 735)

The rhetorical questions suggest that Wheeler holds his presuppositions about fraud to be true, if not commonsense knowledge to be acted on in due course and with appropriate policies. At the same time, refugees who have to be kept out are clearly identified here as coming from the Third World. Especially people of other cultures and colors are associated with bogus applications, forgery, and crimes. In news headlines, stereotypical metaphors of "flow" (words such as *waves, floods, streams,* and *tides*) are routinely applied to asylum seekers. They are perfidiously appropriate metaphors for persuading public opinion in the British Isles. Explicitly using this populist appeal, his colleague Terry Dicks will later in the same debate qualify Tamil refugees as "liars, cheats, and queue jumpers" who will "anger thousands of people in this country" (March 3, 1987, column 737). This, then, is the dominant elite voice of the conservative mind and the reliable expression of the underlying social representations of Others as refugees in the rich Northwest of Europe. Instead of the buzzword "economic refugees," we find here what is really meant: They are frauds and liars. Hence we need not let them in. The logic of the ensuing policy is as clear as the rhetoric of its persuasive parliamentary recommendation by Tory members of Parliament (or, more than a decade earlier, by Labour members of

Parliament when they were in power and enacted immigration restriction bills).

By describing Western countries as "democracies," it is suggested that such tidal waves from the South are a threat to our democracies that have to find ways in which to stem the tide. In other words, immigration restriction is not a policy decision but a "natural" necessity to protect white Britons from the hordes from the South. In summary, there are many stylistic and rhetorical ways in which to describe the situation so that the preferred policy answer from the government is predictable: Restrict the immigration of refugees. This has indeed happened since 1985, both in the United Kingdom and in all other Western European "democracies."

Yet, there also may be evidence of political oppression in other countries. After all, everybody knows about the treatment of Kurds in Turkey. The accusation of being an economic refugee, and the concomitant denial of political persecution, obviously is weak against the background of such facts (as supplied by Amnesty International, the United Nations High Commission for Refugees, and other international organizations). So, the next move in the argumentative strategy must be to deny or mitigate such facts, as Renton indeed does when he speaks about Turkey: "We are well aware that the human rights standards in Turkey still fall somewhat short of which we consider acceptable" (May 26, 1989, column 1268).

Massive arrests, torture, execution, and all-out war against Kurds thus euphemistically come to "fall *somewhat* short of human rights standards." We see that the categorization into political and economic refugees has little to do with the facts. Refugees are classified as a result of financial, political, and other opportunistic criteria, not on the basis of the human rights situations in their own countries. And if, under international pressure (e.g., from the UN High Commission for Refugees), countries are officially declared to be seriously infringing on human rights, then other strategies, except flat denials or mitigations, may be applied. These include requiring proof of individual persecution or even proof of torture. The main political strategy, however, is to examine whether refugees could not stay "in the regions" of their own countries where they would be close to peoples of their own "kinds" or "cultures." This suggests that ethnic-racial criteria also play a role in the classification and treatment of refugees. Otherwise, as is now European policy, refugees are relegated to the first "safe" country through which they pass, even if they are on their way to the United Kingdom because they may have relatives there or because they already may speak English and consequently can get work more easily.

Overall impression management strategies, rhetoric (such as contrast and hyperbole), lexical style, and the local semantic moves that function as disclaimers reveal not only the underlying social cognitions of the British Conservatives regarding immigrants but also how such social cognitions and their discursive formulations are used persuasively in a political and public relations strategy to garner media and popular support and legitimation for a restrictive immigration policy. Indeed, as Renton's arch-conservative colleague, Sir John Stokes, said a year later in a debate on immigration rules, "British citizenship should be a most valuable prize for anyone, and it should not be granted to all and sundry" (May 15, 1990, column 844).

It is not surprising that such rhetoric claims to be supported by the "vox populi" of a white group that is the secondary (if not the primary) target of such talk; immigration restrictions, said Stokes, "will be welcomed wholeheartedly by the British public" (May 15, 1990, column 844). Thus the elite preformulation of prejudice and the strategies of political legitimation come full circle if "the public" can be persuaded to think and speak like the elite.

Just in case one might conclude that such discourse is applied to all immigrants and that the question of ethnic, racial, or regional difference is therefore irrelevant, we may refer to the remark of Stokes's comrade on the Right, Tim Janman, made a year earlier during a debate on new immigration rules:

> We do not have vast numbers of Americans entering this country on a false basis to secure permanent residency. The whole point of this legislative change is to direct it at where the problem lies—people from west Africa, not from America. . . . We are talking about country of origin, culture, and religion. Those factors are important, and they cause great anxiety to our constituents. (June 20, 1989, columns 292, 294)

In other words, it is "black" immigration that must be stopped. It is this kind of differentiation that is at the heart of British immigration policies and of the populist rhetoric with which political elites sell themselves to the white public at large. Everyone knows it, but only arch-conservatives like Janman say so explicitly, although he is somewhat frowned on by his more moderate colleagues. (The opposition speaks of a "vicious streak of racism.") Americans do not *need* to enter the country "on a false basis." That they will not have much difficulty in being accepted as immigrants in the first place is a presupposition of this statement that is wisely not made explicit by the speaker. The same is true not only for immigrants but also for minorities more generally. That "one in three children born in London today [is] of ethnic origin" is, for Janman, a "frightening concept to come to terms with" (June 20, 1989, columns 293-294). Immigration restrictions thus legitimated are tantamount to a policy of keeping Britain as white as possible.

When challenged, however, Tories will, of course, never admit such an implication but have ways to redefine the categories of people involved. This was the case during another debate (on DNA testing of immigrants) during the same year. Besides the usual prepared statements of representatives, here is a piece of genuine dialogue between a Labour and a Conservative MP:

Mr. Hattersley: Does the home secretary believe that the rule [declaring oneself a "real" student from the outset] should be applied to all students or that it should apply just to students of a particular ethnic origin?

Mr. Hurd: I regard it as reasonable where the mischief has arisen. [Interruption.] If the right [honorable] member for Sparkbrook wishes to remain blind to the facts, he can do so, but if he wishes to study the evidence of the abuse, where it exists, and the proportion of it to be found in those countries where visas are required for entry to this country, we can provide him with it. . . . Large parts of the Third World are in ferment of one kind or another, and many people are suffering as a result of disorder or poverty. (July 5, 1989, column 383)

Hattersley's seemingly factual question obviously presupposes his belief that for the Conservative administration, represented here by Home Secretary Hurd, "bogus" students should primarily be sought among non-Europeans. Hurd does not immediately deny the implicit allegation of racism but cautiously moves around ethnicity and race by referring in abstract terms to the *domain* of application of the rule "where mischief has arisen" and, more specifically although still very generally, to the countries whose citizens need visas to enter the United Kingdom. Hurd's reaction is circular, if not begging the question, by referring to current visa policies that are themselves premised on concepts about the likelihood of immigration abuse from specific countries:

those in the Third World. Only a paragraph later does he actually mention "large parts of the Third World and Eastern Europe" as the geographical area of application for the policies, but he does so with the expected positive style of humanitarian concern ("People are suffering as a result of disorder and poverty"). Again, people from the South (and the East) are literally associated with fraud ("bogus students"), mischief, and abuse, an accusation that is made credible by offering for examination "the evidence" or "the facts," which the opposition refuses to see. These remarks are followed by the well-known story of the middlemen we have encountered earlier.

Even in the style of the more moderate Conservatives such as Hurd, there is ample evidence of a consistently negative portrayal of immigrants, refugees, and Others, especially those from the South. Other Conservative speakers in the same debate thus speak of "illegal immigration," "bogus marriages," and the "birth rate [that] exceeds that of the original population" (Stokes, column 390). Indeed, in such a plainly racist framework, white elite speakers like the right-wing Stokes may even wonder what will happen to "our beloved England" and what will be the effect of immigration on "our religion, morals, customs, habits and so on? Already there have been some dangerous eruptions from parts of the Moslem community" (columns 390-391). The differences are merely of degree. Right-wing Tories explicitly formulate what is presupposed or otherwise implied by more moderate speakers.

Although several of the more blatant expressions of political racism analyzed in the preceding are easy to spot and therefore easy to analyze and challenge, additional characterizations of Others are much more insidious. The moderate MP Andrew Rowe, who "distances" himself from the remarks of his Conservative colleague Stokes, recalls that there still is too much "prejudice" in Britain. Those who know British race relations could not agree more, although some of them would prefer to speak of *racism* rather than use the more innocent sounding term *prejudice.* However, Rowe qualifies the experiences of minorities confronted with racism as follows:

> One must, of course, always be extremely careful about the natural tendency of those who belong to a minority, whatever it may be, that when they do not get what they want, they assume that their failure to do so is directly attributed to their membership of that minority, when that is frequently not the case. (July 5, 1989, column 393)

The "natural" tendency of minorities, about which Rowe wants us to be "extremely careful" and which thus seems to constitute a fundamental problem, is, however, a widespread myth, especially under the more moderate white elites. Minorities, and particularly blacks, often are characterized as having a chip on their shoulder, as being overly sensitive, and as seeing "racism where there is none." This myth is at the heart of what has been called modern (or symbolic) racism (Dovidio & Gaertner, 1986). According to this view, not only do minorities (and especially blacks) make unreasonable demands, they commit the unforgivable sin of accusing "us" of prejudice and racism. This is also the dominant discourse among white elites in the Netherlands in their attacks against those who combat racism in general and against minority researchers and leaders in particular.

That this accusation is based on a self-serving myth is shown by repeated research results that have found that, on the contrary, minorities do not have a natural tendency to blame their own failures on the majority by accusing majority members of racism. They generally are reluctant to make such accusations, even when justified, precisely to avoid white charges of oversensitiveness (Essed, 1991). Underreporting of experiences with racism is the tendency, not overreporting, let alone groundless accusations of majority group members. Blaming minorities for imagining or exaggerating racist events is part of a well-known strategy of marginalizing dissidence and problematizing minorities. No wonder Rowe's colleague, Robert G. Hughes, finds that "we need a drive against discrimination, but not a rerun of discredited, so-called 'antiracist' strategies" (July 5, 1989, column 398). That is, some opposition against discrimination is allowed as long as it does not go all the way and assumes a truly antiracist stance. Obviously, the use of the adjectivized verb *discredited* conceals *who* did the discrediting, namely the white elites who feel uncomfortable with antiracism and whose strategy of reaction is to marginalize antiracist critique.

British Education Secretary Sir Keith Joseph typically rejects well-documented accusations of prejudice and racism among teachers during a discussion of the well-known Swann report on multicultural education:

> The [honorable] gentleman has allowed himself to speak in far too absolute a fashion about what he calls "racism." He does an injustice to the teaching force, whose members are dedicated to the service of individual children and in whom I have seen precious little evidence of any racist prejudice. (March 14, 1985, column 453)

The classic example of racism denial operates through several concurrent moves. First, the very notion of racism is rejected as an acceptable description of the facts, namely as a purely subjective qualification. Second, the use of the expression "far too absolute" suggests the usual counteraccusation of exaggeration. Third, Joseph positively calls to mind the "dedicated service" of teachers, thereby suggesting that if one uses the term *racism,* then one would falsely accuse all such dedicated teachers. And, finally, he provides "personal evidence"—there is no racism because he has not seen it himself—as if he were daily present in the classroom and his observations and experience were on a par with those of a minority child. In summary, the defense against the observation that in education we find racism is simple: It is not true, and those who say it is do not know what racism is and/or exaggerate (see also Mullard, 1984; Troyna & Williams, 1986).

It is crucial to emphasize again that the denial of racism not only is a form of self-serving impression management but also is an attack on Others whose insight, knowledge, and experience are marginalized, not taken seriously, or even qualified as a threat. In the same way as refugees were seen by Tories as making "spurious" applications for asylum, we now find that minorities and white antiracists make "spurious" accusations of racism. That is, they are liars, cannot be trusted, and are a threat to "our system."

Thus those who combat racism may effectively be silenced; racism is not on the public agenda, and those who use the very term will have no access to public debate. This may be less true for extremist, overt racism of the far Right, which is strategically recognized and (weakly) combated by moderate politicians because it deflects attention from their own role in race relations. It is, however, typical for all reactions against analyses of elite racism and of the seemingly "innocent" forms of everyday racism that characterize virtually all situations, organizations, and institutions of white society.

Describing Others in the U.S. House of Representatives

Style, rhetoric, and topics in the U.S. House of Representatives when debating the Civil Rights Bill of 1990 (H.R. 4000 or the Kennedy-Hawkins Bill) are quite different from those in the British House of Commons. Yet there also are interesting commonalities. To attack the bill proposed by the Democrats, which was supposed to make it easier for minorities to fight discrimination in employment, the Republicans also occasionally felt the need to resort to (usually subtle) forms of derogation. The easiest form of attack, not subject to the same norm that prohibits explicit racism, was the attack against those who are seen to profit most from antidiscrimination litigation: the lawyers. Hence the frequent reference to a "lawyers' bonanza" bill. It is even more persuasive to address an alleged breach of U.S. equality norms: This bill is a "quota" bill that will hire minorities "by the numbers" instead of by their qualifications. It is the bill's alleged "quota" property that was used by President Bush as a reason for vetoing the version of the bill adopted by the House later that year (a veto that subsequently could not be overturned by a two-thirds majority in the House). Third, the beneficiaries of the bill, namely minorities, had to be addressed. This meant that they, and especially their role in accusations of discrimination, needed to be characterized in some way.

Contrary to much political and media debate in Europe, U.S. representatives do not generally deny the existence of racism and discrimination. On the contrary, most Democrats and Republicans will first of all emphasize the need for civil rights and continued struggle against racism, citing the background of the civil rights movement of the 1960s and the legislation that has resulted from it. Hence this bill, which was intended to counter some Supreme Court decisions that generally were seen as incompatible with the spirit of earlier legislation. Many interventions in this debate began with the following humanitarian rhetoric. (Quotations are taken from the *Congressional Record.*)

> Mr. Speaker, I rise in strong support of this rule. Discrimination in America today is unthinkable. It is offensive. It should be a relic of history. This bill should pass this House unanimously. (House, James Scheuer, August 2, 1990, H6326)

It is within this complex political framework that we should understand the conservative attacks against this bill, which was seen to grant excessive rights to minorities when suing discriminating employers. Indeed, Republicans primarily saw this bill as an unwarranted attack against the business community and as an indirect way to push for "quotas" because, as they emphasized repeatedly during the debate, employers would rather hire by the numbers to comply with such a law than pay huge litigation costs. Some conservative representatives even saw the consequences of this bill as a national catastrophe:

> This nonsense about quotas has to stop because when we begin to hire and promote people on the basis of their race, we are going to bring to our society feelings of distress, feelings of unhappiness, and these emotions will accumulate and ultimately destroy us. (House, August 2, 1990, William Dannemeyer, H6332)

That the bill was supposed to combat the fact that (white) people in the United States have been, and still are, often hired on the basis of their race is a point ignored in this well-known move of reversal: We are not discriminating, they are. Thus quotas are seen as reverse discrimination, which, according to Dannemeyer's populist appeal, is opposed by "most Americans . . . who overwhelmingly support even-handed policies that treat all individuals equally" (House, August 2, 1990, H6333). More importantly, such "even-handed" policies have the "support of the business community," as Dannemeyer concedes a few minutes later. We see that one of the argumentative moves of the Republicans was to assert the myth of a "color-blind" society, which obviously favors those who already are in power.

Among the many arguments leveled against this bill, we may also expect negative descriptions of those who will benefit from it: ethnic minorities, and especially African Americans. Let us examine how this is done in the U.S. Congress to get insight into the more subtle means used by elites in the United States to convey persuasively negative social representations of such minorities and of those who are firmly with them.

One first move in this strategy of negative Other-presentation is to refer negatively to everybody who would support this bill: "Now a 'no' vote on the bill is bound to be politically unpopular because the civil rights industry—it is no longer a movement but an industry—will demagogue the issue" (House, August 2, 1990, Robert Dornan, H6335). Thus discrediting the civil rights movement as an "industry" (as British Conservatives also do routinely) and as "demagogues" who will force such a bill on us is one of the moves in the conservative strategy of attack against this bill. The choice of the word *demagogue* is, of course, not innocent and suggests that the civil rights movement is incompatible with American values of democracy and political decision making.

Another important move in attacking this law is to suggest subtly that unqualified minorities will be hired under the threat of litigation, as is the case in the following fragment about an imaginary plumbing firm named ABC:

> Along comes Joe Johnson, a black applicant who has not graduated from a trade school and has only six months of experience. He applies to ABC and is turned down. He sues, charging that ABC's hiring practices have a "disparate impact" upon the black community. Instead of having 20 minority plumbers, the company has only 10. (House, August 2, 1990, Bill McCollum, H6781)

Two presuppositions are casually introduced into the debate, namely that minorities tend to be less qualified than other applicants and that minorities are likely to sue falsely employers for discrimination. Both presuppositions are the stock in trade of modern racism; no proponents of this antidiscrimination bill suggested that unqualified people must be hired "by the numbers," nor is there any evidence that blacks tend to make unwarranted accusations of discrimination. It is especially the presupposed lack of qualifications that is a powerful argumentative move because it plays such an important role in white resentment against blacks, commonly formulated in terms of favoritism. Following is what Senator Orrin Hatch said that same autumn during the Senate debate, after President Bush had vetoed H.R. 4000:

> With respect to successful performance on the job, that language means only minimal standards are acceptable. What that means is that employers, if this bill passes, will have to hire on the basis of the lowest common denominator. They will no longer have to hire the most qualified employee for the job. (Senate, October 24, 1990, S16566)

France: The *Assemblée Nationale*

Debates on immigration in the *Assemblée Nationale* in France sometimes are more heated than those in the United States. Especially the far Right, represented by Le Pen's *Front National,* may in that case focus on the alleged negative properties of immigrants (usually North Africans). Most debates during the 1980s, as elsewhere in Europe, were about details of immigration and residence regulations and conditions. Let us just give a few examples to provide the flavor of conservative and right-wing discourse on minorities in France.

Our examples are taken from a debate about a new bill (*Conditions d'entrée et de séjour des étrangers en France*) proposed in July 1986 by the conservative government (a coalition of two parties, the *Rassemblement Pour la République [RPR]* and the *Union pour la Démocratie Française [UDF]*). The bill was strongly attacked by the Socialist opposition. Here, also, the debate begins with the usual rhetoric of positive self-presentation, but soon a more "realistic" approach to those who "refuse to integrate" is proposed (Pierre Mazeaud, July 9, 1986, pp. 3049-3050).

To make sure that negative Other-presentation is not misunderstood as racism, the well-known "rotten apple" argument, which says that the good will suffer from the bad, is used. Examples are taken from the *Journal officiel* and are translated more or less literally to keep the original stylistic flavor of the speeches.

> Indeed, illegal foreigners and those who do not respect our public order cause great damage to those foreigners who wish to integrate themselves into the national community. . . . [Some people come here without any money.] Such a pecuniary situation often leads them to clandestine work or, much more seriously, to acts of delinquency. (Pierre Mazeaud, July 9, 1986, p. 3050)

The restrictions on residence and immigration proposed in this bill are legitimated by criminalizing sections of minority and immigrant populations. Obviously, Mazeaud does not accuse all immigrants of crime but makes sure to distinguish carefully between the immigrant communities as a whole and those illegal and criminal immigrants who spoil the situation for the rest.

Whereas this discourse is still rather moderate, Jean-Marie Le Pen, leader of the racist *Front National,* is more explicit in his derogation of Others. Following are a few fragments of one of his speeches in this debate:

> The increasing number of foreigners implies serious dangers for the security of our country and its economic and social equilibrium. . . .

> [France and the French are under] serious and lethal menace by the continuous development of foreign immigration. . . . [Poor people from other countries only have to come here and,] without working, they make ten to 100 times more than for work in their own country. . . . They only have to write "Mohammed, come quickly! Allah's paradise is not at the other side of death of the glorious soldier, but at the other side of the Mediterranean! Quickly take an Air France flight!" (July 9, 1986, pp. 3061-3063)

It is not surprising that after his last remarks about the fictitious Mohammed luring his Muslim compatriots to France, the Socialist opposition protested forcefully. In these few fragments, one sees the standard racist prejudices against immigrants in Europe: They only come here to take advantage of our social security, they do not want to work, they are a threat to "our" country and "our" people, and so on. The racist prejudices and attacks against Muslims and Islam are classic right-wing rhetoric (see Said, 1979).

> Today, the French people, realist and solidary as it is, knows that it cannot welcome particular foreign communities. Thus, we now observe, on our national soil, a clash between two fundamentally different cultures. Islam, which already represents the second religion in France, is opposed to any assimilation and threatens our own identity, our Western Christian civilization. (July 9, 1986, Jean-Pierre Stirbois, p. 3092)

In line with many other forms of "modern" racism, such right-wing speakers carefully focus on culture instead of on race and articulate the difference, if not the threat posed by Others in terms of religion and other practices that are found incompatible with "our culture." Note also the use of such typically nationalist terms as *soil* (French: *sol*) and the use of "identity" and "Western civilization." Although Islam is presented as the second religion in France and therefore as a threat to Christianity for the speaker, only about 5% of the population is Muslim, and this makes the "threat to our identity" a hyperbole rather than a realistic assessment of the situation. Also, the presupposed condition that *if* immigrants would assimilate, then they would be seen in a more positive light is spurious because even members of minority groups who are French by birth, speak French fluently, and are not Muslims are treated as aliens by the representatives of the *Front National.*

Speakers of the right routinely enumerate cultural differences that allegedly do not allow integration and hence are defined as barriers to immigration:

> The Maghrebian [North African] community remains largely attached to a civilization which is not our own and which even totally distances itself from it on numerous points that we consider to be essential, such as the equality of the sexes or the conception of the family. Hence, the uncontrolled increase of that population in certain sectors will always, beyond certain thresholds, pose unsolvable problems. . . . Finally, the increase of violence with which neighborhoods like mine are confronted, and the important role that certain immigrants play in this delinquency, contribute to maintaining a dangerous combination of immigration and insecurity. (July 9, 1986, Serge Charles, p. 3096)

This routine list of racist prejudices is persuasive because it makes an appeal to generally accepted norms and values in "Western civilization" such as gender equality, birth control, family values, and security. One of the many problems of such passages is the facts themselves, not the values that are at stake, even when these may vary considerably within Muslim, North African, and European cultures. Thus, in the reference to gender equality, which is routine in school textbooks and the media, the presupposition is that gender equality already has been achieved in Europe; this, of course, is hardly true and certainly not in the ranks of the *Front National* or the Right in general. Indeed, the "family values" of the right favor a rather traditional role for women.

Similarly, the familiar racist suggestion about "uncontrolled" reproduction among foreign communities ignores the well-known fact that in a very short time their birthrates become similar to those of the rest of the population (Bisseret-Moreau, 1988). Finally, the familiar association of immigrants with crimes has nothing to do with culture, and this, after all, is the crucial criterion of difference for the extreme Right. Nor does the presence of foreigners, as such, have any relation to crime, although the social circumstances of poor and marginalized people, including poor whites, may be related to criminality.

Racist rhetoric like this is a mixture of assuming general values of "our" civilization that are not general, presenting biased or wrong information, selecting specific forms of deviance that may be associated with immigrants, and so on. As is also the case for everyday "antiracist" practices, there is little point in simply rejecting, let alone counterarguing, such racist argumentation; rather, it should be critically analyzed, and its mechanisms should be exposed. In this case, it is the sequence of faulty argumentative steps, and especially the manipulation of presuppositions as "facts," that is involved and that needs critical analysis.

Despite the many blatantly racist remarks by himself and the other members of the *Front National,* Le Pen repeatedly denounces those who accuse him of racism. He claims only to defend the interest of France and the French: "We are neither racist nor xenophobic. We only wish that, quite naturally, there be a hierarchy in this country, because it concerns France, and France is the country of the French" (July 9, 1986, p. 3064).

In overtly racist discourse such as this, equality is replaced by a "natural" hierarchy between the French and Others, as is also the case in traditional supremacist thinking. At the same time, this claim is prefaced by the familiar disclaimer of the denial of racism. Le Pen's hierarchy is not simply one of nationality or citizenship but essentially one of race and culture. He never opposes immigration from other European countries or from North America but focuses on immigration from the South and especially by Muslims and (other) Africans, that is, those for whom he "spontaneously" sees "differences of behavior and culture" (July 9, 1986, p. 3065). His colleague, Jean-François Jalkh, even rhetorically demands to know why it is so reprehensible that people who naturally are attached to their children rather than to those of their neighbors should not also "prefer French people to others" (July 9, 1986, p. 3070). Discrimination, for the Right, is a "natural" tendency of people: a familiar argument of racist ideologies.

One valid objection against my analysis of these examples of the *Front National* would be that the racist rhetoric of the Right is marginal and thus does not allow us to generalize to political discourse in general. True, I have argued that usually in Western parliaments such overt and blatant forms of racism as practiced by the Front national are (still) rare. However, as we have seen in other parliaments, and as we know from less formalized settings of political talk, other politicians may routinely engage in sometimes indirect or subtle forms of derogation. That African Americans are seen as being favored in affirmative action programs and as having a chip on their shoulder when falsely accusing employers of discrimination is also quite a "respectable" racist belief, even in the U.S. Congress.

More generally, other cultures tend to be presented in a negative and threatening perspective by many politicians. Especially arguments derived from the belief that immigrants engage in unfair competition are routine in populist rhetoric that attempts to limit the rights of minorities, refugees, and immigrants, as we also have seen in the consistently negative definition of "economic" refugees in Europe. In less self-controlled communicative events, many European politicians often made derogatory comments on immigrants or minorities. In other words, the members of the Front national and similar racist parties may not be totally wrong when they openly say what many others think and what many politicians only dare to say in brief moments of enthusiastic populism.

At the present, political discourse on ethnic affairs is becoming increasingly blatant. The social backlash of Reaganomics in the United States and Thatcherism in the United Kingdom has influenced various policies of "no-nonsense" social measures that affect minorities and race relations. An increasing number of racist arguments of the Right have become "respectable," at least among conservatives. In the Netherlands in 1991, Frits Bolkestein, the leader of the conservative party *Volkspartij voor vrijheid en democratie,* started a "national debate" about Islam and Muslims in which arguments were used that were similar to those proffered by representatives of the Front National in France. The liberal press in the Netherlands occasionally features articles that claim to break the "taboos" about "foreigners" and that plead for an "honest" discussion of minority "problems" such as alleged lack of integration or adaptation, minority crime, and Islam.

Concluding Remarks

Common to all these discussions, whether on the far Right or among conservatives in general, is not only disrespect and populist violation of the social facts but also a presentation of "our own" culture and values that has little to do with the vast variety of cultural lifestyles and convictions in "Western" culture or in "alien" cultures, for that matter. The rhetorically populist point in all these discourses always is the persuasive construction of a *threat*—that is, a threat to our norms, values, principles, or religion; a threat to the economy and social structure; and, of course, a threat to our standard of living and our wallets. Cultural differences between "us" and "them" are thus exaggerated, and differences within our group and their group are ignored, as we know from the standard social psychology of (unequal) intergroup relations (Hamilton, 1981; Turner & Giles, 1981). Our own group, culture, and civilization are idealized and uncritically presented as the great example. Even among those liberals who publicly refrain from uttering blatantly racist remarks, we may notice the foundations of this system of intergroup inequality in their occasionally strong nationalist feelings and rhetoric as soon as other ethnic groups, immigrants, or refugees are relevant in observation or discourse. Denying racism, mitigating discrimination, and ignoring Others' perspectives and evaluations of us are common elements in this overall strategy of positive self-presentation, even among the political elites who routinely speak of the "long tradition" of tolerance in their own countries.

Not only do we need to focus on the blatant, and especially the subtle, discursive means of representing and derogating Others when studying elite racism, but perhaps we need to concentrate even more on what Others say about themselves and about our sort of people, our country, our company, our intellectuals, our journalists, and our scholars. In the face of mounting racism, xenophobia, and resentment against minorities and other immigrants, it is this ego defense against explicit or implicit accusations of discrimination and racism that functions as one of the sure signs of group inequality. This is one of the most effective and insidious ways in which to marginalize and problematize Others. Due to such elite denials and mitigations of racism, combating racism becomes very difficult because it presupposes that a problem within white society is first recognized.

True, in most parliamentary speeches, strategies of derogation may be very subtle and indirect, especially among the more moderate MPs. Yet, when we make explicit the presuppositions and implications of such talk, we often discover the beliefs that make up the cognitive representations that are the basis of modern elite racism. Moreover, such talk is not merely talk or merely the expression of underlying social cognitions. It has direct persuasive and thus social functions when targeting other MPs and, more importantly, public opinion. The media and the public at large will make such preformulations of racism more explicit in familiar and less subtle forms of derogation against minorities. Such talk is social and institutional action as constitutive of decision making on immigration, civil rights, and ethnic affairs in general. Its presuppositions, meanings, structures, and strategies thus signal the real social and political functions and consequences of such discourse for ethnic minorities in "our" Western "democracies."

References

Asad, T. (Ed.). (1973). *Anthropology and the colonial encounter.* London: Ithaca.

Barker, M. (1981). *The new racism: Conservatives and the ideology of the tribe.* London: Junction Books.

Bisseret-Moreau, N. (1988). The discourse of demographic "reproduction" as a mode of appropriation of women. In G. Seidel (Ed.), *The nature of the Right: A feminist analysis of order patterns* (pp. 81-114). Amsterdam, The Netherlands: Benjamins.

Domhoff, G. (1978). *The powers that be: Processes of ruling class domination in America.* New York: Random House.

Dovidio, J., & Gaertner, S. (Eds.). (1986). *Prejudice, discrimination, and racism.* New York: Academic Press.

Essed, P. (1991). *Understanding everyday racism.* Newbury Park, CA: Sage.

Fabian, J. (1983). *Time and the Other: How anthropology makes its object.* New York: Columbia University Press.

Gormley, W. (1975). Newspaper agendas and political elites. *Journalism Quarterly, 52,* 304-308.

Hamilton, D. (1981). *Cognitive processes in stereotyping and intergroup behavior.* Hillsdale, NJ: Lawrence Erlbaum.

Herman, E., & Chomsky, N. (1988). *Manufacturing consent: The political economy of the mass media.* New York: Pantheon.

Kalpaka, A., & Räthzel, N. (Eds.). (1992). *Rassismus und migration in Europa.* Hamburg, Germany: Argument.

Katz, P., & Taylor, D. (Eds.). (1988). *Eliminating racism: Profiles in controversy.* New York: Plenum.

Lau, R., & Sears, D. (Eds.). (1986). *Political cognition.* Hillsdale, NJ: Lawrence Erlbaum.

Lauren, P. (1988). *Power and prejudice: The politics and diplomacy of racial discrimination.* Boulder, CO: Westview.

Layton-Henry, Z. (1984). *The politics of race in Britain.* London: Allen & Unwin.

Layton-Henry, Z., & Rich, P. (Eds.). (1986). *Race, government and policy in Britain.* Basingstoke, England: Macmillan.

Miles, R. (1989). *Racism.* London: Routledge.

Miller, A. (Ed.). (1981). *In the eye of the beholder: Contemporary issues in stereotyping.* New York: Praeger.

Mills, C. W. (1956). *The power elite.* London: Oxford University Press.

Mullard, C. (1984). *Anti-racist education: The three O's.* National Association for Multiracial Education.

Omi, M., & Winant, H. (1986). *Racial formation in the United States: From the 1960s to the 1980s.* New York: Routledge.

Reeves, F. (1983). *British racial discourse: A study of British political discourse about race and race-related matters.* Cambridge, England: Cambridge University Press.

Said. E. (1979). *Orientalism.* New York: Random House.

Swanson, D., & Nimmo, D. (Eds.). (1990). *New directions in political communication: A resource book.* London: Sage.

Troyna, B., & Williams, J. (1986). *Racism, education and the state.* London: Croom Helm.

Turner, J., & Giles, H. (Eds.). (1981). *Intergroup behavior.* Chicago: University of Chicago Press.

van Dijk, T. A. (1984). *Prejudice in discourse.* Amsterdam, The Netherlands: Benjamins.

van Dijk, T. A. (Ed.). (1985). *Handbook of discourse analysis.* London: Academic Press.

van Dijk, T. A. (1987). *Communicating racism.* Newbury Park, CA: Sage.

van Dijk, T. A. (1991). *Racism and the press.* London: Routledge & Kegan Paul.

van Dijk, T. A. (1993). *Elite discourse and racism.* Newbury Park, CA: Sage.

Wieviorka, M. (1992). *La France raciste.* Paris: Seuil.

Wodak, R., Nowak, P., Pelikan, J., Gruber, H., De Cillia, R., & Mitten, R. (1990). *"Wir sind alle unschuldige Täter": Diskurshistorische Studien zum Nachkriegsantisemitismus.* Frankfurt, Germany: Suhramp.

Zebrowitz, L. (1990). *Social perception.* Milton Keynes, England: Open University Press.

3

Das Ausland and Anti-Semitic Discourse: The Discursive Construction of the Other

RUTH WODAK

Introduction: The Waldheim Affair

The distinctive quality of anti-Semitic prejudice in Austria today is conditioned by the tension between the legacy of anti-Semitism in Austrian political culture prior to 1945 and the values officially espoused by the Second Austrian Republic, founded after the defeat of the Third Reich. It is not only that the open expression of anti-Semitic beliefs after Auschwitz has been officially tabooed. The official ideology of a new beginning after 1945 in effect obviates the problem of residual anti-Semitic prejudice altogether, either by simply denying its existence or by equating anti-Nazism with anti-anti-Semitism.

The "Waldheim affair," viewed more broadly than Waldheim's personal past, offered both the occasion and the major focus of research for an interdisciplinary study that has concentrated on the form and content of anti-Semitic prejudice in public and private discourse in contemporary Austrian political culture (Gruber, 1991; Mitten, 1992, 1994; Mitten & Wodak, 1993; Wodak, 1991b, 1991c; Wodak et al., 1990, 1994, 1997). The general aim of these studies has been to discover whether, and to what extent, a continuity exists in anti-Semitic prejudice between the present and the First Austrian Republic (1918-1938). Another objective has been to discover specific discursive manifestations of postwar anti-Jewish "angst," that is, the ways in which defensiveness and justifications as well as the projection of anxieties are expressed in language. In other words, I wanted to investigate who speaks when, where, how, and to whom, as well as why and with what effect, in an anti-Semitic way.

The Waldheim affair is the term conventionally applied to the controversy surrounding the disclosure of the previously unknown past of Kurt Waldheim, former secretary of the United Nations, that arose during his campaign for the Austrian presidency in 1986. The affair not only focused international attention on Waldheim personally but also raised broader questions relating to the history of anti-Semitism in Austria. Employing a coded idiom more appropriate to "post-Auschwitz" political debate, the Waldheim camp (the Christian Democratic Austrian People's Party, which had nominated him) helped construct a hostile image (*Feindbild*) of Jews that served both to deflect criticism of Waldheim's credibility and to explain the international "campaign" against him. The central assumption of this *Feindbild* was that Waldheim (or Austria itself) was under attack from an international Jewish conspiracy (*das Ausland*).

The relatively uneventful early phase of the election campaign ended abruptly in March 1986, when the Austrian weekly *Profil* published documents revealing details of Waldheim's unknown past during World War II. *Profil*'s disclosures were followed on March 4, 1986, by nearly identical revelations by the World Jewish Congress and the *New York Times.* Waldheim always had denied any affiliation with Nazis of any kind and had claimed in his memoirs that his military service ended in the winter of 1941-1942 with his wounding on the eastern front. The evidence made public by *Profil,* the World Jewish Congress, and the *New York Times* suggested the contrary: Waldheim had been a member of the Nazi Student Union and had also belonged to a mounted riding unit of the *Sturmabteilung* while attending the Consular Academy in Vienna between 1937 and 1939. Other documents revealed that Waldheim had served in the Balkans after March 1942 in the Army Group E, commanded by Alexander Löhr. This group was known for its involvement in the deportation of Jews from Greece and for the savagery of its military operations against Yugoslav partisans.

For his part, Waldheim first denied any membership in any Nazi organization and claimed to have known nothing about the deportation of Jews from Thessalonika. The general strategy of the Waldheim camp was to brand any disclosures as a "defamation campaign," an international conspiracy by the foreign press and the Jews (*im Ausland*). He later stated that he had just forgotten to mention such minor events in his life because his injury had been the major cause. In the course of the election campaign, the World Jewish Congress became the major object of abuse, and the abundant political invective arrayed by politicians of the Austrian People's Party against it helped promote and legitimate anti-Semitic prejudice in public discourse to an extent unseen since 1945. Waldheim also attempted to identify his own fate with that of his generation and country by claiming that he, like thousands of other Austrians, had merely done his "duty" (*Pflichterfüllung*) under Nazi Germany, an appeal that struck a positive response among many Austrian voters not only of his generation but also of the younger generation (the children of the *Wehrmacht* [armed forces] soldiers). Waldheim finally won the second round of the election on June 6, 1986, with 53.9% of the votes.

Contrary to Waldheim's expectations, however, interest in the unanswered questions about his past did not disappear after the election (see Wodak, Menz, Mitten, & Stern, 1994). Waldheim received no official invitation from any country in Western Europe, and some official visitors even avoided traveling to Vienna because they did not want to call on him. In April 1987, the U.S. Department of Justice announced that it was placing Waldheim on the watch list, further reinforcing his pariah status (see Mitten, 1994, for more details). More broadly conceived, the Waldheim affair symbolizes the postwar unwillingness or inability to confront adequately the implications of Nazi abominations.

In this chapter, I restrict my remarks to the Waldheim affair and to some typical examples of the "we" and "Other" discourse as it has developed since 1986. I also discuss some of the methodological innovations in discourse analysis that the study produced. First, however, I offer some background information necessary to understand the Austrian postwar situation. Then I present some theoretical remarks about how groups are constructed through "discourses of difference." Racism, anti-Semitism, and ethnicism are consequences of such discourses (Matouschek et al., 1995; Wodak, 1996a).

A New Anti-Semitism in Austria?

The year 1945 undoubtedly represented a qualitative break in the history of anti-Semitism in Austria. All discriminatory measures against Jews that the Nazis had introduced were rescinded, and open profession of anti-Semitic beliefs lost its previous normative legitimacy. It would be wrong, however, to assume that the elimination of anti-Jewish legal discrimination necessarily eroded the long tradition of anti-Semitic prejudice in the Austrian population. There are both historical and theoretical arguments that would strongly suggest a continuity rather than discontinuity in anti-Semitic prejudice. Historically, anti-Semitism prior to 1945 can be best understood as having what Mitten (1992, pp. 19-33) has called a "syncretic" character. According to Mitten, mass anti-Semitic prejudice, even under the Nazis, is best understood as a cluster of religious, economic, cultural, and racially inspired beliefs relatively immune to attempts to introduce intellectual "rigor." If one looks at the history of the political parties in the Austrian First Republic, to cite but one example, it is clear that the lines dividing the different currents of anti-Semitism were fluid and that political currents do not fall neatly into those who embraced a "racial" form of anti-Semitism and those who did not. If this is true, then the coming and going of the Nazi dictatorship and its anti-Jewish policies would have left the underlying foundation of prejudice more or less intact. In other words, there has remained a reservoir of anti-Semitic prejudice on which one could (and can) draw as required. Moreover, the legacy of the anti-Jewish policies of the Nazis occasioned additional perceived grounds for hostility toward Jews. To express it in the polemical words of Broder (1987), the Austrians "will never forgive the Jews for Auschwitz" (p. 42).

The collapse of the Third Reich forced many, in Austria as well as in Germany, to confront the extent of Nazi crimes. Doubts, guilt feelings, and the need to justify or rationalize one's behavior encouraged the development of strategies for "coming to terms with this past" (see, e.g., Wodak et al., 1994, 1997). The facts of the persecution were played down, if not denied outright, while the victims of Nazi persecution were made into the causes of present troubles. Moreover, Austria's officially recognized status as the first victim of Hitler's aggression provided many Austrians with a telling argument to deflect any responsibility that went beyond the commission of individual crimes. The search for a new identity involved the validation of Austrian distinctiveness, which at the same time became a negation of all ties with the Nazi past, that is to say, the German past. This in turn reinforced a specific definition of insiders and outsiders, of "us" and "them," and of "the Others" on all levels of discourse.

Anti-Semitism in postwar Austria must therefore be viewed chiefly in relation to the various ways that are used to deal with alleged or real guilt and alleged or actual accusations about the Nazi past. Discursive remedies may be found not only in the large traditional reservoir of anti-Semitic prejudice and in a general discourse of collective experience and attitudes but in several new *topoi* as well. The forms of expression chosen vary significantly; they may be manifest or latent, explicit or very indirect. But each and every one appears to be embedded in a *discourse of justification* (or varieties of justification and defense).

Discourses of Difference: Racist and Anti-Semitic Discourses

In recent research on racism, "discourses of difference" are understood to be racist, according to Hall (1989), when they serve "to establish social, political, and economic practices that preclude certain groups from material and symbolic resources" (p. 913). Hall argues that the association of a differentialist production of meaning with issues of power constitutes, or can constitute, a practice of exclusion. However, I believe that it is necessary to give a more precise definition of racist discourse. "Racism," like "hostility to foreigners," is first of all a concept with negative connotations. Yet there is no unanimity on whether both imply the same thing or both are manifestations of a more profound syndrome to which hostility to foreigners and minorities, marginalization of handicapped persons, hostility to women, and anti-Semitism belong. It is thus essential to differentiate the various phenomena at issue.

According to Taguieff (1991), the term *racism* implies three different ideas: ideological racism (a structured cluster of representations and views), prejudice-based racism (a sphere of opinions, attitudes, and beliefs), and behavioral racism (practices of discrimination, persecution, and even annihilation). The confusing array of ideas circulating as racism today have resulted in two central reductions: between racism (or anti-Semitism) as a negative attitude toward "the Other" and racism (or anti-Semitism) as a system of extermination. The popular use of the word shows hybrid forms that, according to Taguieff, become concrete in one general synthetic definition:

> Racism is an ideology, the hard core of which consists of an asserted inequality. This is founded on natural differences between groups (races). An assumption implying the practices of exclusion, discrimination, persecution and annihilation is ushered in, and accompanied by, forms of hate and disdain. (p. 235)

Regarding the term *race,* Guillaumin (1991) believes that the word lacks "semantic boundaries," be it in ideologies or in the sciences. However, for her, its "field of perception" has not become obsolete. It "resurfaces in different verbal forms, that is, in different words or in circumlocutions or equivalents" (p. 80). Like Guillaumin (who differentiates between four general groups of traits), I can list the following examples of distinguishing features:

1. physical traits (real or attributed ones such as skin, hair color, sex, and physiognomy), for example, the darker skin and hair color of some Rumanians or Jews;
2. spiritual-cultural features or sociohistorically acquired traits;
3. religion (Muslims, Jews);
4. nationality (Americans, Israelis);
5. social traits;
6. socioeconomic features such as the economic system or prosperity (economic refugees, East Germans ["Ossis"]); and
7. politics (Communists).

All of these traits that are attributed to a group of people "merge to form an ensemble that can be defined syncretically. If causal relations can sometimes be established between these various elements, as is the case, for instance, in racist doctrines and theories, it is merely a secondary process" (Guillaumin, 1991, p. 83). In other words, it is an attempt to rationalize or warrant racial thinking.

According to Guillaumin (1991), the elements could be distinguished in analytical terms, but in social perception the ensemble of elements merges to form a singular reality with the group becoming a singular entity. Such an object of perception could be referred to as "race." Of course, various types of traits could appear in clusters as, for instance, in the anti-Semitism of the Nazis. In this particular case, there is a predominance of anti-Semitism based on doctrinary genetic-racist arguments. However, there always has been a more or less pronounced blend of negatively assessed sociocultural traits. (For example, compare Hitler's statement "The Jewish race is above all a community of the intellect" with the sad "proof of the superiority of the intellect over flesh" cited by Taguieff, 1991, p. 247.) The potentially syncretic nature of anti-Semitism (Mitten, 1992) and racism becomes clear in that inherently contradictory distinctive elements are used for the ideological legitimation of exclusion and genocide.

It is important to note that there also are other seemingly restricted groups of characteristics. The hostility of West German citizens vis-à-vis the so-called Ossis cannot, for instance, be accounted for on the basis of physical or religious characteristics. And, naturally, no recourse can be taken to nationality because it is taboo to question the unity of the German nation. Thus primarily the traits related to the social and political structure of former East Germany result in discursive exclusion. Here it becomes clear that an analytical distinction can be drawn between "ethnic" and "racist" (i.e., racial-biological) prejudices.

What individual traits can be selected within a racist discourse or a discourse of difference and what consequences this involves for those affected depend on the greatest variety of historical, social, psychological, and social-ideological factors. The different consequences of the marginalization of the Ossis from the "Wessis" (West Germans), of the eastern "economic refugees" from the Austrians, or of "colored persons" from "whites" in the United States or South Africa will, of course, be different in each particular case. The Austrian discourse on Jews shows that there are even various types of differences on different public levels. Traits that are mainly ethnic and cultural are used for marginalization among the public at large, whereas these characteristics are primarily socioeconomic and religious criteria at the level of politics and the mass media. Discourses of difference in Hall's (1989) sense are thus discourses in the widest (even Foucauldian) sense (as I understand them), ones that make a distinction between "us" and another group. This distinction is made on the basis of a selection of specific traits attributed to one group, traits that are seen, in some sense, as being significant.

Discourse Analysis

The distinctive feature of the discourse-historical approach is the attempt to integrate systematically all available background information in the analysis and interpretation of the many layers of a text. Relating individual utterances to the context in which they were made, in this case to the historical events that were being written or talked about, is crucial in decoding the discourse of the Waldheim affair. Otherwise, metaphors and allusions to the past, to Nazism, and to anti-Semitism would be incomprehensible. To illustrate this context-dependent approach, I now mention some of the many layers of discourse we investigated:

1. documents of the Wehrmacht about the war in the Balkans as well as documents relating specifically to Waldheim's activities there;
2. statements and interviews with other Wehrmacht veterans who served with Waldheim;
3. research by historians on the Balkan war and on Waldheim's wartime role in particular;
4. reports in Austrian newspapers on the Balkan war, on Waldheim's past, on historical research into the war, and on Waldheim's role;
5. reports in newspapers on Waldheim's own explanation of his past and reports in Austrian newspapers on the reporting of all previously mentioned topics in foreign newspapers, especially the *New York Times;*
6. press releases and documents of the World Jewish Congress; and
7. statements of and interviews with politicians and ordinary citizens on all these topics.

Although sometimes tedious and very time-consuming, such an approach allowed us to record the varying perception, selection, and distortion of information. As a result, we were able to trace in detail the constitution of a stereotyped anti-Semitic image or *Feindbild* of the Others as it emerged in public discourse in Austria in 1986.

Our data consisted of both oral and written texts; three newspapers (two Austrian and one American) were examined systematically day by day for the period covering the presidential election campaign (March to June 1986) and then at regular intervals after June 1986. Additional data came from radio and television news, broadcast interviews, televised discussions and debates, lengthier news documentary series, and about 50 hours of video in total. We also recorded discussions in diverse institutional settings and at the vigil commemorating Austrian war victims, especially those who had been killed in concentration camps, that occurred at St. Stephen's Square in Vienna in June 1987. Thus we investigated very different settings and degrees of formality.[1]

Although the specific methods were dependent on the genre of discourse (e.g., news story, spontaneous discourse), all data were analyzed along three dimensions: the *anti-Semitic contents* expressed, the *argumentation strategies* employed, and the *linguistic realizations* on all levels of language. This study, then, addressed the problem of "anti-Semitic language behavior" in contemporary Austria, that is, any linguistic manifestation of prejudice toward Jews. It is important to emphasize that the term "anti-Semitic language behavior" may not always refer to explicitly held and/or articulated hostility toward Jews, but it does imply the presence of prejudicial assumptions about Jews as a group. For example, the slogan "Kill Jews" painted on the Sigmund Freud monument in Vienna in 1988 does clearly contain an explicit, although anonymous, imperative call for the most hostile of actions against Jews. On the other hand, a Jewish joke, which like all jokes is to some extent ambiguous, also forms part of what we termed "anti-Semitic language behavior," but only in circumstances in which the joke expresses anti-Jewish prejudice.

Our study suggests that the context of an utterance is indispensable in determining whether or not an utterance expresses anti-Semitic prejudice. Which anti-Semitic contents were expressed depended on the setting (public, private, mass media, etc.), the formality of the situation, the type of participants, the topic, and the presence or absence of Jews, among others. Second, this study suggests that anti-Semitic language behavior covers a wide range of speech acts, from explicit remarks or appeals for action to mere allusions. Anti-Semitic language behavior includes all levels of language, from text or discourse to an individual word or even to sounds (e.g., the Yiddish intonation of certain words or phrases).

Strategies of argumentation involve the linking of discrete but related contents in a given text that serve to convey prejudice while simultaneously seeking to disguise it. Such strategies include the following.

1. *Strategies of group definition and construction.* These strategies constitute and construct a discourse of difference, a "we-discourse." An essential and relevant function of such a discourse is the rejection of responsibility of guilt and its displacement onto the Other group as a whole.

2. *Strategies of justification.* These strategies enable speakers to make evaluations and to assign responsibility and guilt. The aim of such a discourse is to present the speaker as free of prejudice or even as a victim of so-called reverse prejudice. A typical justification strategy is the *division of the world into a dichotomy*—into good and bad, black and white. The contrast between "we" and "they" is emphasized. A similar strategy is the *disavowal of guilt* or responsibility. Other persons are cited as having prejudiced opinions, or their narratives are related.

Both allow the speaker to evade responsibility for the content of the discourses. *Scapegoating* imputes culpability exclusively to Others. This involves a projection of one's own aggression or guilt onto other persons. In the *victim-victimizer reversal,* the victims of prejudice are held responsible for the very attacks on them. Finally, there is the *strategy of distortion.* The opponent's views can be trivialized or exaggerated, both at the word level (vagueness, predication, assertion) and at the text level (stories, unreal scenarios, comparisons).

Anti-Semitic Stereotypes

With the exception of prejudice dealing with sexuality, virtually every imaginable prejudice against Jews appeared somewhere in our material. Here I list only a few of the most frequent from 1986 and indicate the contexts in which they were most often expressed.

The first category of prejudice is subsumed under the term *Christian anti-Semitism.* According to this ancient but still salient prejudice, Jews are regarded as murderers of Christ and/or as traitors. The character of "Judas" provides everlasting "proof" for the unreliability and lack of credibility of Jews. In 1986, Christian anti-Semitic motifs were found most frequently in newspapers and semipublic realms (e.g., in television discussions).

Although the stereotype of the "dishonest," "dishonorable," or "tricky" Jew has its origins in Judas's betrayal of Jesus, the corollary to this is economic stereotypes that date from the Middle Ages. Jews were forced into certain economic occupations, such as lending money, principally because they were excluded from most others. The clichés of the Jewish commercial spirit and the suspicion that Jews did business dishonorably in principle were both employed in various ways during 1986.

The most pervasive anti-Jewish cliché, however, was that of the international Jewish conspiracy: The Jews throughout the world, so it is said, dominate or control the international press, the banks, the political power, and the capital, and they amass awesome power against their foes. In the rhetoric of the Waldheim election, the term *campaign* became virtually synonymous with an international Jewish conspiracy against Waldheim and/or Austria.

Yet another prejudice common in 1986 was that the Jews are more privileged than other people. Although such a belief traditionally was identified with the idea that all Jews were rich, this particular cliché has taken on an additional significance since the Holocaust. Those Jews who "emigrated" and thereby escaped a far worse fate (especially the many rich Jews), so the argument goes, had no reason to complain; nothing had happened to them.

As mentioned earlier, the collapse of the Third Reich in 1945 gave rise to several additional reasons for fearing the wrath of the "vengeful Jews." One was the fear of the discovery of war crimes and the persecution and conviction of war criminals. Another was the fear that the stolen (so-called "Aryanized") property could be demanded back. Finally, there was fear that the exiles would merely wish to return to their homeland. Not only would they probably want their property back or take legal action against their former persecutors, but they might also become dominant and again "over-Judaize" certain professions.

Feelings of guilt can easily be transformed into aggression toward those whose mere presence is an implicit "attack." One reacts defensively or by turning the tables on the victims themselves. The discourse of justification is thus characteristic of Austrian postwar political culture.

How Are Jews Labeled and Categorized?

Predication and *assertion* ascribe characteristics to individuals and to groups of people. They are important linguistic devices for constructing a dichotomous world, which in turn functions to make judgments concerning "insiders" and "outsiders" or "them" and "us."

In the Austrian daily newspaper *Neue Kronen Zeitung,* which is the most widely read newspaper in its area of circulation, one columnist wrote the following:

> That whippersnapper, General Secretary Singer [of the World Jewish Congress]. . . . The private club with that bombastic name, World Jewish Congress. . . . The wheeling and dealing of the first president of the club, N. Goldmann, with the Arabs, the arch-enemy of the Jewish state. (April 2, 1986)

An excerpt quoted from a press conference of the official institutional representative of Austrian Jews in Vienna on June 18, 1986, represents a collage of statements by spokespersons of the Austrian People's Party and can serve as an example of the device of predication and the content of dishonesty:

Untrustworthy and dishonorable methods. Dishonorable members of the World Jewish Congress. Untrustworthy, dishonorable, and full of hate. Lies—deception and breaking promises—having no culture and simplistic and unfounded hate. (*Zeit im Bild II,* Austrian Broadcasting Company, June 18, 1986)

Christian Anti-Semitism: We (Christian Austrians) and They (Jews)

One of the questions debated most intensely during 1986 and 1987 was the recommendation of the U.S. Justice Department's Office of Special Investigations that Waldheim's name be placed on the U.S. government's so-called "watch list" of undesirable aliens, a move that effectively would bar him from entering the United States as a private citizen. After an initial deferral of the decision in 1986, Attorney General Edwin Meese eventually did place Waldheim on the list in April 1987. The World Jewish Congress and its president, Edgar Bronfman, had been a strong advocate of such a measure since March 1986. Carl Hödl, at that time deputy mayor of Linz and an enthusiastic supporter of Waldheim, wrote on May 12 an open letter to Bronfman that was full of religious anti-Jewish allusions. Following are the sections of the letter most relevant to my point:

It is difficult for an Austrian not to employ a polite phrase in the salutation. In your case, my tongue would indeed balk. As an Austrian, a Christian, and a trained lawyer, I must protest against your biased, unqualified, and most infernal attacks on our president and thus on us Austrians. . . .

You, my dear Mr. Bronfman, probably lived in a safe country during the Second World War, or perhaps had then just outgrown your [diapers]. Otherwise you would remember that millions of innocent civilians were senseless victims of bombings, especially in the German city of Dresden. . . .

Thus your allegations are to be judged as those of your co-religionists 2000 years ago. These allowed Jesus Christ to be condemned to death in a show trial, because he didn't conform to the thinking of the [masters] of Jerusalem. And I should like to make another comparison. Just as then it was left to a Roman to pronounce the judgment, so now were you able to find the "culprit" in the American Department of Justice, which is [now] to place Dr. Waldheim on the watch list. . . .

I only hope that the members of your association will call you to account [for your actions], which have damaged Jews in Austria, Germany, Hun-

> gary, and God knows where else. An eye for an eye, a tooth for a tooth, is not our European conception. I leave it to you and your ilk to advocate this talmudic tendency in the wider world. I can merely take note of this, but with the deepest horror and shock. (*Salzburger Nachrichten,* May 12, 1987)

Hödl begins by immediately constructing two mutually exclusive groups: on the one hand, the Austrians, Christians, lawyers, and Austrian president; on the other hand, Bronfman and his "ilk" (i.e., Jews). Hödl's demarcation, simultaneously normative and ethnic, is reflected in the "we-discourse" he employs, and this in turn serves as the basis for his anti-Jewish remarks. The use of "infernal" itself implies the religious ambience; Bronfman is associated with hell and the devil. Another religious motif, although indirect, may be inferred from Hödl's attempt to criticize Bronfman for having survived the war; apart from implying that his avoiding the fate of the Jews in Europe somehow morally disqualifies any statement he might make against Waldheim, the nonsequitur introduced by Hödl contrasting Bronfman's ostensible secure living environment with the civilian victims of Dresden seems also designed to underline Bronfman's lack of proper "Christian" virtues such as charity.

Presumably uncertain as to Bronfman's age, Hödl complements this argument with one invalidating the right of the postwar generation to pass any verdict on the Nazi past. On a more explicitly religious note, Hödl recalls the traditional story of Christian salvation as an allegory explaining Bronfman's actions during the 1980s with Waldheim as Jesus Christ; Meese as Pontius Pilate; and the World Jewish Congress, like its forbearers thirsting for vengeance, urging on Christ's crucifixion. In its current epistolary form, of course, Hödl's biblical morality required an assumption of Jewish power that is far more contemporary and that makes sense only as part of the conspiracy to "get" Waldheim and Austria.

Das Ausland: The Discourse-History of an Allusion

There were even more direct associations made that suggested that the World Jewish Congress had assumed a representative function, which Mitten (1992, 232 ff.) has termed "political synecdoche," both for the Jews as a whole and for the more vague but equally evocative German expression *das Ausland* (abroad).[2]

The discursive manifestations of this idea were varied and could be more or less explicit. For example, Kurt Vorhofer, a journalist for a provincial newspaper, wrote, "Of course it was necessary to answer the monstrous attacks which came from the Jewish side" (*Neue Vorarlberger Tageszeitung,* May 13, 1986). Because the World Jewish Congress was by consensus the principal author of the "monstrous attacks," Vorhofer's description left little doubt that it was conceptually interchangeable with the Jews. After the first round of the election, the newspaper of the Socialist Party in Carinthia, *Kärtner Tageszeitung* (May 13, 1986), asked in a banner headline, "Is Waldheim Beholden to World Jewry?" In the context of the election campaign, the implication of the headline, even though (or perhaps because) it had come from a Carinthian newspaper that opposed Waldheim, was unmistakable. In a similar vein, Kurt Markaritzer of the *Neue Volkszeitung* (May 28, 1986) in Kärnten, Osttirol, [Carinthia, East Tyrol] wrote, "Now it is not easy to counter Jewish attacks. Spokesmen of this people have a right to excessive tolerance, in light of the frightful horrors of the Nazi period. One need not and should not take what they say too literally." In other words, they do not know what they are doing.

Similar examples could be found of the direct and explicit association of the World Jewish Congress with world Jewry or simply Jewry, but it probably is not accidental that they tended to be found in provincial newspapers, where familiarity with the preferred forms of linguistic etiquette might have been less developed. In fact, the World Jewish Congress also came to stand for the forces from "abroad," as head of an international campaign against Austria. The Waldheim camp deployed this theme skillfully in its electoral propaganda, and in appealing to Austrians to unite against the foreign (Jewish) danger it could call on equally potent sources of national identity such as Austrians being the perpetual victims of international dictate. The amalgamation of the World Jewish Congress with *das Ausland* gave rise to a kind of coded language (allusions) in which the attacks from "abroad" could become synonymous with criticisms "from the Jewish side." If these prejudices were not formulated explicitly, then the authors could very well reject any accusations of being prejudiced. The coded language became the language of the "in-group," the coded terms receiving the function of a specific sign indicating the Others. In 1986, the German word *Ausland* lent itself particularly easily to such an amalgamation. A word for which there is no exact equivalent in English, *Ausland* is a singular noun describing everything that lies outside the boundaries that define the country. In some usages, the word *Ausland* could connote an idea of "those out there," but the normal translation as "foreign countries" implies a plurality of subjects that the singular *das Ausland* simply obliterates. In the debate on the Waldheim affair, das Ausland frequently was described as though it possessed capacities of action normally associated with more differentiated individual units but that in this case could only have helped forge the link between *das Ausland* and the World Jewish Congress.

For example, Dieter Lenhardt of the conservative national newspaper *Die Presse* (March 27, 1986), alluding to the disclosures that the World Jewish Congress had made, wrote of the "now completely unvarnished foreign intervention in the Austrian presidential election." More concretely, a spokesperson of Waldheim's campaign office referred to the disclosure of documents as the "meddling of *das Ausland* " (*Salzburger Nachrichten,* March 27, 1986). This statement not only assumed that *das Ausland* was capable of intervening in the election (the phrase was not "from abroad" [*aus dem Ausland*] but rather "of abroad" [*des Auslands*]), it connected an amorphous and undefined group with actions that, according to general agreement, the World Jewish Congress had been carrying out.

Other references to *das Ausland* or some variant that, in the context, could only have referred to the World Jewish Congress also helped forge the chain of associations. The second president of the National Assembly, Marga Hubinek of the People's Party, asked rhetorically "whether it is, then, still necessary . . . to elect the president by popular vote if a few [foreign/ausländish] functionaries believe that they can decide who will become Austrian president" (APA dispatch, March 27, 1986). The only "functionaries" who were mentioned in connection with Waldheim and influence on the election were those from the World Jewish Congress. The conservative party newspaper *Neues Volksblatt* (May 22, 1986) printed an article under the headline "Agitators in New York in the Final Push Against Waldheim." Party General Secretary Michael Graff was quoted in the article as denouncing the "hectic activities of the lobby of the World Jewish Congress," which not only made the World Jewish Congress into such an important organization that it required its own lobby but also signaled to those listening the relevant coded allusions: "The stronger the foreign interventions become, the more the second round in the election becomes an act of patriotism and Austrian self-respect" (*Neues Volksblatt,* May 22, 1986). One week later (*Neues Volksblatt,* May 29, 1986), Walter Salzmann concurred:

> The fact remains that *das Ausland,* and especially the World Jewish Congress, was consciously engaged in this campaign and has unfortunately not understood that they [could] not have done their organization and thereby their Jewish "fellow citizens" [*Mitbürger*] in Austria a greater disservice than to have taken over and to continue leading the chase [*Jagd*] after Kurt Waldheim.

This is a clear application of the victim-victimizer reversal strategy.

Perhaps the most compelling evidence of the explicit association of the World Jewish Congress with Jewry as a whole, however, was visual. In its April 1, 1986, issue, the independent weekly newsmagazine *Wochenpresse* contained a long background article on the World Jewish Congress and an interview with Simon Wiesenthal in which he expressed sharp criticism of the organization's handling of the Waldheim affair. The article on the World Jewish Congress was not in itself excessively tendentious. The editors of the magazine apparently were conscious of the perils of publishing an article on this subject. After much consideration, they decided to run it but were determined to avoid, as journalist Gerald Freihofner (*Wochenpresse,* April 1, 1986) wrote, "in any way providing ammunition for latent antisemitism, which is still widespread in the Austrian population." The cover story, titled "Waldheim's Adversaries: The World Jewish Congress," was accompanied by a photograph whose semiotic significance was obvious.

This photograph showed the back of a man's head covered with a yarmulke. In the middle of the yarmulke was an embroidered star of David. An anonymous male figure with a yarmulke could be related to the World Jewish Congress alone, however, only if it were an identifying feature of the organization or its members. In the popular imagination, of course, a yarmulke is the characteristic that marks off not the World Jewish Congress but "the Jews." The message this cover photograph conveyed was a simple but powerful one: When we say World Jewish Congress, we mean Jews.

The Amalgamation of Others: Jews, Turks, and Bicycle Riders

In 1989, the "Iron Curtain" dividing Europe was torn down. In Austria, as in other Western countries, these changes were greeted euphorically by politicians and media alike. Armed with wire cutters, Austria's foreign minister, Alois Mock, was shown doing his part—literally as well as symbolically—to open the border between Austria and Hungary. The end of 1989 witnessed the success of the Romanian "revolution," and the fall of Eastern European Stalinist regimes (or the death of Marxism, according to taste) was everywhere exuberantly acclaimed. As the first waves of refugees and immigrants seeking asylum and work made their way westward, however, this enthusiasm soon dampened.

In the wake of the democratic revolutions in East Central Europe, the distinctions between "political" and "economic" refugees quickly elided. Indeed, the patronizing, condescending tolerance in Austria of political refugees from Communist Eastern Europe seems to have veiled more profound ethnic hostilities toward these same groups. The uncertainties of this new political configuration in Europe occasioned the emergence in Austrian public life of xenophobic discourses, fed by and couched in the terms of social anxiety. Those who even a few months earlier would have been warmly welcomed as heroic refugees from tyrannical regimes suddenly became socially more threatening "economic immigrants," "spirit and salami merchants," and "criminals"—violent, dirty, too lazy and selfish to remain in their countries and solve their own problems. The negative discourse on foreigners in Austria nowadays includes Poles, Romanians, Turks, Serbs, and Gypsies. Although Jews from Russia also immigrate to Austria, they usually are not mentioned in antiforeigner speech.

An indication of the political implications of this transformation was given in the campaign preceding the 1990 elections to the Austrian National Assembly. Confronted by the obvious success the *Austrian Freedom Party (Freiheitliche Partei Österreichs)* and the *Austrian People's Party (Österreichische Volkspartei)* quickly accommodated their own electoral strategies and general political propaganda to the new climate of resentment and anger (cf. Wodak, 1991a). Not surprisingly, the kinds of ethnic stereotypes that the studies of Helsen (1990), Jäger (1991), and van Dijk (1984, 1987, 1991) had registered in other political cultures found their equivalents in contemporary media discourse and politicians' statements in Austria (Matouschek et al., 1995; Wodak, 1966a).

The text I discuss in the following stories was recorded during an election rally of the *Freiheitliche Partei Österreichs* held on November 11, 1991. The populist right in Austria, represented by Jörg Haider's Freedom Party (similar to the movement in France led by Le Pen), has gained much popularity and won votes with its antiforeigner propaganda, especially in districts where many workers live and that until recently regularly returned Socialist majorities. At this rally, three people (two men and one woman) were standing together involved in a discussion. They first exchanged bad experiences about foreigners of Turkish or formerly Yugoslav origin (with the general label *Tschuschn*). Because of the criminality of the Turks, the old mother of one of the speakers was too afraid even to go out in the park alone. Her son had to accompany her (first story). Suddenly, the discourse switched to the subject of the Jews. This anti-Semitic phenomenon, which we term the *Iudeus ex machina* strategy, frequently is encountered when a general scapegoat is needed. The coherence seemed clear to all participants, and no explicit transition was felt to be needed. Then the discussion continued, again without transition, about foreigners and bicycle riders. (In the stories, E = elderly male, Y = younger male, and F = female.)

Story 1

E: They chased my mom out of the park. They said this is a [Turkish park] and she can't go there anymore. She's 86, and when the weather's nice I have to go with her to the park, see, if you want her to have any peace
. . . .)

Story 2

Y: Yeah, he inherited from his uncle, from a Jew, yeah, well, and where did the Jew come by it?
F: They work just like we do
Y: Yeah, and you know what, hey, your Hillinger, yeah, you've also lived
E: (. . . . .) just like
Y: a long time, yeah, you've lived a long time in this world you live in
E: Hitler (. .) with the Palestinians, understand? They're no good
Y: in Vienna, just like the Jews, I've seen the Jews firsthand, I've seen it firsthand, it was like this
Y: but they used us again and again, and I'll tell you something, I grew up in the country. This Jew came, we didn't have anything to eat, nothing to wear,

my parents had to go into debt to buy clothes for me and food. Jew came at harvest time (. .) and took everything, in summer, and this then we we once again didn't have anything left to eat, that's the way he was, the way the Jew is, my dear lady, well, I ask you now

F: well, I worked for Jews as a young

Y: I lived through it myself. I lived through it myself, didn't I? Boy

F: girl(. . . . .)

Y: did they have it good. What I heard about what had happened to

F: (. . . . .)

Y: the Jews. I have a lot of friends, and they told me that they used them

F: (. . . . .)

Y: again and again, too, used them again and again, good there was a good one, look, there are good and bad everywhere, but I can but, but

F: exactly (. .) most Jews, they are really honest (. . . . .)

Y: but but there were in fact many bad ones and this Jew he he let them that, didn't he? He didn't didn't till it himself there and that (. . .) he skimmed it off from somewhere, didn't he? Well, then, you the Jews

F: they work hard

Y: The Jew is a businessman, he doesn't work himself, he lets others work for him

F: well, all right, he just

E: The Jew has it here, my dear lady [pointing to his head]

F: (. .) but today's young people don't want to work, either

E: Listen, if I got 7,000 schillings from the dole [unemployment], I wouldn't go to work either—what do you think?—you see, they are right not to go to work

(. . . . .)

Story 3

Y: A bike rider (. . .) on the sidewalk, yeah, really, one of them recently ran into me in the park—do you hear?—(. . .) my wife
and I were walking hand in hand, a Tschusch, a Tschusch, a Tschusch it was—do you hear?—at 9:00 in the morning [laughter],
like I'm walking through the park with Wally [his wife]—do you hear?—he rode down on his bike (. .) rode between us
I got all dirty, my wife, my wife fell down, he fell down himself, that's the the children the Tschuschs
bike riders (. . .) bike riders (. . . .)
(. . . . .)

The first story is short; it has neither an orientation section nor a disclaimer but starts immediately with the complication. Thus the mother of the speaker, an old lady, was chased out of the park by "them." The perpetrators remain anonymous and vague. The resolution is clear, however: The mother cannot visit the park alone anymore because it has become "Turkish." The beliefs implied that Turks are criminal and violent, especially toward women, may be assumed as a given for the other participants. The implication is equally obvious: The Austrians have to defend themselves. This stereotype implicitly claims that Turks are different and violent, but no biological relationship is assumed.

The second story begins with an orientation section. One speaker mentions a rich Jew who seems to have inherited money. The first generalization that appears, "the Jew" (*der Jude*), is used as a predication. "The Jew" (singular) was the common currency of all anti-Semitic propaganda, and it is to this ideological tradition that this speaker clearly alludes. The topic is then explicated: Jews are rich, but they come by their wealth by chance rather than through work. The second speaker posits a moral equivalent between the Jews and the Nazis: Hitler acted the same toward Jews as the Jews do toward the Palestinians. This serves to deny or justify any guilt anti-Semites might have been expected to feel.

The second introduction to the story is a generalization: Jews are not good. As in the previous example, the speaker feels no need to introduce any initial disclaimer. The complication that follows, an apocryphal story about the village Jew, is very similar in structure and content to many other stories we found in 1986 and 1987. Again we find the victim-victimizer reversal: The Jew was responsible for the loss of property of the farmers. A woman present tries to defend the Jews. She has had her own experience with these people, she claims, as she used to work for a Jewish family. But she is not able to persuade the two men, because they continue the anti-Semitic discourse. Again generalizations and general conclusions arise from the empirical evidence of one example: Jews are exploiters and let other people work for them. Although there "are good and bad everywhere," as the disclaimer suggests (the first disclaimer introduced), Jews are and remain businessmen. The speaker claims to have heard "what happened to the Jews," but even those left over are bad. The sentence itself is internally contradictory: Because there are "good and bad everywhere," some good persons must be presumed to have survived, yet the use of the generic "the Jew" suggests that all Jews are bad. Often enough, such contradictions are not noticed but are nonetheless typical of prejudiced discourse. No resolution is felt to be needed; the story ends with another generalization. Pointing to his head, the speaker says "The Jew has it here." The precise character of this statement is not entirely clear: He might have meant that Jews are innately intelligent or that their intelligence is learned. Whether Jewish intelligence is generally or culturally acquired is, however, less important than what it signifies for the speaker, namely, because Jews are intelligent, they do not have to work themselves. The attempted reply of the woman, that "they [do] work hard," is not even noticed.

The third story is short. The generalization at the end claims this one example to be typical of the "Tschuschs" (the general label for all foreigners): They are reckless and do not care about other people. Many people dislike bicycle riders in public places, but here this dislike is associated with foreigners.

The story about the Jew possesses several functions related to its specific context. It is supposed to underline Austrians' bad experiences with foreigners in general (Jews apparently being foreigners). Moreover, it serves as the premise for the generalizations that follow. It establishes group solidarity between the two men who share the same opinions on more than one out-group. Finally, this passage suggests that prejudiced discourse about foreigners has not taken the place of anti-Semitic discourse during the Waldheim affair; rather, it has only elaborated and augmented it. The general conclusion of these texts could be that "real" Austrians are total victims, whereas foreigners are criminal, are reckless, and/or steal jobs. And even if one should have a job, he or she will be exploited by the Jews.

Conclusions

It was possible in this study to describe and expose the range and quality of anti-Semitic discourse in contemporary Austria. "The Jews" form the archetypical Other; anti-Semitic discourse constitutes the model for xenophobic and sexist discourse, although certain argumentation patterns were found that form part of a new "discourse of justification." Anti-Semitic prejudice clearly is present in everyday life, in all settings, even in the most public ones. Anti-Semitism is part of the collective tradition and memory in Austria, is used by all political parties, and has this very specific function in societies that the German philosopher Theodor Adorno mentioned in his concept of the authoritarian personality: Anti-Semitism is the basic typology of the Others; the archetype explains everything that otherwise remains incomprehensible (Adorno, 1968).

The linguistic tools developed, however, have an analytical value as diagnostic measures that extend beyond their inception in the Austrian anti-Semitic context. We are now able to detect more effectively anti-Semitic and racist meaning in various contexts as well as the impact of certain contextual features on the quantity and quality of anti-Semitic remarks.

But many questions remain unanswered, especially the following: How is all this possible after 1945? It is possible because of an internationally accepted *Lebenslüge* (lie) of Austria and Waldheim personally, because of the possibility of claiming to be a victim oneself without having to face the responsibilities of having been a participant. The Waldheim affair has at least allowed us to speak and write about the taboos and pose the question of *vergangenheitsbewältigung* (coming to terms with the past), a question that is raised nowadays in many Eastern and Western European countries.

Notes

1. For each genre of discourse, we applied a different method of analysis. In analyzing "prejudice stories," for example, we developed a narrative scheme drawing on the work of van Dijk (1984). The newspaper analysis differs substantially from conventional content analysis. Argumentation, lexicon, metaphors, and other linguistic strategies played an important role. The descriptive taxonomy employed in interpreting the interviews with politicians stems from the specialized literature on "political language" (Dieckmann, 1969, 1981; Wilson, 1990). Finally, for the spontaneous discussions, we had to integrate categories of conversational analysis as well as those of discourse analysis (Wodak, 1989, 1996b).

2. I thank Richard Mitten for the opportunity of using the materials from his book (Mitten, 1992). His works as well as his comments and criticisms have been extremely important for the writing of this chapter and the project on Waldheim as a whole.

References

Adorno, T. (1968). *Studien zum autoritären Charakter.* Frankfurt, Germany: Suhrkamp.

Broder, H. (1987). *Der emige Jude.* Frankfurt, Germany: Suhrkamp.

Dieckmann, W. (1969). *Sprache in der Politik: Einführung in die Pragmatik und Semantik der politischen Sprache.* Heidelberg, Germany: C. Winter.

Dieckmann, W. (1981). *Politische Sprache, politische Kommunikation: Vorträge, Aufsätze, Entwürfe.* Heidelberg, Germany: C. Winter.

Gruber, H. (1991). *Antisemitismus im Mediendiskurs: Die Affäre "Waldheim" in der Tagespresse.* Wiesbaden, Germany: Deutscher Universitätsverlag.

Guillaumin, C. (1991). Rasse, das Wort und die Vorstellung. In U. Bielefeld (Ed.), *Das Eigene und das Fremde: Neuer Rassismus in der alten Welt?* (pp. 65-90). Hamburg, Germany: Junius.

Hall, S. (1989). Rassismus als ideologischer Diskurs. *Das Argument, 31,* 913-921.

Helsen, J. (1990). *Flüchtlinge im Diskurs.* Master's thesis, University of Amsterdam.

Jäger, S. (1991). *Rassismus im Alltag.* Duisburg, Germany: Duisburger Institut für Sprach und Sozialforschung.

Matouschek, B., Wodak, R., & Januschek, F. (1995). *Notwendige Massnahmen gegen Fremde.* Vienna, Austria: Passagen.

Mitten, R. (1992). *The politics of anti-Semitic prejudice: The Waldheim phenomenon in Austria.* Boulder, CO: Westview.

Mitten, R. (1993, January 2). Die "Judenfrage" im Nachkriegsösterreich. *Zeitgeschichte,* pp. 14-34.

Mitten, R. (1994). Waldheim affair. In *Encyclopaedia Judaica decennial book 1983-1992* (pp. 387-389). Jerusalem: Encyclopaedia Judaica.

Mitten, R., & Wodak, R. (1993). On the discourse of racism and prejudice. *Folia Linguistica, 27,* 191-215.

Taguieff, P. (1991). Die Metamorphosen des Rassismus und die Krise des Antirassismus. In U. Bielefeld (Ed.), *Das Eigene und das Fremde: Neuer Rassismus in der alten Welt?* (pp. 221-268). Hamburg, Germany: Junius.

van Dijk, T. (1984). *Prejudice in discourse.* Amsterdam, Netherlands: Benjamins.

van Dijk, T. (1987). *Communicating racism.* Beverly Hills, CA: Sage.

van Dijk, T. (1991). *Racism and the press.* London: Routledge.

Wilson, J. (1990) *Politically speaking.* Oxford, England: Basil Blackwell.

Wodak, R. (Ed.). (1989). *Language, power, and ideology.* Amsterdam, The Netherlands: Benjamin.

Wodak, R. (1991a). Der Ton macht die Musik. *Werkstattblätter, 4,* 16-22.

Wodak, R. (1991b). Turning the tables: Anti-Semitic discourse in post-war Austria. *Discourse & Society, 2,* 65-84.

Wodak, R. (1991c). The Waldheim affair and anti-Semitic prejudice in Austrian public discourse. *Patterns of Prejudice, 24*(2-4), 18-33.

Wodak, R. (1996a). The genesis of rascist discourse in Austria since 1989. In Caldsas-Coulthard, C. R., & Coulthard, M. (Eds.). *Texts and practices* (pp. 107-128). London: Routledge & Kegan Paul.

Wodak, R. (1996b). *Disorders of discourse.* London: Longman.

Wodak, R. De Cillian, R., Reisigl, M. Liebhart, K., Hofstätter, K., & Karge, M. (1997). *Zur diskursiren Konstruktion der Nationalität.* Frankfurt, Germany: Suhrkamp.

Wodak, R., Menz, F., Mitten, R., & Stern, F. (1994). *Die Sprachen der Vergangenheiten: Öffentliches Gedenken in österreichischen und deutschen Medien.* Frankfurt, Germany: Suhrkamp.

Wodak, R., Nowak, P., Pelikan, J., Gruber, H., De Cillia, R., & Mitten, R. (1990). *"Wir sind alle unschuldige Täter!": Diskurshistorische Studien zum Nachkriegsantisemitismus.* Frankfurt, Germany: Suhrkamp.

4

Who Are They? The Rhetoric of Institutional Policies Toward the Indigenous Populations of Postrevolutionary Mexico

TERESA CARBÓ

The Rhetoric of President Salinas

In December 1990, President Carlos Salinas introduced a constitutional reform designed to declare Mexico a multicultural country.[1] As part of the legislative process, he authorized what is technically termed a presidential legal initiative, explaining the scope and rationale of the law to the Chamber of Deputies, whose task was to debate and ultimately to ratify the law. In the opening pages of this chapter, I want to concentrate on two paragraphs from the argumentative section of the Salinas initiative, using this text as a point of departure for a discussion of the ways in which the indigenous peoples of Mexico have been constructed in institutional discourses over the greater part of this century.[2]

The approach I take to this material is a syntactically based form of discourse analysis. For the purposes of this chapter, I base my comments mainly on an analysis of four texts from a period of 70 years. It should be pointed out, however, that these texts were chosen from a much larger archive covering debates in the Chamber of Deputies from 1920 to 1990, and all the generalizations made can be abundantly confirmed from this larger corpus (Carbó, 1996).

Text 1

Following are excerpts from the presidential legal initiative, December 7, 1990, regarding the issue of constitutional reform to declare Mexico a multicultural country. The author of the text is the Presidential Office of Carlos Salinas de Gortari. Italics are added for emphasis.

> *Indigenous peoples and communities of Mexico* live in conditions that are far from the general justice and well-being that the Mexican Revolution set as a goal and included in the constitution. The principle of equality before the law, the most essential one, does not always apply to *our indigenous co-citizens*. Such a situation is incompatible with the modernization of the country, with justice, and, finally, with the defense and the strengthening of *our sovereignty*.
>
> *Indigenous peoples and cultures* bring in the deepest roots of *our history and nationality. We are proud of them* [feminine] and *we want to take them* [feminine] *on fully*. The decisive contribution of Mexico's indigenous peoples to the greatest historical episodes that made *our nation* has repeatedly shown that cultural difference and specificity by no means weaken but rather strengthen *their commitment* to the national interest. The daily efforts of *our indigenous co-citizens* to be productive in difficult conditions; to preserve, defend, and enrich *our natural, historical and cultural heritage*; and to practice a day-to-day solidarity at a local and national level shows *their indissoluble link* to the most deeply rooted values of the people of Mexico.[3]

Many of the ideological moves and discursive forms in this passage, with its typical ways of constructing minorities, will seem familiar to students of institutional discourse (van Dijk, 1988, 1992, 1993). At the same time, there are specific tendencies in the Mexican case that require a more extensive discussion of the immediate context and situation and the histories that have contributed to the emergence of these precise forms.

This text is marked as the discourse of the president, an institutional source and voice that has a specific meaning in the Mexican context. Mexico has been characterized as a strongly presidentialist political regime (Carpizo, 1978; Meyer, 1976a, 1976b) within a system of government where one party (at present the Partido Revolucionario Institucional) has been continuously in power since 1919, with a few minor changes in structure and name. This system has ensured the formal legitimation of a single political and social regime that has reproduced itself with extraordinary efficiency over this extended period. Although the postrevolutionary Mexican political regime traces its origins from the peasant-led uprising of 1910 and bases its claims to legitimacy on this foundation, in practice a small elite group has achieved an extreme concentration of wealth and power that today underlies the so-called "Mexican miracle" as it has for the past 60 or 70 years. In fact, the authoritarian inclinations of the political practices in the country are widely known. In an extremely inegalitarian society, indigenous peoples belong largely to the peasant sector of the population, which in the long run has been the real loser in the postrevolutionary process.[4]

Within the Chamber of Deputies constituted under this system, a presidential initiative is destined to be passed in the majority of instances, and this was the case with the preceding text. This discourse, then, is not destined to persuade or convince, given that those who hear it have views that are preempted in advance. Nor, however, is it intended to be overheard by the majority of the population, given that the chamber is filled by representatives who are drawn largely from a small segment of the population, the ruling elite.

All the materials in my larger archive share this characteristic. They seem curiously without any specific political effect, yet they constitute important discursive events. The Chamber of Deputies in Mexico is a route to power, not an irrelevant discursive enclave (de la Garza, 1972). Van Dijk's (1992, p. 100) observation that parliamentary discourse typically performs the function of being discourse for the record clearly applies to the Mexican case. Salinas's speech shows another characteristic that van Dijk has also found to be typical of parliamentary discourse in general; it attempts to portray the legislators in a positive, altruistic light, emphasizing their concern for all groups within the nation (pp. 110-111). In this text, we have no less than the president himself acknowledging and lamenting the injustice and poverty suffered by the indigenous populations and celebrating those people's contribution to the culture of the nation.

This text performs the function of recording an exemplary degree of concern on behalf of the state for its "indigenous co-citizens." In the process, it constructs a past in which that care was not always shown but in which the nation was still fundamentally united. The injustices of the past should be rectified, in terms of this scheme, but there is no impediment or lack of resolve that will prevent the remedy that has been promised for the present. History is about to be healed.

In this scheme, we can see clearly an ideological motif that is insistently present throughout the institutional discourse of the post-revolutionary period. Whereas in van Dijk's (1992) materials, drawn mainly from European countries, there is a tendency for the dominant political elites to minimize the contribution of minority groups to political organization and the national culture, in the Mexican case the opposite is to be found. That is, it is regularly highlighted as in Salinas's text. Part of the explanation for this is to be found in "reality," the 500 years of magnificent history of peoples whose level of culture at the time of the conquest was in many respects superior to that of the Spanish conquerors. This heritage has proved to be too obvious to ignore and too splendid to waste as an ideological theme.

But "reality," of course, never determines ideological forms. In this case, history and culture as well as economic and social conditions provide themes and materials that are turned to specific use in the discursive and ideological forms produced by the elite. In fact, the ideological work that has to be done in the discursive construction of indigenous peoples of Mexico is to invert the celebration of their qualities and turn it into the legitimation of a ruling elite that always has been concerned with its own wealth and power at the expense of the interests and needs of indigenous peoples, among other exploited social sectors.

A basic premise in this ideological structure has been the concept of *mestizaje,* whose literal meaning is "mingling" or "mixture" but which has acquired a powerful ideological connotation as applied to the ethnic components of the national group. The term proclaims a total and irreversible mixture of European and indigenous elements in the national culture and the national identity. The function of this proclaimed unity has been to legitimate a sense in the European elite that all components of this "mestiza" culture and nation are their own inheritance. This projected unity also has justified a policy of Castilianizing contemporary indigenous peoples, incorporating them into a "common" culture that masks the continuing inequality and discrimination that have been a feature of the past 70 years, as they have been of the whole period since the conquest.

It is against this background that we must read Salinas's use of the phrase "our indigenous co-citizens," even though this precise way of constructing indigenous peoples has its own specificity, associated with the contemporary discursive forms that are different from the forms that would be found at earlier stages of institutional discourse in this century. The functions of the ideological forms are stable and continuous, but the precise discursive structures through which they are realized show a systematic pattern of development.

Salinas's words can be juxtaposed to the realities of the life of indigenous peoples in Mexico and criticized from this point of view as ideologically motivated misrepresentations, even though he incorporates precisely that countertext in his own discourse. In my understanding of the project of discourse analysis, such a practice of situating a discourse in its full social context is essential to sound method. However, in this chapter, I want to emphasize another aspect of method. In the syntactically based form of discourse analysis that I follow (Carbó, 1984; Hodge & Kress, 1993), the syntactic component of discourse is understood to carry decisive elements of the ideological force of discursive events. The form of analysis is not to be understood as independent of political, social, and historical forms of analysis. On the contrary, it requires the kind of information that I already have sketched out, organized by a thoroughgoing investigation of texts and contexts on a greater scale than I have space to describe here (see Carbó, 1996, for a fuller exposition).

Within this framework, I make the following claim for a syntactically based form of discourse analysis: The contradictions that exist between the external context of Salinas's speech and his actual words are matched by a contradiction between the implications of his words and the implications of his syntax. That is, a study of the relation between syntactic and lexical components of the text is able to identify a determining set of contradictions that may well constitute its primary ideological content and force. That is not in the least to imply that the syntactic component of the analysis recovers the "real" conditions that are being discursively worked over in lexis. On the contrary, those conditions and contexts can only be studied directly by the methods used in the political and social sciences and through various forms of historical inquiry. The play of contradictions between lexical and syntactic forms is not an opposition between ideology and reality but rather an important mode in which contradictions are managed within and by the ideological forms.[5]

In this text, as in many others, the pronominal system is a major site for the connection between ideological and syntactic forms. An account of discourse can easily be anchored by an analysis of the pronominal system.[6] Salinas's text is no exception to this constructive principle in political discourse. His use of "our" and "we" is a seemingly transparent instance that is not without subtleties and complexities.

He uses "our" six times and "we" twice in these two paragraphs. Both "them" and "their" are used twice. "Our indigenous co-citizens" occurs first in the text, and it represents the positive face of *mestizaje* ideology in its clearest form. The syntactic conjunction masks the opposition between "our" and "co-citizens," a phrase in which the noun claims equality between the speaker and his group ("our"), whereas the pronoun tacitly distinguishes the speaker's group from the Others who are "co-citizens" with them, although they are marked by the grammatical form as Others.

The first-person pronoun in its plural form (*nosotros, nos* in Spanish) is perfectly designed to perform this kind of ideological work because the same word is employed for both inclusive uses ("we" including speakers and hearers plus objects of discourse) and exclusive uses (where "we" is opposed to a "they" who are the object of the discursive act). There are some languages that systematically mark the difference between inclusive and exclusive plural pronouns, but even the European languages that do not mark the difference are well adapted to the task of blurring the boundary around "us" so that the solidarity group can seem to be broad and generous. However, the function of the distinction between inclusive and exclusive forms of the pronoun is still carried equally effectively, displaced from a marker attached to the pronominal form onto forms of the third-person plural pronoun. Formally speaking, "we" and its various forms are given boundaries that exclude Others when they occur in environments where the third-person form also occurs. In addition, there are other instances in which the context sufficiently implies an Other outside the boundaries of the "we."

I do not want to imply that the use of the third-person forms acts in any simple and consistent way to disambiguate the uses of the first-person form. On the contrary, the form is used to create a field of reference by ideologically motivated shifts and indeterminacies involving kinds of inclusion and exclusion. At one extreme in this text is "our indigenous co-citizens," where there is a maximum effect of fusion between "us" and "them," within a form that projects a "them" that is separate from but co-equal to "us." At the other end is the next occurrence of "our" in "our sovereignty," where the scope of the reference shrinks to include only the elite group through whom and on behalf of whom sovereignty is exercised.

A central instance of this form is the key phrase at the beginning of the second paragraph, "We are proud of them" (*Estamos orgullosos de ellas*), and the following clause: "we want to take them on fully" (*asumirlas*). The English translation is misleading in one crucial respect because "them" most obviously would be referring to "indigenous peoples." However, that would require a masculine pronoun. Salinas has used the feminine form, so that "them" may be "culture" or "roots" (both feminine) but cannot be "indigenous peoples."

This displacement is as surprising in Spanish as it is in English, given that the apparent focus of Salinas's legislative gaze is people, not "roots" or "cultures." However, precisely that shift is a basic move in his ideological strategy. Indigenous peoples need to be transformed into roots and/or cultures to be worthy of the grandiloquent profession of respect and veneration that is habitual to the rhetoric. Salinas's grammatical transformation of people into attributes, represented by a third-person pronoun, is the mirror image of his ideological work.

In Spanish, Salinas has the further choice of two forms of the pronoun, unassimilated (*ellas*) or assimilated (*as,* attached to the infinitive). He uses both, and the forms are arranged along a continuum from explicit and foregrounded to implicit and taken for granted. Pecheux (1978) argues that taken for grantedness is a definitional quality of ideology. In this case, both forms slip over the shift in reference so swiftly that many readers or hearers may hardly notice that it has happened. The real effect of this form can be seen if we use the full form with a human object: "We are proud of the indigenous races and cultures" and "we want to take on/over the indigenous races and cultures." The first phrase is either obviously patronizing or actually wrong. "We" are not proud of the indigenous peoples; it is only their culture that we are proud of. More strongly, the Spanish verb *asumir* (meaning something like take on, take over, or add to an inventory or account) reveals a directly acquisitive attitude that at this period, in the context of this kind of rhetoric, would strike a jarring note in the explicit form. In the form used by the speaker, the claims are made so unobtrusively that they are easier to accept and feel "naturalized."

The form has another effect that is equally important in terms of the ideological economy of the text. As has already been indicated, the scope of the first-person plural pronominal form is fixed, however loosely in specific instances, by oppositions with third-person pronominal forms. The group referred to by "we" continues indefinitely until it reaches the boundary formed by another group marked by "they." In this instance, if "them" refers to indigenous peoples, then "we" must be unequivocally exclusive. It cannot include "them," whoever else it may include. However, indigenous peoples have been removed from any determinate place in this part of the text. They no longer are marked by "they/them" as the Other to (be appropriated by) "we," but neither are they specifically included in the "we."

To put this in terms of patterns of inclusion/exclusion, we can say that the transformation that emptied "them" of specific human reference has simultaneously allowed indigenous peoples as "they" to be incorporated into the dominant "we" that is the subject of these utterances. That is, "they are we." More precisely, it is grammatically possible that "they are we." However, the converse is not true. "We" are not "they." The movement works only in the one direction; "we" can be proud, but "they" cannot be except insofar as they are incorporated into "us." More decisively, "we" can take over their qualities and contributions to national history and culture, but they cannot—again, except insofar as "they" become "us."

In this text, Salinas does not use the explicit pronoun *nosotros,* which is required in English but not in Spanish. This has the effect of shifting the pronominal group along the continuum toward the unstated and implicit pole, so that the "we" whom "they" may be part of are not referred to explicitly in the text but are incorporated into the verb ending *amos.* Thus both "we" and "they" are removed from a position of prominence in the text, but the effect of this is quite different in the two kinds of instance. "They" are removed from the text and replaced by "their culture" and other attributes. "We" (*nosotros*), on the contrary, are established so deep inside the text that such a presence is taken for granted there.

In early formulations of critical linguistics (especially in Kress & Hodge, 1979), the operation of what were called "transformations," and which would include the operations I have identified here, were seen as having a single invariable effect of mystification and concealment. The present example, among many others that could be cited, shows that there can be at least two very different effects of operations that seem to have in common a partial or complete deletion of material from the text. One is indeed suppression, a form of symbolic or semantic annihilation such as has been exercised on the indigenous peoples in Salinas's text. The other corresponds to what Barthes (1970) has termed "ex-nomination," in which elements or agents are removed from the words of the text not so as to be excluded from thought but rather to be included in the ideological substratum that is immanent in the text.

The complex operation of inclusion-exclusion that we have seen at work in this instance is a basic ideological form employed in the discursive construction of indigenous peoples in institutional discourse. It operates with a basic binary structure of "us" and "them" to position "them" strategically, together with "us" or not, in terms of a shifting definition of "us" that allows the ruling elite maximum scope to claim that they represent the whole of Mexico or any convenient part of it.

The other major recurring ideological-discursive strategy employed by Salinas in this text and by the ruling elite over this period is a division that operates on the indigenous peoples themselves. We can see the rhetorical and syntactic exponents of this strategy clearly in the organization of these two paragraphs (the first two of the presidential initiative). Both begin with the same emphatic phrase, "indigenous peoples," but the first is collocated next to "communities" and the second next to "cultures." The distinction corresponds to a basic split in how indigenous peoples are constructed in this discourse: on the one hand, as people living today in communities, suffering many difficulties and constituting social problems; on the other, as carriers of a culture that is ancient and venerable and of which "we are proud."

Van Dijk has observed how immigrant and other minorities typically are constructed as problems in the dominant institutional discourse, and this observation clearly applies to the Mexican case. The important difference in the Mexican materials is that the splendor of the archeological heritage has to be acknowledged as well, but not in a way that disrupts the construction of living indigenous peoples as demonstrating a lack of culture, a deficiency that the state, in its beneficence, will labor to remedy insofar as it can.

Rhetorically, the split is managed in this instance by devoting one paragraph to each element. There also are syntactic differences in the representation of agency between the two paragraphs, evidence of two major modes of representation. In their role as problems, indigenous peoples are represented as the subject of one intransitive verb, "live," and the object of an abstract action by the agent "principle of equality." The representation of agency in the second ideological mode is more complex. After the second sentence, in which indigenous peoples do not play an active or initiating role, it appears that they are represented in the rest of the paragraph as acting effectively in a way that has positive value.

After closer inspection, however, we have to modify this judgment. Salinas expands the scope of the history to which he is referring so that it includes potentially the whole of Mexican history, presumably postindependent Mexico as well as earlier periods. The weakness of the verb "contribute to" (which is present in a nominalized form) can be seen if one remembers all the unhappy ways in which indigenous peoples have been involved in Mexico's history. For instance, they made a "decisive contribution" to the conquest of Mexico by being so decisively conquered. It is not "indigenous peoples" but rather "cultural difference and specificity" that initially are a threat to the "national interest" (which is thus distinguished from their specific interests). This threat is canceled and replaced by a positive action.

It is true in the final sentences that living Indians and their conditions of life are reintroduced, but even here what is foregrounded is their efforts, not their accomplishments. They are represented as problems who can be commended for their efforts, but they endure and survive rather than act and create. We can generalize. In terms of this double construction, Indians of the past are celebrated for their accomplishments, not their efforts, and for their culture, not their economic or political actions.

Historical Roots of the Construction of Indigenous Peoples in Mexico

Salinas's gesture toward a consensus history of Mexico was not a gratuitous or isolated discursive move. The multiethnic composition of Mexican society has been a frequent and persistent theme in the discourse of the ruling elite, and the topic included an obligatory mention of the debt that the postrevolutionary regimes owed to the indigenous peasant sectors that had participated decisively in the armed uprising of 1910 that precipitated the revolution.

Although the revolution was taken over and managed by various powerful interests, its status as a revolution was dependent above all on its recognition of the claims for justice of the peasantry. In this sense, it was not possible to construct them simply as the helpless and passive objects of administrative benevolence. To some extent, it was necessary for any regime claiming revolutionary credentials to appear to satisfy the most strongly felt aspirations of these indigenous peoples and to acknowledge their legitimacy.

One of the most important planks in the policy of the postrevolutionary regime was radical land reform, breaking up the large estates and enshrining the rights of peasant farmers to their land in the constitution itself. These rights remained sacrosanct through successive regimes until 1992, when Salinas managed to have the constitution amended to allow peasant families to alienate their traditional lands, thus "liberating" them to enter the cash economy more directly and allowing investors to buy land for nonagricultural purposes that might prove more profitable.

The other main motif in the official recognition of indigenous peoples has been the creation of a series of government agencies designed specifically to provide the indigenous populations with specific educational institutions and general welfare programs. The documents that record this history provide a major source of data for investigating the different ways in which indigenous peoples have been constructed during the 70 years since the postrevolutionary regime stabilized in 1919. In this section, I try to identify some main phases of this ideological and discursive process, indicating the continuities that have led from 1919 to the present and the distinctive forms that have been manifested in different periods.

At the beginning of the period, the program and outcomes of the revolution were neither clear nor secure. The position of president had great power but not yet the institutional authority of the later presidentialism, and the ruling party was divided into vocal factions that debated fundamental issues of social and political policy. The election of President Lázaro Cárdenas with a radical political program in 1934 marked a new phase in the administration of indigenous peoples at the same time as it put in place an exemplary form of presidential power that later presidents built on to construct the apparently seamless fabric of Mexican political regimes that Salinas inherited on his election in 1988.

To illustrate the forms of discourse associated with these three main phases, I have chosen three texts. One comes from the debate in 1920 that established the first department that dealt with indigenous peoples, the Department for Culture and Education of the Indigenous Race (*Departamento de Educación y Cultura para la Raza Indígena [DECRI]*). The second comes from Cardenas's initiative establishing his more radical body, the Department of Indigenous Affairs (*Departamento de Asuntos Indígenas [DAI]*) in 1935. The third comes from the initiative of President Miguel Aleman, in the postwar period (1948), establishing the body that still controls the field of indigenous affairs in

Mexico along ideological lines that remain in force up to the present: the National Indigenous Institute (*Instituto Nacional é Indigenista [INI])*

In 1920, the establishment of the *DECRI* was not part of the original plan of President Obregón and his influential minister of education, Jose Vasconcelos. Vasconcelos's intention was to set up a major program of public education that would have incorporated Indians into standard schools as soon as possible, following a general curriculum whose primary aim would be Castilianizing the indigenous populations, introducing literacy in Spanish. Vasconcelos's project constructed Indians as the same as the Spanish-speaking population, lacking only the ability to speak and write in Spanish. His common education policy, filling this indigenous deficiency with Spanish content, would be the compensation of the state for the efforts of the Indians during the revolutionary period.

This legislative proposal eventually was modified to a degree that would not have happened in later periods when presidentialism managed all disagreements more effectively within the Chamber of Deputies before they emerged into the public gaze. A group from the Left within the majority party proposed that indigenous peoples warranted specific attention in their own right and that they should be represented in the new ministry through a department of their own. This model carried the day and became the model for later administrative solutions. Its basic premise was the notion of difference and deficiency, in contrast to Vasconcelos's premise of homogeneity and deficiency, although in practice the two contradictory assumptions have coexisted in government policy until the present.

Text 2

Following are excerpts from a parliamentary session, August 16, 1921, regarding the issue of creating the present national Ministry of Education (*Secretaría de Educación Pública*) and, within its administrative structure, the *DECRI*. The speaker is a member of the majority party (*Partido Liberal Constitucionalista [PLC]*). He is the spokesperson for the smaller group in the *PLC* that proposed the additional department. The president is Alvaro Obregón. Italics are added for emphasis.

> Speaker 5: I request the floor only to make some further clarifications. *Those within the [PLC]* have had in mind not only the creation of [the *DECRI*] but also the creation of a true Ministry of Culture for the Indige-

> nous Race, attending to all that concerns *this race*. . . . It is quite unbelievable that successive governments in Mexico have done nothing in this respect. . . . The *members of this party* find it surprising that a whole Executive Department exists devoted to the production of ammunition, which is not necessary because we are not in a state of war, while there is no department concerned for the welfare and culture of *five million inhabitants* who are a deadweight on *our civilization,* one of the causes of *our backwardness,* and who could instead be factors and elements instrumental in the progress of the country.[7]

This speaker comes, in fact, from the Left, and, as can be seen from this speech, he constructs himself as the revolutionary consciousness of the majority "revolutionary" party. He is concerned that the interests of what Salinas was to call "our indigenous co-citizens" are not neglected or overlooked. Those concerns, as I have said, were effective in influencing the course of the legislative process, so that they have a representative status for the period, even though this speaker and his group did not occupy the center of power within the party. They show a progressive point of view that is at the same time a dominant one in the party and the ruling elite. Its structures and its limits, then, provide us with the first outline of the basic discursive forms at play.

There are two syntactic features to which I want to draw attention for purposes of this discussion. The first is his use of the first-person pronominal form, where we can see a significant contrast to Salinas's usage. In this passage, he uses "we" only once and "our" twice ("our civilization" and "our backwardness"). On these two occasions, the third-person form is used with indeterminate boundaries and as an inclusive form. It does not specifically include indigenous peoples but does not exclude them either.

This speaker does, in fact, have an exclusive form of reference to his own group; however, this is realized not by the first-person pronominal group but by a distinctive use of third-person forms: "those within the *PLC*" (by which he means himself and his group) and "the members of this party" (ostensibly a more inclusive "we," referring to all members of his party, but in fact again referring only to his dissident group). That is, he uses a form of words that functions as an exclusive first-person plural to identify his own group and exclude all others in the majority party and in the political elite, but the use of the simplest form available in the grammar, "we," seemingly is not allowable for him to use in this context. Tactically, we may suppose that if he had identified the integrity and difference of his faction in this debate, then it would have been divisive and counterproductive. This indeed is the normal tendency of the exclusive use of this pronominal form.

Although his use of the first-person plural form is less insistent than is that of Salinas, this is largely because he is foregrounding the complex internal structures of the ruling group including his own group's position within it. "We" in his text is still the undivided nation that is held back by the "five million inhabitants" who are a "cause of our backwardness," not a part of the "us" who are backward. A deficiency that is a problem to the nation is attributed to this large population, as is also the case in Salinas's initiative.

A second syntactic feature in this text is the use of singular forms. The object of the legislation is "the indigenous race," and this speaker repeats the singular form that is part of the title of the proposed (and passed) department. Salinas, by contrast, used plural forms for the peoples, cultures, and communities, grammatically recognizing the differences that indigenous groups and communities themselves insist on as important.

The crucial singularity here is the unity of "race," which lumps together all the differences of the Other into a single grand category, founded on the essentialist basis of racial identity.[8] It hardly needs pointing out that this is the ultimate premise of racism. This racist premise is built into the title of the department that was introduced to promote a more positive response to the needs of indigenous peoples. The revolutionary consciousness at this time was not as indifferent to these needs as was the mainstream of the party, but it still was built around a contradiction, and the policies made on behalf of indigenous peoples hardly recognized them as part of civil society. Salinas's rhetoric is more sophisticated, but in many respects it is built around the same contradiction.

The *DECRI* established in 1920 a department whose primary concern was with education, anticipating the split between material and cultural interests that still is present in Salinas's discourse. The election of Cárdenas as president in 1934 meant a decisive shift in policy in this area. The creation of a new department, the *DAI,* was heralded in advance as a project that was strongly backed by Cardenas and implemented with extraordinary speed. In his introduction to this initiative, Cárdenas wrote the following.

Text 3

Following are excerpts from a presidential legal initiative, December 27, 1935, regarding the issue of creating the former Department of Indigenous Affairs. The author of the project and text is the president, Lázaro Cárdenas. Italics are added for emphasis.

> The direct knowledge possessed by *the Executive Office I hold at present* concerning the harsh conditions of life of the vast majority of *our indigenous population,* who are sunk in the worst poverty and in many cases form isolated groups completely separate from the rest of the country, *has made me search* with dedication for the most effective means whereby governmental and administrative action of the revolutionary government may be suitably focussed and enhanced so as to be translated into genuine improvement for *the autochthonous races.* Before I assumed charge of the Executive Office, I indicated the desirability of creating a Department of Indigenous Affairs, so that it could attend directly and exclusively to such important issues.[9]

In this text, Cárdenas uses "our" once in the same patronizing manner as used by Salinas. However, what is distinctive here is his extensive use of the first-person singular; "I" occurs three times in this short text (plus once in the form "me"). Whereas Speaker 5 in the previous text was unable to identify himself and his group directly, the president is able to speak as an individual from this privileged space.

But Cárdenas is, of course, constructing a discursive identity here; he is not speaking as an ordinary individual. The effort that has been required in the process is visible in this text; the locution "the direct knowledge possessed by the Executive Office that I hold" is strained in Spanish, imputing knowledge to the Presidential Office while referring to the private citizen who had this knowledge before he acceded to the office. The point of the claim can be understood in the light of knowledge that is not contained in this text. Cardenas claimed Indian as well as Spanish forebears, although his immediate origins were far removed from peasant life. Through this claim to possess *mestizo* identity, Cárdenas was able to represent himself as the savior and champion of indigenous peoples of Mexico. The president himself was thus able to focus the diversity of the nation in his own personal history. It was a powerful way in which to mobilize the ideology of *mestizaje* that Salinas, in his own way, also used.

Cárdenas's proposal was for a strong Department of Indigenous Affairs, a proposal that resolved the split between cultural life as opposed to economic and social conditions that is the normal construction of indigenous peoples in Mexico over this period. His text foregrounds the deficiencies of contemporary indigenous peoples in more stark terms than does Salinas or the proposer of the *DECRI.* In fact, there is a total polarization here between a presidential "I," who has concentrated in himself an almost godlike certainty of knowledge and power, and pluralistic Indian populations that not only live in degraded conditions but are isolated from each other and from the rest of Mexican life, unable to participate as knowing actors in the general life of the nation.

Cárdenas was a radical president who achieved more reforms on behalf of indigenous peoples than Salinas has attempted. Thus his negative construction of their state of life can be seen as a necessary opening move in his legislative project. Nonetheless, it is the case that the precondition for this reformist stance is to construct the Indian populations as helpless victims whose powerlessness is the other face of his pretensions to absolute power. That is, their powerlessness is a function of his own power, and vice versa. The Mexican institution of presidentialism, with its concentration of power in the center (located in the hands of the president and his immediate circle), can be seen to require the construction of a population that is passive, marginal, suffering greatly, and unable to help itself. In Mexico, this role has been recurrently (although not exclusively) filled by indigenous peoples. Although Cárdenas's political program was to the left of that of Salinas, it was Cárdenas who articulated most clearly the construction of indigenous peoples as helpless victims that underlay all later legislative proposals.

The Modern System of Surveillance

The body that currently presides over this area is the National Indigenous Institute (*INI*), founded under the presidency of Miguel Alemán during the 1940s according to ideological principles that still have force. My final text comes from the presidential preamble to the legal initiative that established this body.

Text 4

Following are excerpts from the presidential legal initiative, September 24, 1948, regarding the issue of creating the present *INI.* The author of the text is the Presidential Office of Miguel Alemán. Italics are added for emphasis.

> *The Executive Office I hold* at present, by virtue of the powers assigned to it by Section 1 of Article 71 of the Political Constitution of the Republic, and considering:
>
> *First.* That there exists in the country a number of *indigenous groups,* more than *four million people,* who still in varying degrees show *specific cultural traits that give them a peculiar physiognomy, different from* that of the Mexican peasant in general;
>
> *Second.* That *these indigenous groups,* organized in communities, *need special study* so that they may receive more attention than has been devoted to them until now;
>
> *Third.* That in the culture of these indigenous groups there remain characteristics that can be used to benefit the national culture, since they will continue to give it the physiognomy that distinguishes it from other countries in Latin America and the world in general.[10]

We may note in passing the different way in which Alemán constructs his identity as president. This is consistent with the fact that this text was issued from the Presidential Office but is not marked in any way as authored by Alemán himself. This project reverses the tendency introduced by Cárdenas, who emphasized material conditions and aimed at a unified approach. There is no invocation of the revolution and no pretense that this is in any way a radical project. Alemán historically is closer to the actual revolution than is Salinas, but this does not show in his text. The focus now is on indigenous culture as an object of knowledge. The text uses the curious word "physiognomy," which makes these cultural characteristics seem like physical marks of racial identity, not under the conscious control of these people or something that they might be expected to understand.

In practice, the establishment of the *INI* was intended to lend support to the disciplines of anthropology and archeology as sciences whose task was to put the surveillance of indigenous populations on a firmer basis. This "special study" is presented as something that these people "need," and it replaces other material needs that Salinas and Cárdenas identified. In fact, it represents the other pole in the binary structure that underlies all these proposals, the split between cultural forms that are celebrated (and appropriated) and economic and social conditions that are regretted (and sometimes ameliorated).

In Alemán's text, the impulse to cultural appropriation is especially clear. What is different about Mexico's indigenous cultures is what gives "them" value as a commodity on the world market. The "need" that will be served by special study is not hard to see; it is the need to market aboriginality better than has been done before. This includes a double dimension: on the one side, to improve the country's international image through the ideological usage of cultural difference and of the institutional attention that is devoted on the part of the state to the living carriers of that interesting specificity; on the other, to incorporate ample masses of the productive population into the national economy and the modern development of the country. The *INI* has from 1948 to the present dutifully served the goals that were initially established for it, creating schools in indigenous areas, introducing drinking water and roads to isolated communities, and stabilizing a repertoire of discursive uses of the indigenous populations.

Conclusions

The four texts I have used can do no more than indicate the range of positions and the complex developments revealed by the full corpus covering the whole period. Nonetheless, there are a number of points to emphasize about the Mexican example in relation to a more global study of the construction of minorities in institutional discourse. First, over the period of 70 years, the dominant elite constructs the indigenous peoples in a variety of ways that represent different methods of mediating the same contradictory set of relationships between the ruling group and these exploited peoples. Culture and economics, present and past, and celebration and deficiency are regularly split from one another, and one aspect or the other is emphasized within this common ideological scheme.

A contemporary text such as that produced by Salinas offers a new arrangement of the given elements but the underlying structures remain the same. Indigenous peoples are presented as a scandal *and* a bedrock in the construction of national identity by the elite. More than is the case in most European examples, this gives rise to an inflated rhetoric in which the principles of *indigenismo* and *mestizaje* are central elements in a discursive practice that is systematically misleading about the material conditions of life of indigenous peoples in Mexico. In such a situation, there is a need for the kind of discourse analysis that I have used, one that attempts to identify contradictions and structural continuities in a wide range of texts.

Notes

1. It is worth noting that the constitutional amendment did not declare Mexico a multilingual country, regardless of the fact that nearly 60 different Amerindian languages are spoken regularly. The presidential initiative reduced the change to the vanishing frontier of "cultural" phenomena. Nonetheless, an official training program for legal interpreters is on the way for the different national ethnic groups. It is a long way, to be sure, to a situation of the sort implied in Berk-Seligson's (1990) description of court interpreters' exercise of power.

2. The title of this chapter deliberately echoes a formulation by van Dijk (1988) on ethnic minorities. I particularly thank van Dijk for his suggestions concerning a repertoire of typical ways in which to construct the Mexican indigenous peoples along time. Bob Hodge has been helpful in the difficult process of writing; he not only dealt with (most of) my syntactic peculiarities but also discussed, to my great benefit, substantial parts of the argument.

3. The untranslated Text 1 follows:

> Los pueblos y las comunidades indígenas de México viven en condiciones distantes de la equidad y el bienestar que la revolución mexicana se propuso y elevó como postulado constitucional. La igualdad ante la ley, el principio essencial e indiscutible de nuestra convivencia, no siempre se cumple frente a nuestros compatriotas indígenas. Esa situación es incompatible con la modernización del país, con la justicia y, finalmente, con la defensa y el fortalecimiento de nuestra soberanía.
>
> Los pueblos y las culturas indígenas aportan las raíces más profundas de nuestra historia y nacionalidad. Estamos orgullosos de ellas y queremos asumirlas con plenitud. La contribución decisiva de los indígenas mexicanos a las grandes gestas históricas, constitutivas de la Nación, ha mostrado reiteradamente que la diferencia y la especificidad cultural, lejos de diluir, fortalece su compromiso con los intereses nacionales. El cotidiano sacrificio de nuestros compatriotas indígenas para producir en condiciones adversas, para preservar, defender y enriquecer nuestro patrimonio natural, histórico y cultural, y para ejercer la solidaridad comunitaria y con el país, expresa hoy su indisoluble vínculo con los valores más arraigados del pueblo de México.

4. For a comprehensive review of Mexican politics during the past 70 years, see Meyer (1976a, 1976b). For a clear assessment of recent economic changes that have accentuated the inegalitarian profile of the system, see Lustig (1992). For an overall critical view of official programs for bilingual-bicultural education, see Coronado (1992).

5. The concept of ideological complexes developed by Hodge and Kress (1988, p. 5) expresses quite well the function and usefulness of certain sets of contradictions for the practice of domination, as will be observed in our case.

6. The field of personal pronouns, interesting in itself as an intriguing and complex linguistic category, has proved most productive at the level of textual and discursive phenomena. Revealing analyses of different sorts can be seen in Carbó (1984, pp. 26-30), Kress and Hodge (1979), Leith and Myerson (1989), the journal *Mots* (1985), Seidel (1975), and Wilson (1990, pp. 45-76). For a fuller discussion of the methodological interest of this and other syntactic categories, see Carbó (1996).

7. The untranslated Text 2 follows:

> Pido la palabra: Unicamente para hacer mas aclaraciones. En el seno del Partido Liberal Constitucionalista no solamente se trató del DECRI, sino de la futura creación de un verdadero Ministerio de cultura de la raza indígena, en todo lo que se refiere a esta raza. . . . Parece increíble que los sucesivos gobiernos en México no han hecho nada a este respecto. . . . Llama la atención a los miembros de este partido que exista un departamento enteramente dedicado a la fabricación de municiones, que no se necesitan puesto que no estamos en estado de guerra, y que, sin embargo, no exista un departamento para el fomento y cultura de cinco millones de habitantes que son un lastre para nuestra civilización, una de las causas de nuestro atraso, y que serían factores y elementos de progreso para el país.

8. A striking example of an almost blatant racist approach toward the national indigenous peoples occurred during World War II under the banner of a democratic, egalitarian, and exemplary homage rendered to "them" by the Chamber of Deputies. See Carbó (1987).

9. The untranslated Text 3 follows:

> El conocimiento directo que tiene el Ejecutivo de mi cargo, de las duras condiciones de vida en que se encuentra una buena parte de nuestra población indígena, sumida en la mayor pobreza y en muchos casos formando grupos aislados por completo del resto del país, me ha hecho buscar con ahinco los medios mas eficaces para que la acción gubernamental y administrativa del gobierno revolucionario, intensificándose y afocándose convenientemente, se traduzca en un mejoramiento efectivo de las razas autóctonas. Desde antes de hacerme cargo del Poder Ejecutivo anuncié la conveniencia de constituir un Departamento de Asuntos Indígenas, con la mira de encargarlo directa y exclusivamente de la atención de tan importantes cuestiones.

10. The untranslated Text 4 follows:

> El Ejecutivo de mi cargo, con fundamento en lo que previene la fracción I del artículo 71 de la Constitución Política de la República y considerando:
>
> *Primero.* Que existen en el país grupos indígenas que suman más de cuatro millones de personas que en mayor o menor grado participan todavía de restos culturales que les dan una fisonomía propia, distinta a la del campesinado mexicano;
>
> *Segundo.* Que estos grupos indígenas, organizados en comunidades, requieren un estudio especial para darles mayor atención de la que han recibido hasta ahora;

Tercero. Que en la cultura de estos grupos indígenas se conservan características que pueden ser utilizadas en favor de la cultura nacional, ya que continuarán dándole la fisonomía que la distingue de los demas pueblos de América y del mundo.

References

Barthes, R. (1970). *Mythologies.* Paris: Editions du Seuil.

Berk-Seligson, S. (1990). Bilingual court proceedings: The role of the court interpreter. In J. Levi & A. Walker (Eds.), *Language in the judicial process* (pp. 155-201). New York: Plenum.

Carbó, T. (1984). *Discurso político: Lectura y análisis.* Mexico City: CIESAS.

Carbó, T. (1987). Identité et différence dans le discours parlementaire Mexicain. *Langage et Société, 39,* 31-44.

Carbó, T. (1993). *El discurso parlamentario mexicano entre 1920 y 1950: Un estudio de caso en metodología de análisis de discurso.* Ciesas & El Colegio de México, Mexico City.

Carpizo, J. (1978). *El presidencialismo mexicano.* Mexico: Siglo XXI Editores.

Coronado, S. (1992). Educación bilingue en México: Propósitos y realidades. *International Journal of the Sociology of Language, 96,* 53-70.

de la Garza, R. (1972). *The Mexican Chamber of Deputies and the Mexican political system.* Ph.D. thesis, University of Arizona.

Hodge, R., & Kress, G. (1988). *Social semiotics.* Cambridge, England: Polity.

Hodge, R., & Kress, G. (1993). *Language as ideology* (Rev. ed.). London: Routledge & Kegan Paul.

Kress, G., & Hodge, R. (1979). *Language as ideology.* London: Routledge & Kegan Paul.

Leith, D., & Myerson, G. (1989). *The power of address.* London: Routledge & Kegan Paul.

Lustig, N. (1992). *Mexico: The remaking of an economy.* Washington, DC: Brookings Institution.

Meyer, L. (1976a). El primer tramo del camino. In *Historia general de México* (Vol. 4, pp. 227-249). México City: El Colegio de México.

Meyer, L. (1976b). La encrucijada. In *Historia general de México* (Vol. 4, pp. 251-283). México City: El Colegio de México.

Mots. (1985). (Ordinateurs/Textes/ Sociétés). Le 'nous' politique [Special issue] No. 10, March 1985, Annie Geffray & Pierre Lafon. Paris: Presses de la Fondation Nationale des Sciences Politiques.

Pecheux, M. (1978). *Hacia el análisis automático del discurso.* Madrid, Spain: Gredos.

Seidel, G. (1975). Ambiguity in political discourse. In M. Block (Ed.), *Political language and oratory in traditional society* (pp. 205-231). New York: Academic Press.

van Dijk, T. (1988). How they hit the headlines: Ethnic minorities in the press. In G. Smitherman-Donaldson & T. van Dijk (Eds.), *Discourse and discrimination* (pp. 221-262). Detroit, MI: Wayne State University Press.

van Dijk, T. (1992). Discourse and the denial of racism. *Discourse & Society, 3,* 87-118.

van Dijk, T. (1993, May). *Political discourse and racism: Describing Others in Western parliaments.* Paper prepared for the International Conference on "Others" in Discourse, Toronto.

Wilson, J. (1990). *Politically speaking.* Oxford, England: Basil Blackwell.

5

Discourses of Exclusion: The Irish Press and the Travelling People

JANE HELLEINER
BOHDAN SZUCHEWYCZ

Within critical discourse studies, much attention has been focused on the role of the mass media in the construction and reproduction of dominant ideologies of sexism, classism, and racism. The ideological characteristics of newspaper discourse have been particularly well documented (e.g., Fowler, 1991; Kress & Hodge, 1979; Trew, 1979a, 1979b). In a number of publications, van Dijk (1987, 1991, 1992, 1993) has focused specifically on the central role of the press in the reproduction and communication of racism in Western capitalist democracies.

In this chapter, we extend van Dijk's discussion to the Republic of Ireland.[1] The application may at first be surprising because of a widely shared perception of the republic as culturally homogeneous and free of racism. Although the concepts of ethnicity and racism frequently are employed in discussions of the sectarian division in Northern Ireland (Brewer, 1992), they rarely are used in the South. An exception is found in discussions of the "Travelling people." Although the Travelling people (also referred to as "tinkers" or "itinerants") were explicitly denied "ethnic" status during the 1960s (Commission on Itinerancy, 1963, p. 37), they have since been described by some scholars (Gmelch & Gmelch, 1976) and increasingly by Travellers themselves and their advocates as an "ethnic group" (Dublin Travellers Education and De-

AUTHORS' NOTE: Articles cited from the *Galway Observer* are used by permission of the publisher. Articles cited from *The Connacht Sentinel, The Connacht Tribune* and *The City Tribune* are used by permission of The Connacht Tribune Ltd.

British spelling was maintained for the word *traveller* and related phrases.

velopment Group [DTEDG], 1992). The "ethnicization" of Travellers has been accompanied by the recognition of widespread anti-Traveller racism. For example, antihatred legislation introduced in the Irish Parliament during the late 1980s specifically named the Travellers as a category of the population in need of protection (Helleiner, 1995a). In this chapter, critical discourse analysis provides insight into the processes through which anti-Traveller racism becomes reproduced through the Irish press. This in turn contributes to the larger project of incorporating Ireland into the literature on comparative racism.

Irish Racism: The Travelling People

The relative lack of ethnic divisions or racism within independent Ireland has been variously attributed to a reaction against racialized colonial subordination, the removal of the Protestant minority from the southern state through partition, or a semiperipheral economy that has yielded a pattern of emigration rather than immigration (Brown, 1981, pp. 17-18; Lee, 1989, pp. 10, 77; van Dijk, 1993, p. 63). This "imagined community" (Anderson, 1983) of Ireland as a homogeneous state recently has been challenged by studies emphasizing the diversity and inequalities associated with gender, region, religion, and class (e.g., Curtin, Jackson, & O'Connor, 1987; Curtin & Wilson, 1989; Silverman & Gulliver, 1992). However, ethnicity and racism remain largely unexplored. In the case of the Travelling people, recognition of ethnicity and the experience of racism raise interesting issues for the comparative literature in part because of their putative origins.

Outsiders' constructions of Traveller origins can be traced back to the late 19th century, when they emerged in the context of scholarly debates over the origin of Gypsies. At that time, linguistic evidence was used to assert that the Irish tinkers were linked to ancient Ireland and therefore were distinct from the "true Gypsies" believed to have originated in India (Helleiner, 1995b).

Another account of Traveller origins that has become dominant since the 1950s portrays them as having a more recent genesis as descendants of Irish peasants forced into landlessness and mobility as a result of the famines and evictions suffered during the centuries of British domination. During the 1980s and early 1990s, however, Travellers and their advocates have reasserted the earlier claim to a much deeper history in Ireland (DTEDG, 1992).

The point of interest here is that Travelling people are not constructed as immigrants or as an encapsulated indigenous minority; rather, they are racialized as Irish and distinguished from other European Gypsies and Travellers on this basis. One result is that, within Ireland itself, Travellers have only rarely been differentiated from other Irish on the basis of signified phenotypical or genotypical characteristics (Miles, 1989, p. 75). In contrast to past and present discussions about Gypsies in Britain (see Acton, 1974; Mayall, 1988; Okely, 1983), notions of race and blood have remained minor themes in Traveller-related discourse within Ireland.

Travellers more frequently have been constituted as a category distinct from other Irish on the basis of a (negatively evaluated) cluster of class and/or cultural features including itinerancy, trailer living, specific occupations, and poverty. More significantly, they also are distinguished on the basis of putative endogamy and descent, which allows for the attribution of "naturalized" difference despite allegedly common origins with other Irish.

Although it is important to recognize the specificity of Traveller-related discourse in Ireland, including the absence of racialization, it also is necessary to recognize this discourse as racism. In making this argument, we are following not only recent discussions of discrimination against Travellers in Ireland that have employed the concept (DTEDG, 1992) but also those that reject the utility of maintaining a distinction between categories and ideologies of dominance based on signified physical/biological features (race, racism) and those based on signified cultural features (ethnicity, ethnicism) (e.g., van Dijk, 1993, pp. 22-23). One recent commentator argues that such a distinction actually serves to "naturalize race" by distinguishing it from "culture" (Wade, 1993). As the following discussion reveals, analyses of anti-Traveller discourses in Ireland share similarities and benefit from comparisons with other racist discourses.

Although the focus in this chapter is on discourse, it is important to note that this is integrally linked to numerous "exclusionary practices" (Miles, 1989, p. 77) whose cumulative effects on Travellers include disproportionate levels of poverty, unemployment, low life expectancy, and poor living and health conditions relative to those of the Irish population as a whole (Barry & Daly, 1988; Rottman, Tussing, & Wiley, 1986; Travelling People Review Body, 1983).

Since the mid-1960s, Travellers have been the targets of a state settlement program aimed at eliminating their way of life through the provision of accommodation, education, and employment. In the course of the settlement program, Travellers have been subjected to ongoing harassment and evictions from encampments, denial of basic rights, and differential treatment and segregation in the provision of social services (e.g., social welfare, education, accommodation). In addition to exclusionary practices on the part of the state, Travellers are the victims of routine discrimination in labor markets and the service sector (e.g., they are regularly denied service in pubs, cinemas, and shops) as well as unsanctioned (i.e., illegal) attacks on their camps (DTEDG, 1992).

Travelling People and the Press

The concern of this chapter is to demonstrate the role of the press in the reproduction and legitimization of such discriminatory practices in Ireland. Van Dijk has argued that the media warrant particular attention from those interested in analyzing the reproduction of racism because they constitute the most influential of several elite discourses (including scholarly and state discourses) when it comes to shaping and changing social perceptions. The production of news is largely accomplished by members of dominant groups and reflects their interests; moreover, other elite discourses are widely communicated only after being filtered through media (van Dijk, 1993, p. 243). In the case of Ireland, a focus on elite discourse is important because discrimination and antagonism toward Travellers is commonly attributed to an unenlightened public or, more specifically, to the working class. By contrast, our analysis aims to demonstrate how the powerful discourses of the press contribute to the creation of an ideological context that legitimates coercive state policies, everyday discriminatory practices, and ultimately, violence against Travellers.

The larger database on which this chapter is grounded consists of more than 2,000 articles including references to Travellers gathered from the Galway City press for the period covering 1922 to the end of the fieldwork period in 1987.[2] Galway City has had a high national profile in the area of Traveller-state relations. Besides being the scene of several well-publicized confrontations between Travellers and non-Travellers, it is the location of a variety of projects geared toward Traveller settlement including a special group housing project and two training centers. Since 1987, the city also has provided a limited number of hardstands (i.e., serviced campsites).

The database of articles from the local Galway press includes news reports, reports of court cases, commentaries, letters to the editor, and editorials. Over the course of the time period surveyed, the frequency of press reporting on Travellers varied greatly, as did the types and content of press reports. The reportage reveals both continuity and change in portrayals of Travellers as a negatively defined Other, suggesting the need to situate analyses of exclusionary discourses within a wider context of historically specific political and economic relations. Only a small portion of this material is referred to here to provide a historical context for the analysis of a particular editorial from 1986.

Presettlement Discourse of Exclusion

Throughout the first half of the 20th century, there were infrequent but gradually increasing references in the Galway City press to a rather amorphous population referred to by a diversity of terms including tinkers, Gypsies, nomads, itinerants, wandering tribes, and vagrants. The press and other archival sources also reveal that this population was increasingly identified as a threat to private property, public health, and the general economy of the city and region by the local propertied classes (i.e., landowners, private homeowners, Chamber of Commerce), who lobbied local government to take greater measures against its Traveller camps and economic activities. The local government and judicial system responded to such pressure by harassing, fining, and imprisoning Travellers in an effort to control and exclude them from the jurisdiction. The press of this period largely reproduced and supported elite statements that associated Travellers with images of dirt, danger, disease, criminality, and an outsider status while excluding Traveller (or working-class) perspectives (Helleiner, 1993).

During the 1950s, press reports began to refer to a more clearly labeled population of tinkers and itinerants who were described as constituting a social problem for the city and for the nation as a whole. The frequency of reporting on the "itinerant problem" increased dramatically as the local elite began to demand that the national government provide them with the legislative means to control Travellers better. The increased pressures coincided with local and national initiatives on the part of the state to encourage "modernization" through foreign-financed industrialization. A government-sponsored Commission on Itinerancy, whose report was published in 1963, advocated a wide-ranging national settlement program as the solution to the "itinerant problem." Central to the new settlement program was the argument that the settlement of itinerants was a necessary part of the larger project of national economic and social development. New discourses of inclusion were disseminated as settlement was described as a means to effect the "absorption" and "integration" of Travellers into the "settled community" (Commission on Itinerancy, 1963).

Settlement Discourse in Galway City

In Galway City, there was increasing concern on the part of the city elite with controlling the Travellers, whose camps lay in the path of commercial and industrial expansion and whose presence was felt to be a hindrance to a city intent on attracting economic investment (Helleiner, 1993). Press reports of source discourse reveal how settlement was increasingly accepted by politicians and other leaders as a solution to the Traveller problem. Settlement advocates promoted settlement through the invocation of religious and nationalist references. For example, the Travellers were compared with the "holy itinerant family" ("The Attack on Camp," 1968, p. 10) that had found "no room at the inn" ("No Room, " 1967, p. 3); detractors were reminded that the Travellers "may have been descendants of our own kith and kin who were evicted during the famine" ("For the itinerant," *Connacht Tribune,* January 12, 1968, p. 10)

Whereas press reports incorporated the new discourses of inclusion, earlier images of dirt, danger, and criminality also were reproduced in discussions of settlement. The alleged degradation of Traveller life, for example, was constantly cited in support of the argument that settlement was in the best interests of both Travellers and the nation as a whole. At the same time, the often reported concern that local provision of accommodation and other services would lead to an "influx" or "invasion" of Travellers from other parts of the country depended on and reinforced negative constructions of Travellers. Thus settlement discourse promoted absorption and integration through settlement while simultaneously excluding Travellers by defining them as outside the "settled community."

A striking example of this new discourse of settlement may be found in a 1967 editorial marking Itinerant Settlement Week in Galway City. The editorial expressed a plea for public sympathy and charity toward Travellers and urged public support for the settlement efforts to facilitate the "ultimate aim of integrating the itinerants into full community life"

("On the Roadside," 1967). Within this context of a plea for sympathy, however, Traveller life and behavior were characterized as follows:

> Many of their roadside camps and the camp surroundings are filthy; they are an annoyance in the towns as beggars, and farmers will say they are a greater nuisance in the country because of deliberate trespass in fields and gardens and damage to crops and because of a feeling of unease that household clothes put out to dry on a line may disappear when they are about. It is probable that the sweeping generalizations are true in a great many instances—undoubtedly many roadside camps are sickeningly filthy and undoubtedly the begging habit is widespread and annoying. Understandably people do not want to see them about. (p. 10)

Furthermore, the editorial argued that sympathy for Travellers would be forthcoming once people realized that:

> the wretched families among the itinerants are not people who rejected the normal pattern of community life. . . . They were born and reared to the wretched life they lead. . . . They never had a chance to sample the normal pattern of living and to develop to human dignity.

In characterizing Travellers, for example, as having failed to develop human dignity and as having "wretched" and abnormal lives, the dominant settlement discourse provided ideological support not only for assimilation through settlement but also for the continuation of discrimination and violence against Travellers. The role of the press in providing impetus to continuing exclusionary ideologies and actions became most evident within the context of disputes over Traveller settlement between and within political jurisdictions.

As the settlement program began to be implemented within Galway City, the press supported the program through its portrayal of the Traveller way of life as a problem that required eradication. At the same time, however, it also reproduced the regularly articulated argument that services to Travellers should be minimized for fear of prompting an "influx" to the city. The undesirable nature of Travellers suggested by this argument also legitimized the more active harassment of Traveller encampments aimed at forcing Travellers out of the city.

Such exclusionary actions were reproduced within the city as members of the "settled community" echoed and reproduced the press images of dirt, danger, criminality, and economic threat in their efforts to block or restrict the provision of accommodation to Travelling people in their respective neighborhoods. In the class-stratified urban political economy of Galway City, the implementation of the Traveller settlement program was met with class and neighborhood-based resistance. For example, initial plans to provide serviced camps faltered in the face of outcry from landowners, and early attempts to house Travellers in public housing estates encountered a series of organized protests by tenants (Helleiner, 1993). The press, although sometimes critical of such resistance, uncritically reproduced allegations regarding the nature of Travellers and Traveller life, thereby legitimizing such actions on the part of tenants and residents.

Whereas press reports of the 1960s and much of the 1970s were explicit in their portrayal of the Travellers and the Travelling way of life as problematic, during the 1980s overtly racist discourses were increasingly replaced by more sophisticated discourses of exclusion. The shift in elite discourse from explicit to implicit exclusion can be seen clearly in press editorials. As van Dijk (1993) suggests, editorials provide particularly useful texts for critical discourse analysis:

> because they formulate most explicitly the position of the press in the white elite management of ethnic affairs . . . [and although] news reports may partly be based on source discourse . . . this is not the case with editorials [whose] content and formulation are wholly controlled by the editors themselves. (p. 266)

To demonstrate the persistence of racism in the Irish press, we examine editorials that comment on the more dramatic acts of violence against Travellers (and, therefore, presumably those most likely to be censured)—vigilante attacks on Traveller camps.

Vigilante Attacks

Galway City has been the scene of several attacks on Traveller camps. One of these in 1969 prompted an editorial that, although ostensibly criticizing this vigilante action, also denied that this was an example of racist action and proceeded to attribute the blame to the Travellers themselves:

> This was not the case . . . of a harmless unoffending people being attacked. The itinerants bring filth wherever they go; they bring fear to many people,

> and they cause damage to the property of others. . . . They spread fear, damage, and dirt. And yet they deserve a sympathy they did not get in Rahoon [location of the attack]. ("The Itinerant," 1969, p. 10)

The reproduction of racism is transparent in the editorial, repeating as it does the typical associations of Travellers with dirt and criminality. Stating that "it is recognized that the adults cannot be integrated into a [*sic*] ordinary life of the community," the editorial argued that Traveller children cannot be brought "into ordered ways of living" if "the parents are to be molested by people of the locality where they are settled" (p. 10). Travellers are explicitly excluded from the dominant community, and their way of life is characterized as something from which their (innocent) children must be "rescued."

Whereas the text of the 1969 editorial combines condemnation and justification of the attack in a fairly obvious manner, the articulation of the two becomes much more sophisticated in editorials that follow a similar attack on a Traveller camp in 1986. In August of that year, a large group of armed local residents attacked a Traveller encampment, dragging trailers out of a field and onto the roadside. The Travellers had entered the field following a court case in which they lost the right to camp in an area where Travellers had been camped for more than two decades. In the absence of any official campsites within the city or county, these Traveller families had asked that the city provide an alternative place to park their trailers. The decision to move into the field had followed informal assurances by a city official that they would not be disturbed if they did so. The resulting attack, carried out at night, received a great deal of national media attention. The attack was the subject of three editorials in the local press, which provided their readers with explanations and interpretations of the event and defined its significance. The remainder of the chapter focuses on the first published, and most substantial, of these editorials (published in the *Connacht Sentinel* [see Appendix]), with supporting evidence drawn from the other two (published in the *Galway Advertiser* and the *Galway Observer*).

Editorial Analysis

The editorial "Consultation Not Confrontation" (1986, p. 4) in the *Connacht Sentinel* reveals a number of lexical, syntactic, and semantic strategies for dealing with the attack and its perpetrators. These include

(a) terms and syntactic patterns used to refer to and characterize the event itself and the larger context within which it is interpreted; (b) terms used to identify and characterize the participants and their roles in the event; and (c) semantic strategies of mitigation, reversal (i.e., blaming the victims), and apparent concession used in the assignment of responsibility. As will become clear, the editorial is critical of the event and through these strategies shifts the ultimate responsibility for the violence from its actual perpetrators (i.e., local residents) to the city officials' handling of the situation and ultimately to the Travellers themselves. Mitigating information also is provided for the behavior of both of these groups; however, its effect, as we will see, reinforces the exclusion of Travellers through what van Dijk terms "negative other-presentation," and, although it criticizes the city's handling of the situation, it constructs an overall positive presentation of the city, its officials, and its residents.

The title itself, "Consultation Not Confrontation," provides a catchy summary of the editorial's attitude toward the attack as well as a prescription for future action regarding the settlement of Travellers. It also is very revealing of the editorial's attitude toward the participants and their roles in the events. In spite of the apparent symmetry implied by contrast (*X* not *Y*) and parallel structure (both *X* and *Y* are nominalizations and phonetically similar), the actual participants in these processes of consultation and confrontation are not the same. Consultation, according to the editorial, must continue to take place between the city officials and residents; indeed, the editorial makes reference to "hours of talks in other difficult situations *regarding the itinerants*" (emphasis added). Travellers, it seems, need not, cannot, or should not take part in this process. The confrontation to which the editorial refers involved local residents "confronting" the Traveller families.

Defining the Context

A primary function of editorials is to interpret and articulate the significance of specific events for their readers (Fowler, 1991; van Dijk, 1993). The editorial opens with the following statement:

1. The tragedy of the most recent incidents surrounding the five traveller families moving on to land . . . is that many months, or even years, of patient effort to resolve the problem have been endangered.

It closes with the following statement:

2. It is to be hoped that last week's incidents and the ongoing situation do not have a long-term detrimental effect on settlement plans, for the city is building up for itself a dangerous and major social problem if it does not produce answers to Irish people living on the sides of the roads.

These statements reveal a number of significant features that are discussed subsequently; however, the present focus is on their contextualizing function.

Both statements situate the event in terms of the much broader issue of the "problem" (or the "question" as implied by the need to "produce answers") and its solution, that is, "settlement plans." The perception of Travelling people constituting a problem—indeed a "dangerous and major social problem"—is continually reinforced throughout the editorial. In addition to the examples already cited, reference is made to the following:

"the problem of settling the travelling families";
"solv[ing] this difficult question";
"the city's most intractable social problems";
"difficult situations regarding the itinerants"; and
"a problem the size of which is not easy to tackle."

An important aspect of the "problem" is that it has been "borne" and "put up with" unequally by members of the settled community. The editorial strongly urges that to achieve a more equitable balance, each area of the city must take its share of itinerants; that is, the problem and the negative aspects associated with the process of its resolution must not be confined to particular (working-class) neighborhoods. Furthermore, the efforts of the city officials in implementing the settlement policy are described as "work" requiring "great perseverance and determination" and "years of patient effort." In this regard, the editorial reproduces the dominant and popular perceptions of Travellers as constituting a problem in Irish society, and it unquestioningly accepts the state policy of settlement and eventual integration as the only solution. However, the ultimate inclusionary aims and rhetoric of the settlement policy are undermined and contradicted by the characterization of Travellers as a problem to be borne and shared by the larger community.

Emphasizing the problematic nature of Travellers not only reinforces their exclusion from Irish society but also serves as a general semantic strategy of mitigation with respect to the actions of the residents. It provides the background against which it becomes possible to shift responsibility for the attack to the Travellers themselves (i.e., blaming the victims) and, to a lesser degree, to the "botched" efforts of city officials in this particular instance.

The Event

The lexical representation of the event itself in the editorial is significant. The national press uniformly reported the event as an "attack" by a "mob." For example, a headline in the *Irish Independent* read " 'Calm' Plea After Mob Attack on Itinerants" (1986). The *Irish Times* described the attackers as "a vigilante-style mob wielding slash-hooks, pitchforks, iron bars, and hurleys" ("Galway Travellers," 1986, p. 1). However, both of these terms—*attack* and *mob*—are conspicuously absent from the editorial in the local press. Relying on the assumption of shared knowledge of the event on the part of its readers, the editorial in general uses vague and neutral terms to refer to the attack. It is termed *the incident* and *an occurrence,* and the events are summarized as "a number of things happened which should not have occurred."

Several other terms are used that did suggest the violent nature of the event; however, in each of these cases, semantic agents and/or patients are deleted through the use of nominalization and passive constructions. The effect of these transformations is, first, to obscure causality and responsibility (Kress & Hodge, 1979) and, second, to call into question, minimize, and/or trivialize the degree of violence involved. For example, "confrontation" is used, but readers must interpret for themselves who confronted whom. The term also implies a less serious situation than, for example, "attack"; indeed, in other contexts, to confront an opponent (e.g., a bully, a criminal) constitutes a positive course of action.

Passive constructions are used to provide the most specific details of the event; in these instances, not only are the agents of the action left unspecified, but doubt as to the actual nature of the event is suggested: "There is room for argument about the level of 'violence' offered on the night the itinerant families were 'moved out.' " The degree of violence reported is explicitly questioned, and this is furthered by use of quotation marks around the term *violence,* which insinuates that the term is inappropriate in describing the event. Two agentless passives are used—"violence offered" and "families were 'moved out' "—with the former creating a convenient ambiguity as to who precisely was responsible for whatever degree of violence that did occur. Crucially, the attacking local residents never are explicitly specified as agents of the violence.

Where agents and patients both are present, the editorial uses the same abstract term *group* for both: "no groupings [*sic*] is entitled to belabor any other as happened that night, and any group so set upon is entitled to the protection of the law." Here we have a group set on and belabored by another group, yet the precise identity of the groups remains implicit. Two other terms are used to refer to the event when the actual perpetrators are discussed; the residents are described as "rebel[ling]," and their actions are described as constituting a "protest." Both of these contribute to the more global semantic strategy of mitigating the actions of those residents initiating the attack.

The Participants

The editorial goes to considerable lengths to present a positive image of the residents of the area in which the attack occurred and to account for their behavior. They are characterized as people who are "proud of their area," who "value their privacy," and who "do not wish to see unofficial camps cause problems from litter to just plain unsanitary conditions." Furthermore, these residents "have had to put up with the brunt of one of the city's most intractable social problems," and "they have been left to bear the problem . . . too long." Their area "has suffered more than most from itinerant encampments" and has "borne [its] share of the settlement effort." The residents themselves are in fact portrayed as victims of Travellers and the settlement program, and it thus follows that "it is perfectly understandable" that these people would "rebel eventually" against those camps. Their actions, although criticized in the editorial, are understandable and are interpreted as a protest. The value of designating the event in this manner is clear in that protests, when carried out appropriately, are legitimate forms of political expression in democratic nations.

The term *protest,* although consistent with the mitigating scenario presented in the editorial, does not map easily on to the event at hand.

The semantics of protest include some individual or group, *X*, protesting to some other individual or group, *Y*, concerning some particular issue or situation, *Z*. Given this meaning, it is unclear to whom the residents' supposed action of protest was addressed. The implication in the editorial is, of course, that the residents were protesting to the city's officials regarding the presence of Travellers in their area. Given the absence of city officials during the incident as well as the facts that it took place "under the cover of darkness" and that the Travellers were more than just "an issue," this interpretation is particularly strained.

The actions of the attackers also are mitigated by placing responsibility for the attack, first, on the city officials and, second, on the Travelling families themselves. The editorial is explicit in its criticism of the city officials, who are described as having "thoroughly botched" their role in the situation. Although asserting that "incidents like last Thursday's are inexcusable and must be condemned in the strongest terms," the editorial proceeds to excuse the actions of those residents responsible for the attack: "But utter lack of consultation, and a sudden move such as that made in the early hours . . . was simply asking for trouble, or tempting fate to the point where worse may well have happened."

The city officials are responsible because, in this case, there was no prior consultation with the residents of the area, and thus "misleading information . . . was bound to get out in such circumstances and all kinds of rumour was [*sic*] bound to 'fester' in the atmosphere of uncertainty." In such circumstances, the editorial presents the attack as inevitable—a strategy that submerges the question of the personal responsibility of those individuals who initiated the attack.

It is important to consider here that although the editorial places the responsibility for the attack on the shoulders of the city's officials, it does so in a context of high praise for the city's efforts in general with regard to the "Traveller problem." Again, a semantic strategy of mitigation serves to create a very positive image of the elites involved in the settlement issue. The city council is described as having devoted "many months, or even years, of patient effort," as having "shown great perseverance and determination." Members of the council have "shown their faith in the process (of consultation) by many special meetings" and "hours of talks in other difficult situations regarding the itinerants." City officials are credited with having accomplished "remarkable work in settling itinerant families," and a number of these "forgotten" efforts are named in the editorial.

In spite of the condemnation of the city's actions, or rather its lack of action in the form of consultation with the area's residents, one of the primary objectives of the editorial is defending the reputation of the city, that is, a face-saving strategy of positive self-presentation (van Dijk, 1993). Concern with the image of the city was explicit in the two other editorials concerning the attack published at the time. An editorial in the *Galway Advertiser,* titled "The Righteous" (1986), criticized the national media for their "obsession with how Galway tries to handle its Traveller situation" and voiced the concern of the community "that the good name of the city be taken at once from the pages of the righteous national media" (p. 6). Aside from blaming the nonlocal media for damaging the reputation of the city, this face-saving strategy involved a positive presentation of the residents of the area, a condemnation of the attack and the mitigation of its perpetrators, and the emphasis of the city's past successes with respect to settlement. A third editorial published in the *Galway Observer,* titled "A Night of Shame" (1986, p. 2), also referred to how "the events of last week at Rahoon have once again soured the name of Galway and its people . . . and blackened the reputation of [the] area." In sharp contrast to the *Connacht Sentinel,* however, this editorial referred to the perpetrators of the attack as constituting an "unruly mob" and as "bully-boys" engaged in "thuggery" and violence. In this case, the perpetrators were at least temporarily excluded from the larger community in order that the community might preserve a positive self-presentation. Although the strategy was different, the intended effect was the same, that is, to distance the newspaper and the community from the event.[3]

Returning to the main editorial published in the *Connacht Sentinel,* we see that the Travellers who were the victims of the attack are held responsible for precipitating the violence against themselves. Indeed, this strategy of reversal or blaming the victim commences in the initial sentence, where the topic of the editorial is specified as the "incidents surrounding the five traveller families moving on to land." It was thus the actions of the Travellers—their moving on to land—that gave rise to the attack. Later in the editorial, their "sudden move" onto the field is characterized as "simply asking for trouble, or tempting fate." Here, the implication is that the actions of the Travellers provoked a degree of anger (which is seen as understandable and justifiable) in the local residents that inevitably led to the violence; again, the issue of the responsibility of the residents for their actions is not raised.

As is the case in most contemporary mainstream press, the overt expression of racist ideology no longer is socially acceptable, and strategies of blaming the victim such as those that have been described cannot be explicit. To maintain an image of tolerance and even concern for Travellers (an important aspect of the discourse of settlement), the editorial makes a number of apparently positive statements about Travellers who were the victims of the attack. First, the editorial commented that "worse might well have happened but for the fact that . . . the itinerants sensibly moved without much resistance." Although the individuals are positively portrayed as "sensible," the use of "much" implies that they did indeed offer some resistance and hence share in the responsibility for the violence.

Second, and of greater significance for the issue of Traveller exclusion in general, is the characterization of the Travellers' families as being "specially selected" by the city, all of whom were "non-drinkers" and some of whom had been in the area for "five years or more" and had "only seven children in all between them." The implications of such a characterization with respect to the larger Traveller population are clear, as it evokes some frequent negative stereotypes of the group. The implied contrast to these "specially selected" families is that Travellers in general are drinkers with a "proliferation of large families" (which leads to unsanitary conditions). Furthermore, the reference to sustained residence—that these were Galway Travelling families—both counters and evokes the frequent accusation that Travellers from other parts of the country "invade" the city.[4]

In two other instances, the editorial includes Travellers with the majority Irish population. Again, given their local semantic roles and the overwhelming negative representation of Travellers in the editorial, these may be seen as what van Dijk (1993) terms an "apparent concession," a form of disclaimer whose function is "not primarily intended to emphasize the good qualities of the [minority] community, but rather as an argumentative ploy to more credibly convey the message about its bad qualities" (p. 261). In the first instance, an explicit comparison is made between the Traveller and settled communities: "Itinerants, like all of us, are not angels, and left without basic sanitary facilities they are likely to be a nuisance in an area as the residents say." The rhetorical effect of this apparently inclusionary statement is one of exclusion. The fact that a comparison is made between "us" and the itinerants emphasizes that they are not included with "us." Furthermore, the editorial adopts and thus legitimizes the perspective of residents who view Travellers as a nuisance in the area.

The second example occurs in the final sentence, where the editorial cautions about the "dangerous and major social problem" that the city will face "if it does not produce answers to Irish people living on the sides of the roads." Although the term *Irish people* is inclusive of Travellers, the fact that it is used at all is evidence of their profound exclusion in the minds of the public and the press.

Conclusion

To conclude, the editorial functioned on a number of interrelated levels, all of which contributed to the maintenance and reinforcement of existing racist perceptions and actions vis-à-vis the Travelling people. First, it expressed support for the government policy of settlement by interpreting the significance of the attack in terms of its potential threat to that policy. Second, Travellers consistently were characterized as a "problem" and, furthermore, as a problem whose solution must be found through the consultation among various groups within the settled community (i.e., the state and local residents). Finally, the editorial acted to protect the city's reputation. It did so by praising the past efforts of its officials, by denouncing the attack while excusing the actions of the attackers, and by placing the ultimate blame for the attack on the Travellers themselves.

Critical discourse analysis, through its focus on language use in situations of inequality and injustice, attempts to "uncover and de-mystify certain social processes . . . to make mechanisms of manipulation, discrimination, demagogy, and propaganda explicit and transparent" (Wodak, 1989, p. xiv). In this chapter, critical discourse analysis has revealed the applicability of work on racist discourse to the situation of Travellers in Ireland. Given the conventional view of Ireland as a nonracist state, the analysis of anti-Traveller discourses contributes to the larger comparative project of mapping the features and dimensions of racism as a social phenomenon. At the same time, critical discourse analysis makes it possible to demonstrate something of the processes through which anti-Traveller racism is developed and promulgated within Ireland itself. In this chapter, we have focused on how one of several influential elite discourses—that of the press—uncritically reproduces the state ideologies of settlement and incorporation while actively contributing to the inferiorization and exclusion of an Irish minority. The consequences of these processes are not merely symbolic but have concrete effects on the material conditions of Traveller life and the nature of their social relationships with their fellow citizens.

Appendix

Following is the full text of the *Connacht Sentinel* editorial, titled "Consultation Not Confrontation" (1986, p. 4), critiqued in this chapter:

> The tragedy of the most recent incidents surrounding the five traveller families moving on to land at Circular Road is that many months, or even years, of patient effort to resolve the problem have been endangered, tempers have frayed, and at least in the short term, difficulties may be harder to overcome.
>
> There seems little doubt that though the five families involved were not told to go into the site directly, someone certainly gave them the impression that if they did go onto the land newly-acquired by the corporation, then they would be left there, while a court order was in existence governing the site on which they were camped up to then.
>
> For whatever reason, a lot of talking, behind-the-scenes work towards finding sites for parking, and some courageous tough-talking by city councillors and officials have been placed at risk—for the confrontation of the past few days has put a sharp new emphasis on the problem of settling the Travelling families and "raised the temperature" of the issue.
>
> A number of things happened which should not have occurred, and though we must now move on from there, having attempted to understand why these things happened, we must be firm in our attitudes to occurrences like last Thursday's and the role of the City Council and the forces of the law must play if we are not to have near-anarchy to trying to solve this difficult question.
>
> The people of the area involved—and by that we mean all those living near the long-serving unofficial camping area along the Seamus Quirke Road, and near the flats at Rahoon Park, have had to put with the brunt of some of the city's most intractable social problems for many years they have seen the camps and caravans proliferate and without even the most basic of facilities; and they have put up with it.
>
> It is perfectly understandable that people who are proud of their area, who value their privacy, and who do not wish to see unofficial camps cause problems from litter to just plain unsanitary conditions, would rebel eventually against them. They have been left to bear the problem on unofficial

sites too long. But any such protest must be within the law, it must be done in a democratic fashion, and not under the cover of darkness.

There is room for argument about the level of "violence" offered on the night the itinerant families were "moved out," but the point is that no groupings [*sic*] is entitled to belabour any other as happened that night, and any group so set upon is entitled to the protection of the law, something they are now, thankfully, getting.

The city has done remarkable work in settling itinerant families, work that at times like these can be forgotten. It ranges from housing in estates to housing travellers in the special village complex. Very vexed housings in the past that have been insisted upon through the force of the law and with all the authority that the city council could command, and they have in many cases proved successful.

The city council, both in the shape of elected members and officials, have [*sic*] shown great perseverance and determination in getting on with the settlement, but on this occasion the job was thoroughly botched, there was no consultation, [and] misleading information about the ownership of the land involved was bound to get out in such circumstances and all kinds of rumour was [*sic*] bound to "fester" in the atmosphere of uncertainty.

Many hours of talks in other difficult situations regarding the itinerants should have shown the importance of consultation, and indeed the elected members of the Corporation have shown their faith in the process by many special meetings on plans to set up permanent parking sites around the city in an effort to make real headway against a problem the size of which is not easy to tackle.

Incidents like last Thursday's are inexcusable and must be condemned in the strongest terms. But utter lack of consultation, and a sudden move such as that made in the early hours of Thursday last, was simply "asking for trouble," or tempting fate to the point where worse might well have happened but for the fact that the confrontation was quickly over and the itinerants sensibly moved without much resistance.

The real tragedy was that in these cases, the five families involved say they had been specially selected by the Corporation; all of them were non-drinkers, some of them had been five years, or more living in the area, and if the residents feared a proliferation of large families living without proper sanitary conditions, the families had only seven children in all between them.

Guarantees on proper servicing and supervision of the site, discussions on whether it might be permanent, a guarantee that an end would be put to unofficial sites and the closure of the Seamus Quirke Road shantytown might well have resulted in agreement from an area which has suffered more than most from itinerant encampments—and itinerants, like us all, are not angels, and left without even basic sanitary facilities they are likely to be a nuisance in an area as the residents say.

The key to this problem lies in each area or district of the city taking its share of the itinerants who need settling—places like Bohermore, Ballybane, and Rahoon (through Seamus Quirke Road), have borne their share of the settlement effort. Patently last week's move had no such balance to it, taken in isolation and without any consultations.

It is to be hoped that last week's incidents and the ongoing situation do not have a long-term detrimental effect on settlement plans, for the city is building up for itself a dangerous and major social problem, if it does not produce answers to Irish people living on the sides of the roads.

Notes

1. The ideas expressed in this chapter are the result of collaboration between the coauthors. Press reports and information on the historical and contemporary context for such reports were gathered by Jane Helleiner in the course of doctoral field research into the position of Travelling people in Ireland. Analysis of the editorial texts was done by Bohdan Szuchewycz.

2. References to Travellers (i.e., Gypsies, tinkers, vagrants, itinerants) in the major press source, the *Connacht Tribune,* varied dramatically over the 1922-1987 period. There was a gradual increase in reporting, beginning with 3 or 4 references per year from the 1920s to the mid-1940s. This increased to 16 or 17 annually by the 1950s. The result was a total of 220 articles prior to 1960. The 1960s saw an explosion of such articles, as annual reporting ranged from 70 to 140 articles relating to Travellers. The 1970s averaged about 60 articles annually, and a further decline was evident during the 1980s when the pattern was closer to 30 articles per year. During all decades, however, there was substantial fluctuation from year to year.

3. This interpretation draws on van Dijk's (1993) discussion of how the implications of racist attacks on minority group members sometimes are downplayed through the attribution of such violence to "social out-groups, such as football hooligans or skinheads" (p. 250).

4. A similar strategy is at work in this case. The metaphor of invasion is interesting because of the parallels with xenophobic discourse surrounding immigrants in other European countries and North America. Indeed, van Dijk (1993) identifies "immigration, with a special emphasis on problems, illegality, large numbers, and demographic or cultural threats" (p. 248), as one of the most frequent topics in the press concerning ethnic affairs. Although Travellers are not seen as foreign immigrants, and indeed their Irishness is stressed in settlement discourse, they certainly are perceived as outsiders to the local community—they always are from somewhere else—and thus are not its responsibility.

References

Acton, T. (1974). *Gypsy politics and social change.* London: Routledge & Kegan Paul.
Anderson, B. (1983). *Imagined communities.* London: Verso.
The attack on camp. (1968, November 1). *Connacht Tribune,* p. 10.

Barry, J., & Daly, L. (1988). *The Travellers' health status study.* Dublin, Ireland: Health Research Board.

Brewer, J. (1992). Sectarianism and racism, and their parallels and differences. *Ethnic and Racial Studies, 15,* 352-364.

Brown, T. (1981). *Ireland: A social and cultural history, 1922-79.* Glasgow, Scotland: Fontana.

"Calm" plea after mob attack on itinerants. (1986, September 27). *Irish Independent,* p. 5.

Commission on Itinerancy. (1963). *Report of the Commission on Itinerancy.* Dublin, Ireland: Stationery Office.

Consultation not confrontation. (1986, September 30). *Connacht Sentinel,* p. 4.

Curtin, C., Jackson, P., & O'Connor, B. (Eds.). (1987). *Gender in Irish society.* Galway, Ireland: Galway University Press.

Curtin, C., & Wilson, T. (Eds.). (1989). *Ireland from below: Social change and local communities.* Galway, Ireland: Galway University Press.

Dublin Travellers Education and Development Group. (1992). *Irish Travellers: New analysis and new initiatives.* Dublin, Ireland: Pavee Point.

Fowler, R. (1991). *Language in the news.* New York: Routledge & Kegan Paul.

Galway travellers decide to defy mob. (1986, September 27). *Irish Times,* p. 1.

Gmelch, S., & Gmelch, G. (1976). The emergence of an ethnic group: The Irish tinkers. *Anthropological Quarterly, 49,* 225-238.

Helleiner, J. (1993). Traveller settlement in Galway City: Politics, class, and culture. In C. Curtin, H. Donnan, & T. Wilson (Eds.), *Irish urban cultures* (pp. 181-201). Belfast, Ireland: Queen's University of Belfast.

Helleiner, J. (1995a). Inferiorized difference and the limits of pluralism in Ireland: the 1989 anti-hatred act. *Canadian Journal of Irish Studies,* 21, 63-83.

Helleiner, J. (1995). Gypsies, celts, and tinkers: Colonial antecedents of anti-Traveller racism in Ireland. *Ethnic and Racial Studies, 18,* 532-554.

The itinerant [Editorial]. (1969, September 5). *Connacht Tribune,* p. 10.

Kress, G., & Hodge, R. (1979). *Language as ideology.* London: Routledge & Kegan Paul.

Lee, J. (1989). *Ireland 1912-1985.* Cambridge, England: Cambridge University Press.

Mayall, D. (1988). *Gypsy-Travellers in nineteenth-century society.* Cambridge, England: Cambridge University Press.

Miles, R. (1989). *Racism.* London: Routledge & Kegan Paul.

A night of shame [Editorial]. (1986, October 1). *Galway Observer.*

No room at the inn. (1967, May 12). *Connacht Tribune,* p. 3.

Okely, J. (1983). *The Traveller-Gypsies.* Cambridge, England: Cambridge University Press.

On the roadside. (1967, September 29). *Connacht Tribune.*

The righteous [Editorial]. (1986, October 2). *Galway Advertiser,* p. 6.

Rottman, D., Tussing, A., & Wiley, M. (1986). *The population structure and living circumstances of Irish Travellers: Results from the 1981 census of Traveller families* (Paper No. 131). Dublin, Ireland: Economic and Social Research Institute.

Silverman, M., & Gulliver, P. (Eds.). (1992). *Approaching the past: Historical anthropology through Irish case studies.* New York: Columbia University Press.

Travelling People Review Body. (1983). *Report of the Travelling People Review Body.* Dublin, Ireland: Stationery Office.

Trew, T. (1979a). Theory and ideology at work. In R. Fowler, B. Hodge, G. Kress, & T. Trew, *Language and control* (pp. 94-116). London: Routledge & Kegan Paul.

Trew, T. (1979b). "What the newspapers say": Linguistic variation and ideological difference. In R. Fowler, B. Hodge, G. Kress, & T. Trew, *Language and control* (pp. 117-156). London: Routledge & Kegan Paul.
van Dijk, T. A. (1987). *Communicating racism.* Newbury Park, CA: Sage.
van Dijk, T. A. (1991). *Racism and the press.* New York: Routledge & Kegan Paul.
van Dijk, T. A. (1992). Discourse and the denial of racism. *Discourse & Society, 3,* 87-118.
van Dijk, T. A. (1993). *Elite discourse and racism.* Newbury Park, CA: Sage.
Wade, P. (1993). "Race," nature, and culture. *Man, 28,* 17-34.
Wodak, R. (Ed.). (1989). *Language, power and ideology.* Philadelphia: John Benjamins.

6

Racial Intimidation: Sociopolitical Implications of the Usage of Racist Slurs

PHILOMENA ESSED

Over the past decade, discursive representations that justify white dominance have gained increasing scholarly attention. An important terrain of research involves the ideological reproduction of racism in the media (Bogle, 1991; Jewell, 1993; van Dijk, 1991), the social sciences (Barkan, 1992; Chase, 1980; Duster, 1990), school textbooks (Mok, 1990; van den Berg & Reinsch, 1983; van Dijk, 1987b), children's books (Redmond, 1980; Stinton, 1979), and everyday conversations (van Dijk, 1987a). These and other studies indicate that condescending and hostile perceptions of the Other are (unwittingly) accepted as "normal" despite routine disclaimers and official appeals to tolerance. Moreover, conformity to the norm of tolerance generates a range of face-saving strategies. Researchers who interviewed whites about their views on racial issues found that participants made few, if any, supremacist statements in their conversations with the interviewers (Blauner, 1989; Terkel, 1992; van Dijk, 1987a; Wellman, 1977). But when confronted with racist hate messages, speech, epithets, graffiti, or propaganda, the typical reaction of non-target groups is to consider these incidents an aberration (Matsuda, 1989). Thus a rich vocabulary of racially insulting epithets has remained alive and well (Allen, 1983; Greenberg, Kirkland, & Psyszczynski, 1988). The media, politicians, and other authorities explicitly denounce racist slurs and hate messages as the product of "sick" personalities while arguing that the rest of society is decent and basically "nonracist" (van Dijk, 1993). This disassociation of hate statements from other forms of racism is part of a denial of the systemic nature of racism in society (Feagin & Feagin, 1993).

The link between microevents of racist slander and the macrostructural context of racial injustice is crucial to understanding that racism permeates all levels of the social order. From the point of view of those who are harmed by racism, slurs coincide with numerous racist constructions of Otherness and with the practices of exclusion and inferiorization these representations legitimate (Brand & Bhaggiyadatta, 1986; Essed, 1990, 1991). Voices of the victims constitute a rich source for studying the social-political implications of incidents of racist slurs (see also Razack, 1993).

This chapter focuses on the usage of racist slurs in everyday situations, the nature of these situations, and how the participants involved interpret and react to the event. In this chapter, I show that offenders are not ideologically constructed "sick" personalities but rather are ordinary people including fellow students, friends, and neighbors. Although it often is tacitly assumed that race or ethnic labels are "things they say behind your back," as the title of one book about such labels suggests (Helmreich, 1982), racist comments, including slurs, are in fact often made straight to black people's faces or at least loud enough for them to overhear.

Background of the Study

This focus on the usage of racist slurs is a continuation of two earlier cross-cultural projects on everyday racism (Essed, 1990, 1991). Illustrative materials to be used in this chapter were collected during the second study (Essed, 1991). The data consist of accounts derived from in-depth interviews conducted in the United States and the Netherlands during the mid-1980s with two comparable groups of black women. In total, about 50 interviews were made with black women who were students or professionals between the ages of 20 and 45 years. The systematic analysis of accounts of the daily reality of racial oppression was instrumental in the conceptualization of racism as a process located in everyday life. It was shown that racism operates as a cumulative force in multiple relations and practices—from education to the labor market, from private homes to the media, from neighborhood to policymakers. Mechanisms of racial exclusion and the repression of other cultures are integrated in the mundane and routine practices of everyday life. In this process, the dominant group comes to perceive and experience the marginalization and problematization of the Other as "normal."

Many of the American women I interviewed agreed that significant changes had occurred in the racial landscape during the past three decades but that the basic structural position of blacks is the same (Moss & Reed, 1990). Despite an increase in opportunities for (middle-class) blacks in white institutions during the 1970s and 1980s, blacks and whites continue to live mostly segregated lives (Hacker, 1992). Racism penetrates politics, culture, and economic life with obvious consequences for the lived experience of individuals. African American women are regularly confronted by racist slurs. The aim of the dominant group in using racist slurs as a form of intimidation is to repress black opposition to racial injustice.

In the Netherlands, race and ethnic relations have a different history than they do in the United States. During the period after World War II, migrations to the Netherlands took place from the overseas colonies of Indonesia, Suriname, and the Dutch Antilles. Indonesians, who came during the late 1950s and early 1960s, were subjected to assimilation policies, the repressive effects of which were made public only years later (Cottaar & Willems, 1984). The arrival of many of the Surinamese and Antillian immigrants coincided to a large extent with the economic depressions of the 1970s and 1980s. Racial discrimination in housing and in the labor market has taken on dramatic proportions. Unemployment numbers among Antillians and Surinamese exceeds 30%, whereas the Dutch average is 8.5% (Roelandt, Smeets, & Veenman, 1993; van Beek, 1993). Judging from newspaper articles and opinion letters, more and more white Dutch openly resent the presence of people of different color and culture, who make up 5% to 6% of the population. Yet the term *racism* is a taboo and is considered inherently un-Dutch. The word *racism,* let alone the system of oppression it represents, is trivialized and ignored. Unlike women in the United States, those in the Netherlands less frequently encounter overtly racial name-calling or hate statements. But covertly racist talk in the form of semijokes, negative comments, ridicule, pestering, and verbal forms of sexual-racial harassment is common practice (Essed, 1991, 1992, 1993).

Needless to say, any person who becomes the target of scolding, slurs, insults, or any other abusive language may feel hurt or offended as a person because insults undermine and refute the Self of the Other (Perinbanayagam, 1991). From our human experience, however, we have learned that racist insults are special. This knowledge is reflected in the universal acceptance of the evil of doctrines of racial supremacy. The universality of the rejection of racial supremacy and race hatred can be considered a mark of collective human progress (Matsuda, 1989). But we have to be alert to the fact that the universal denouncement of doctrines of racial supremacy often is overemphasized to obscure the fact that racism comprises more than the overt support of "white supremacist" ideas. Furthermore, racial hate statements go beyond the hurt caused by derogatory words themselves. The function of racial slurs is to reconfirm and/or mobilize existing racial contempt or anger against the target (Allport, 1954; Greenberg et al., 1988). The usage of racist slurs indicates the offender's apparent consent with existing racial injustice and inequities. In other words, the statements aim to hurt not only in a personal sense but also in a structural sense.

Method

The data were gathered in nondirective interviews. This method, simulating a "natural" conversation, has been successful before as an instrument for conceptualizing personal experiences. It allows for the narration of events that are likely to remain unexpressed within the format of a questionnaire (Finch, 1984; Graham, 1984; Reinharz, 1983). The nondirective interviewer serves primarily as a catalyst for the comprehensive expression of the participant's feelings and beliefs in a relatively free and detailed way as he or she tries to reveal, rather than to impose, interpretations. Because an interview is only a moment of reflection, there are some limitations to the use of nondirective interviews as data. The amount of information gathered is restricted by, among other things, the factors of time and memory. Furthermore, the interviewer steers the conversation only minimally, which in our case means that the interviewer did not ask the informants to search their memories extensively for experiences of racial name-calling. The information made available concerns experiences they voluntarily disclosed. The empirical basis of the analysis consists of 33 extensive accounts (24 from the United States, 9 from the Netherlands). Given the small numbers, the findings cannot be generalized. With a few exceptions, all of the events occurred during the 1970s and 1980s.

Finally, some words are in order to explain the concept of "experience" and the analysis of accounts. Although the notion of experience often is used to refer only to "personal" experiences (e.g., Larsen,

1988), the concept as used in this chapter has a broader meaning. It includes (a) direct experiences (acts of racism directed against oneself) and (b) vicarious experiences (acts of racism directed against identified others). Discussing in detail the use and analysis of accounts goes beyond the immediate aims of this chapter. It is sufficient to mention that accounts of racism are reconstructions of past events. The concept of accounts of racism, as developed in Essed (1988, 1991), draws partly from narrative theory (Labov & Waletzky, 1967) and thus comprises the following five elements: *context* (featuring time, place, and participants), *complication* (describing problematic, unexpected, disturbing, and/or exceptional acts), *evaluation* (explaining whether these acts are evidence of racism), *argumentation* (further supporting arguments with respect to the evaluation), and the *decision* (planned or executed reaction). Not all of these categories are equally salient in accounts. With respect to accounts of covert manifestations of racism (i.e., when the racist intentions are implicit or hidden), the argumentation category ("Why do you think it was racism?") is crucial for understanding the event. Because this chapter addresses only one form of racism, the use of racist slurs, the evaluation (that it concerns racism) is obvious within the act, thus making more or less superfluous any further argumentation in support of that opinion. My main attention is directed to the context of the event ("Where did it happen?," "Who was the offender?," "What was the nature of the situation?"), to the social implications of the complication (linking microevents to macrodimensions of racism), and to the decision ("What did you do about it?").

Racist Name-Calling in Everyday Situations

Information about the situation tells us when and where the event took place as well as who was involved. No relevant differences were found between the two countries with respect to the locations of racist slander. It can happen in the street or on public transportation (7 examples), where someone calls a black person a "N——r."[1] Racial insults occur in classrooms, in neighborhoods, on football teams, and in campus dormitories (13 examples). As one American woman explained, the derogatory label "N——r" is being used "for the simplest things, like you'd be in a car and they want you to move out of the way, and then they just resort to that" (c25).[2] One Dutch woman recalled, "When I was a child, I was forever being threatened and called a black 'N——r' " (s1), and another Dutch woman added, "We were the only blacks in the neighborhood and in school. Sometimes they pestered me, you know, like calling me a "*roetmop*" [Dutch equivalent of 'N——r'] or a 'Sambo' " (s14). However, one woman, who grew up in the South of the United States, reported, "I have not been called 'N——r' to my face since I left the South" (c13), and another woman, who moved from the East Coast to California, said she has been called that name "a couple of times, but very seldom" (c25). But the same does not hold true for her son, who frequently is the target of racial harassment. Several other women confirmed this problem in stories about their own children.

In addition to the questions of when, where, and how often racist slurring occurs, the context category of accounts also contains information as to who is involved, in particular, who the offenders are. One interesting characteristic is gender differences in the usage of racial slander. In both countries, the large majority of the perpetrators are adolescent white males, who use racial slurs both in same-gender and in cross-gender situations. It seems plausible that the salience of this specific category can be attributed to an aspect of masculine identity (Gottlieb, 1992), such as the need to prove oneself as a "white man." However, a hasty conclusion may not do credit to the complexity of gender-related determinants of aggression in race and ethnic conflict (Cock, 1992; Hall, 1974; Vickers, 1993), a topic that is not investigated in this chapter.

Apart from gender, offenders also differ by age and social position. Many of the perpetrators are classmates or fellow students. In rare cases, clients or patients engage in racial slandering. One woman in the medical profession reported,

> I went for a 2-year program at the Veterans [Administration] [VA] Hospital in [name of place]. This was in '69 and '70 when the first group of veterans came back from Vietnam. On the top floor of the VA hospital, they have wards for diseases they had no orientation to. . . . I had come down from one of the floors, drawing blood that morning, and I could hear one of the patients calling down the elevator all types of black obscenities to me, because I had to draw his blood. (c3)

Virtually none of the women had colleagues who used racist slurs. In the Netherlands, however, less blatant verbal forms of racial intimidation prevail in the workplace, including "racial jokes" and "silly racial comments" of a seemingly nonaggressive nature (Essed, 1991, 1993).

Objections are likely to be countered with indignation, if not aggression, while offenders complain that the other parties "cannot even take a small joke once in a while."

Interblack Name-Calling

The word *N——r* is still a racial epithet when used by whites, but it cannot always be interpreted in the same way when blacks refer to each other by that label. In black rap today, "N——r" actually is a term of positive endearment (Smitherman, 1977). However, among black children, norms of color and culture are applied with less compassion, as explained one American woman, who was called "black and ugly" at home (c13). But at the same time, it is not accepted either that "light-skinned" group members think themselves superior, one woman said, referring to her "light-skinned" daughter: "She was called 'Red Bone,' walking down the streets of Washington, D.C., where she went to college, and she heard, 'You think you cute because you're light' " (c27). Another woman, raised in an otherwise completely white community, recalled that she only became aware of her racial identity when she was placed in a high school with a substantial number of black students who called her "white girl" and "Oreo" (c28) when they felt she was acting "white." In all, accounts of racial tongue-lashing among blacks were few compared to stories about verbal racial abuse from whites. The data, of course, do not give any reliable information about the actual frequency of intraracial insults relative to interracial ones.

Racialized Situations Become Racist Situations

The use of racial slurs changes ordinary situations into racist ones. This does not mean, however, that "race" or "ethnicity" was completely absent from the situations until the acts of slander took place. In fact, many dimensions of social life are by definition racialized because of the racial- and ethnic-based allocation of positions and access to sources of power (Anthias & Yuval-Davis, 1992; Essed, 1996; Omi & Winant, 1986). The racialized dimensions of social relations constitute part of the macro framework within which everyday interactions take place.

Because race and ethnicity are fundamental dimensions in occupational relationships, even blacks and whites who occupy similar organizational positions or professions cannot be equated with each other, a matter that also holds true for gender (Apfelbaum, 1993). Race, ethnicity, and gender shape the experiences of the individual. This is not to imply, however, that racism is bound to occur in all occupational relationships. Yet, because the racial and ethnic dimensions of social relationships are activated through contiguous acts of racism, racist events inherently link micro- and macrodimensions of racism.

To illustrate this point, three selected cases are discussed. In the first two examples, an ordinary student quarrel and a fight among peers evolve into racist situations. In the third example, an ordinary neighborhood conflict turns into a racist event when one party resorts to racial slurs to argue her case. Quarrels and fights are interesting modes for illustrating the integration of racism into ordinary situations because the people involved are prone to lose control over their emotions. As a result, hidden racist attitudes surface that would not likely have been voiced otherwise.

The first example, from the United States, involves a black student who shared her apartment, two separate rooms and a common bathroom, with a white student. The context is as follows. The black student was having a party with some (black) friends. After using the bathroom, one of the guests shut the door with a bang. The noise vibrated through a wall, against which the white dorm mate had her record player. The record was scratched. The white girl, furious, ran out of her room to blame the black dorm mate for that. I quote the latter in the following:

> She came over to my front door and banged on the door: "I am sick of you stupid N——rs. You look like apes anyway." . . . The next day, when she was sober . . . she said, "I was drunk. I really didn't know what I was saying." (c7)

The other party did not accept this as a valid argument: "If she was drunk and she was driving and she hit somebody, she would go to jail anyway, so you are still accountable for it" (c7).

As the story illustrates, an ordinary situation, a conflict among dorm mates over noise and banging doors, evolved through specific acts (the complication, i.e., the use of a racist slur) into a racist event. This could only happen because the situation was racialized from the start. Being undergraduate students, both women occupied equal functional positions in college. However, putting aside personal differences in talent or intelligence, their lived realities were structured by unequal positions in the matrix of race relations (and economic opportunities if one were to have a scholarship and the other a rich family to cover her expenses). The black student, acutely aware of the racialized dimensions of dorm sharing, was troubled by the fact that the element of "race" could be activated any day, for instance, when fellow white students get drunk. She clarified,

> Living on campus with those parties and all those white people getting drunk, you get kind of nervous [about] how they are going to act when they get drunk. Are they all going to start chasing me or something? So I worry. (c7)

Adding further to the anticipation of racism, she explained that she always was conscious that things might "get out of hand" and that it was no luxury to take precautions:

> Now I live off campus, but [when] I lived in the dorms and I stayed for the weekend to catch up with some studying, and everybody else was outside partying, you got kind of scared to walk down the hall, where everybody was drunk. Me and my [black] friends used to get together . . . to spend the night [alternately in each other's dorms]. It was like, "This weekend, let's go over to your dorm room, bring your books or whatever." It was almost like we were locking ourselves in, which is really bad, kind of scary. (c7)

The second example illustrates the *cumulative* nature of everyday racism; a new racist event triggers memories of (similar) past events and may even revitalize the effects of these earlier situations.

One American university professor reported about her teenage son, the only black among peers from the neighborhood: "If he had a fight with his friends, his friends would write 'N——r go home' or something in the driveway with spray paint or something" (c9). The slur activates underlying patterns of racial inequality among the members of the peer group. Furthermore, the act revives other experiences of racism. After he and his mother moved from the East Coast to California, he entered high school. At his previous junior high school, he had been in the college stream of classes. But when he entered the new school,

> He was immediately downgraded. . . . When they saw him, . . . they made an assumption that if he was a black child, he couldn't handle college track. In addition to the negative attitude from the school administration, he also had to deal with aggressive hostility from peers; the first week that he was at that high school, the school was leafleted with Ku Klux Klan literature.

> The school denies knowing where it came from or anything, but it tells you who is in the area. He went through times when he was beaten up, physically hurt, hit by kids who were neo-Nazis. (c9)

In addition to violence and hostilities in school, there was "this one kid [from the neighborhood] that really harassed him, who was the head of a neo-Nazi group, the young neo-Nazis." The police patrolling the same neighborhood further exacerbated the situation.

> He was constantly harassed by the police. We live in an area where there's not a lot of blacks. He would be walking home from high school and the police would stop him at least once a week and say, "What is your business in this neighborhood?" And he said, "I am walking home from school," and the officer said, "Why are you taking this route," and he said, "Because my house is on this route." But he was constantly stopped by the police. (c9)

On top of all that, even whites just happening to pass through the neighborhood joined in similar aggressive hostility against the woman's son.

> One time he was standing on the corner of our street, talking to a girlfriend, who happened to be white. A white guy drives up in the car, jumps out of the car, and says to the girl, "Would you like me to take care of this N——r for you?" And the girl, luckily, says, "No, we're friends and we're talking." (c9)

Against the background of rejection in school (you do not belong in the college stream of classes and do not belong in "our" school at all), police harassment, and other hostilities within the same neighborhood, the racial slur of "N——r go home" on their driveway cannot be dismissed as a childish, albeit malicious, reaction by peer group members with whom the son happened to have troubles. The message in the driveway symbolizes the structural and experiential differences between the two parties; one party enjoys the safety of dominant group protection, whereas the other experiences the unsafe conditions of his "race," a group subjected to violence and discrimination. Moreover, with their spraying, the perpetrators appeal to the relative consensus among the dominant group that blacks "do not belong" in certain places.

In light of the preceding, racist slander also may be seen as an *ultimate discursive weapon.* The slur in the driveway links the microevent of peer group fighting to the macrostructure of race relations. Repudiating the struggle of blacks to achieve more justice, perpetrators communicate the wish that they could go back to the time when racial segregation was legal and blacks would have been kept out of the neighborhood altogether. In that sense, racial slurs represent the translation of situational forces into a sense of structural power.

The third example concerns a Dutch neighborhood. The illustration is interesting because it involves the Dutch elite. The context is as follows. Having overcome many (artificial) obstacles in terms of city regulations and permission for buying property in the area, the first black family moved into one of the most expensive and elite neighborhoods in the Netherlands. Later, the family finds out that one of the families on the same street had initiated a petition (which was unsuccessful) to prevent "the black family" from moving in. This prior event is relevant for understanding the case, which involves the black family's adolescent son.

The story is told from the point of view of the mother. Her teenage son, true to his age, had the habit of turning the music on full blast when the parents were not at home. The neighbors on their left already had complained a few times, urging him to decrease the volume, without any luck, however. On the contrary, the son got annoyed and decided to "teach them a lesson." He sneaked out at night and stained their fence with an ugly color of paint. The following day, the police, alerted by the neighbors, found some of the same paint inside the black family's yard. They contacted the mother at her workplace, and she returned home immediately. Very cross with her son and embarrassed by the situation, she decided to go over to the neighbors to apologize and to discuss how to take care of the damage. The woman neighbor answered the door and, upon seeing the visitor, "begins to rave. Imagine, this is upper class talking, and she starts to act up like a fishwife: 'You N——rs.' This is what you get when you let 'N——rs' into your neighborhood" (s22). The other party responded calmly, saying that she had only come to apologize but that she would be willing to return when the neighbor was prepared to address her in a decent manner. In this example, the woman neighbor activated with the slur the racialized dimensions of the situation (white neighborhood, street with a history of restrictive action to keep out blacks). Calling the black woman by that racist name, the neighbor literally expressed the wish that the street could have kept blacks out after all.

To cut short a long story, later when the mother returned to the neighbors, the woman neighbor, now joined by her husband, had calmed down. But she did not apologize for the earlier insult. The black woman ignored it as well. She explained that she had an insurance policy to cover the damage, but she hoped that the neighbors would agree with her that it would be pedagogically more instructive to have her son repaint the fence all by himself. This is what he ended up doing after school for 3 weeks.

To conclude, racist slurs, representing more than merely appalling words, reach beyond the ethical side of the situation. The usage of slurs activates structures of racial inequality beneath the situation as the words express the wish that blacks "stay in their (oppressed) place."

Slurs as Intimidation

Slurs can be directly and indirectly intimidating. The "white guy," who jumped out of his car to physically violate a black youngster spotted in the proximity of a white girl, directly aimed to intimidate the target. One does not need too much imagination to envision the hate accompanying the wish to prove his white masculinity when he threatened to "take care of this N——r."

The following two examples involve indirect intimidation. One American woman with a teenage son stated, "We had rented an apartment in [name of place], and there was nothing but rednecks out there. [My son] would play with the kids, and they would call him 'N——r' all the time" (c25). The idea of "rednecks doing a lot of crazy things in the apartment complex" felt intimidating. The woman was afraid to send her son to "a school in the area" and eventually had to move out because, as she explained, her son's safety had a determining influence on the neighborhood in which they could afford to live:

> A lot of times I think about moving to an area that may be, in terms of real estate, financially wise for me. But, I wonder about my son, who is coming to manhood, and how he is going to be able to deal with dating and problems with white men and things like that. (c25)

Accounts of threats and other verbal intimidation against sons form a salient category among the data. Several of the women mentioned the fact that black men always have been particularly prone to becoming the object of police violence (Berry & Blassingname, 1982; Kerner Commission, 1968). Moreover, centuries of social-economic deprivation, inhuman social conditions, and impoverished housing also contributed to a high level of violence within black communities, the largest number of victims being among black men (Reed, 1992). These and other factors are used to stigmatize black men as inherently violent (Cheatham & Stewart, 1990; Lawrence, 1982; Wilkinson & Taylor, 1977). In addition, ideological constructions of "sex and race," which fuel the image of the black man as a potential rapist of white women, have been used to legitimate hate, lynching, and other physical violence (Blackwell, 1977; Hernton, 1965). Several women, during their youth, had witnessed (near) killings when white mobs attacked male members of their families: fathers, uncles, and cousins. One contemporary version we have seen earlier: the "white guy," motivated by racist chivalry, who wanted to "beat up" the black youngster because he was talking to a white girl.

The final example addresses in a more general sense the socialization of American black children in a predominantly white neighborhood that is "becoming more multiethnic slowly" (c34). The woman, a university professor, was jogging one day when "two little kids, ages maybe about 7 and 9," shouted "N——r" at her (c34). As mentioned before, the alteration of an everyday situation, jogging, into a racist one is significant because the racist slur represents more than "just two little kids harassing passers-by." Consequently, the mother worried, "Are things like this going to happen more often? What does it mean for my child to grow up in such a neighborhood?" The racial slur symbolized, in her view, the general lack of sufficient structural and emotional safety for a black child in a white community. To explain her point further, she compared the present situation to her own youth in a black community:

> It is different from the area I grew up in. There is not even a black church here. I always had a black church that was . . . like an extended family. My grandparents were always around, both sides. There were other older black people around in the community that were like surrogate parents, that my son would not have out here. So I have been thinking a lot about building some kind of racial consciousness and feeling for black community while living in a place like this and wonder whether it is possible, . . . whether or not we should move to some other state or place. (c34)

De- and Reracializing Slurs

This section addresses the contradiction between the normative rejection of racial slurs and the lived reality in which tolerance of racism prevails. Earlier it was mentioned that the dominant group, aspiring to keep up a nondiscriminatory self-image, often trivializes and denies racism. One would expect that denial is hardly feasible when racist intent is overtly included in the act, which is the case with racist slurs. The data belie this expectation, however. We will see shortly that even the racism involved in the usage of racist slurs can be denied. This may be explained as follows. Usually, racist slurs denote open conflict. The conflict situation may be a result of the usage of a racist insult, but it may also be the case that conflict over another matter turns into a racist conflict when one party uses the weapon of slurring. Strategically, dominant group members will acknowledge that there is conflict but then proceed to ignore totally the racist element involved. This specific form of denial, which I call the "deracialization" of racist situations, is in itself a form of racism; when the event is deracialized, it subsequently can be dealt with as if it concerns an ordinary conflict in which both parties involved can be held responsible. With the redefinition of the situation, the reaction of the victim of racist slander is problematized, not the act of the offender, the racist slurring. Several women testified about dominant group members who first ignored the racist epithets and then retaliated when the victim struck back.

One Dutch woman recalled that a male classmate had called her a *roetmop*. Highly offended, she declared that to her he did not exist any longer, and she pursued this "death declaration" rigidly. The first complication (the slur) was followed by a second one when she was ordered to see the principal, who did not agree at all with her attitude. Rather than problematizing the boy for his behavior, he started to criticize her instead. "The principal told me it was wrong to remain angry . . . because it was damaging the classroom climate" (s18). The student did not agree: "*He* started the whole thing" (emphasis in original). The principal demanded, however, that she literally shake hands with the classmate and resume normal relations. If this did not happen within 2 days, he said, either she or the classmate "might have to look for another school" (s18).

Before proceeding with the case, it is relevant to highlight the difference between the student's and the principal's definitions of the issue. The student problematized the classmate for using a racist slur. The principal, on the other hand, problematized her "stubbornness." He deracialized the situation when he blamed both students equally ("One of you may have to go to a different school"). But in fact, he put full blame on her and forced her to solve the problem on a personal level

("If you do not give in within 2 days, you will be thrown out of this school"). Faced with this threat, she felt she had no choice but to give in. The implications are, however, that school authorities sanction tolerance of racist slurring; the other students, who did not reject the boy's behavior in the first place and who, like the principal, felt that the black student was "only making a scene," are reinforced in their belief that racist epithets are not any different from other slurs except that they are racial.

Deracialized events can be "reracialized" in an antiracist sense when assertive witnesses explicitly problematize the racist elements of the situation. One American woman reported that her son was suspended from school for having hit a white girl who had called him "N——r." The mother demanded to see the principal, a woman, and rhetorically asked whether the girl was suspended too and, if not, what other action had been taken. Her worst fears were confirmed. "Nothing!" she exclaimed. "You don't think being called a 'N——r' by a white girl is a form of attack?" (c19). Upon hearing this, the principal immediately dropped the suspension.

One of the most astute political interpretations of the use of a racist slur came from a 20-year-old American student. One afternoon, she was driving with a girlfriend, who also is black. They were waiting for the traffic light to turn green when "these two white boys came on a motorbike, they were two on one bike," and began to stare conspicuously into the car. The window on the passenger's front seat, where the girlfriend was sitting, was partly down. When the two women began to wonder what the boys were looking at, one of them said something incomprehensible and added to that "you N——rs" (c5).

The woman who first told me the story was the driver: "Something clicked and all the blood rushed to my head and something said kill him" (c5). When the light turned green, she started to chase down the motorbike with her car. "I did not realize I had done it until after I had done it, but I was kind of pushing him over into the oncoming traffic." The girlfriend tried to calm her down, saying "Slow down. What are you doing?" But the woman said,

> I didn't hear her. I really couldn't think. I was just trying to hurt this person for saying that to me [because] that hurt me so deeply. That was the first time anybody had ever had the nerve to say that to my face anyway, and I just lost control. (c5)

When I asked her why she was hurt so deeply, her answer revealed her acute understanding of the *macro*structural implications of the insult:

> Because I know the attitude behind that word. It is racist, a degrading term calling me worse than dirt. When I heard it, I just—I remembered everything I've ever read in my history books, everything everybody ever told me about slavery or what I have seen on TV. And I said they can't do this to me. Not in 1985 or whatever year it was. I said no, no, this is for everybody who has been called this and been hurt by it, I'm going to hurt you because of it.

Fortunately, the boys escaped before she could really "hit back with her car," which, of course, could have brought her tremendous problems. I also interviewed the girlfriend who was in the car. For both of them, it was the first time they had been called a racist name. I did not intend to make a linguistic comparison of the two accounts; rather, I wanted to compare the impact the event made on them. Because the girlfriend was sitting at the side of the car where the boys were, she could fill in some of the details the driver had missed: "He kept looking [at us], so I just stared back at him. And then he said, "What are you looking at, N——r?" Both women understood that the boys tried to intimidate them, but their reactions were different. Whereas the woman behind the wheel took the situation as a severe insult that needed to be challenged immediately, the other one was too horrified to react: "I really didn't react like wanting to run him over. Her reacting that way made me get more upset. . . . It was a shock to be called that."

Reactions

Racial slurs are symbolic weapons, words that wound because they hit the individual member of a racially oppressed group with the macrostructural reality of racial injustice. This may cause the other party to feel powerless for lack of access to a "weapon" of the same magnitude. In the previous example, the force of the car engine and the security of the wheel in the woman's hands became a situational source of power for her to express the idea that she did not accept "the attitude behind that word."

Reactions to racial slurs probably depend on factors such as the personality of the individual involved, the means or resources available, and the interests at stake. One determining factor also has to do with the interpretation of the situation. As was shown, the driver recognized instantly the political implications of the slur, whereas her friend did not. This difference may be due to many factors, one of which is related to the availability of relevant knowledge of racism that makes the wider implications of the situation understandable (Essed, 1991; Tizard & Phoenix, 1993). The driver comes from a politically committed family. Her mother had made it a point to inform her daughter about "race" in the United States on relevant occasions, for instance, during certain television programs or when the daughter specifically asked questions. The mother had saved "all the clippings" from the civil rights movement to be used as instructive materials. The daughter said,

> She brought them out and we looked at them together. I guess by the time I looked at them, I already had learned a little bit from school—not much, because they don't tell you that much about things like that in school. . . . She had all this visual knowledge because she [saw it on television]. (c5)

The other woman, who is the same age, did not have the same educational opportunities at home. It was not until she was leaving home to go to a (white) college that her father "started talking," telling her to:

> be prepared for all types of stuff. He did not [mention] particular things, except for the staring and the looks. . . . I remember this one main thing he told me. . . . It had to do with name-calling. He said probably one time out of your life you are going to get called a "N——r." And I was like, oh, that is old, no way. Nobody is going to do that, that is all in the past now. He was like, well, I am telling you, just be prepared.

Referring to the incident in the car, she concluded, "And last year, it happened for the first time. . . . I didn't know how to react" (c6).

Some women decided to *ignore* the offenders completely. In other cases, victims *attacked* the offenders physically or *intimidated* back. One interesting example of counterintimidation comes from Holland, where, as several women testified, it is not uncommon in public situations for whites to engage in (covertly) racist conversations or racist comments. Witnesses pretend to be "deaf and blind." One woman put it like this: "You want to know what the Dutch do? They look the other way. They act like they don't see or hear it" (s24). One 24-year-old woman recalled the following about a bus ride:

> Two drunk guys got on, and they said to me, "Stupid black, what did you come here for? Why didn't you stay in your own country? Came here to steal our jobs, huh?" . . . I couldn't say anything, I was really dripping wet. . . . No one did anything. But they were all looking, you know. A Turkish boy got up and came to stand next to me. I found that really something, the solidarity. (s23)

Transcending gender and ethnic differences, the young Turkish man, himself a member of an ethnically discriminated group in the Netherlands, took sides with the black woman. With his firm act of solidarity, he successfully scared off the other men.

One final issue needs to be mentioned, although it deserves more attention than the available data allow. Studies on strategies against discrimination support the view that racial problems on a micro level can be solved more effectively when relevant authorities take a firm stand against racism (Essed & Helwig, 1992; Shaw, Nordle, & Shapiro, 1987). One woman, herself a school principal, related anecdotally that one of the teachers sent a white boy to her because he had used a racial slur against a black girl. She said. "I could see in his eyes that he wondered what I might do to him, scald him alive? Of course, I didn't do any more to him than what was fair to both" (c25). The data indicate that "race" is a relevant factor with respect to the question of whether or not victims of racism report the problem to the authorities concerned. Anticipating indifference, denial, or retaliation, several women, especially students confronted with racial slurs on campus, preferred to go to black authorities, if available, rather than to white ones. The data underscore their fears, as there were few cases of white authorities who pursued any serious action against racism. In one example, a white student was expelled from campus housing because he had threatened two black women students, housed in the same building, with a baseball bat while wishing they would go "back to Africa" (c5). He claimed that they had been making noise during the night, which had kept him awake.

Conclusions

Blatantly racist remarks are made not only behind one's back but also straight to one's face. The universal condemnation of racist hate statements continues to have only symbolic meaning, however, when society generally tolerates racist discourse and practice. In many cases, non-target members who witness events take a passive stand or, in the case of (white) authorities, deracialize evidence of racial slander, thereby problematizing victims' assertive reactions instead. Anticipating lack of understanding or retaliation, some prefer to ignore the events. Others hit back, or they intimidate back. A point for further research pertains to the gender of offenders. Although none of the findings can be generalized, it seems significant that racist insults, in both same-gender and cross-gender situations, mostly involve white adolescent males. A salient number of cases also involve adolescent black males as victims.

It is important that authorities act firmly against the use of racist slurs, especially in schools, where a substantial number of the incidents occurred. At the same time, it must be kept in mind that procedures against the use of racial slurs can be effective only if embedded in a comprehensive program to fight racism on all levels. After all, it is not the use of offensive words in themselves but the system of injustice they symbolize that makes racist slurs so different from many other insults.

Notes

1. Following the example of Matsuda (1989), this chapter does not spell racial slurs unless this is necessary to be comprehensible.

2. Throughout this chapter, codes for American interviewees are marked by a letter "c" followed by a number. Codes for Dutch interviewees are marked by a letter *s* followed by a number.

References

Allen, I. (1983). *The language of ethnic conflict: Social organization and lexical culture.* New York: Columbia University Press.

Allport, G. (1954). *The nature of prejudice.* Garden City, NY: Doubleday.

Anthias, F., & Yuval-Davis, N. (1992). *Racialized boundaries: Race, nation, gender, colour, and class and the anti-racist struggle.* London: Routledge.

Apfelbaum, E. (1993). *Women leaders within their special cultural contexts: The relevance of social relations between genders in Norway and France.* Unpublished manuscript, UNESCO, Paris.

Barkan, E. (1992). *The retreat of scientific racism: Changing concepts of race in Britain and the United States between the world wars.* Cambridge, England: Cambridge University Press.

Berry, M., & Blassingname, J. (1982). *Long memory: The black experience in America.* New York: Oxford University Press.

Blackwell, J. (1977). Social and legal dimensions of interracial liaisons. In D. Wilkinson & R. Taylor (Eds.), *The black male in America: Perspectives on his status in contemporary society* (pp. 219-243). Chicago: Nelson-Hall.

Blauner, B. (1989). *Black lives, white lives: Three generations of race relations in America.* Berkeley: University of California Press.

Bogle, D. (1991). *Toms, coons, mulattoes, mammies, and bucks: An interpretive history of blacks in American films.* New York: Continuum.

Brand, D., & Bhaggiyadatta, K. (1986). *Rivers have sources, trees have roots: Speaking of racism.* Toronto: Cross Cultural Communication Centre.

Chase, A. (1980). *The legacy of Malthus: The social costs of the new scientific racism.* Urbana: University of Illinois Press.

Cheatham, H., & Stewart, J. (Eds.). (1990). *Black families.* New Brunswick, NJ: Transaction.

Cock, J. (1992). *Women and war in South Africa.* Cleveland, OH: Pilgrim.

Cottaar, A., & Willems, W. (1984). *Indische Nederlanders.* The Hague, The Netherlands: Moesson.

Duster, T. (1990). *Backdoor to eugenics.* New York: Routledge.

Essed, P. (1988). Understanding verbal accounts of racism. *Text, 8*(1), 5-40.

Essed, P. (1990). *Everyday racism: Reports from women in two cultures.* Claremont, CA: Hunter House.

Essed, P. (1991). *Understanding everyday racism: An interdisciplinary theory.* Newbury Park, CA: Sage.

Essed, P. (1992). Alternative knowledge sources in explanations of racist events. In M. McLaughlin, M. Cody, & S. Read (Eds.), *Explaining one's self to others: Reason-giving in a social context* (pp. 199-224). Hillsdale, NJ: Lawrence Erlbaum.

Essed, P. (1993b). The politics of marginal inclusion: Racism in an organizational context. In J. Solomos & J. Wrench (Eds.), *Racism and migration in Western Europe* (pp. 143-156). Oxford, England: Berg.

Essed, P. (1996). *Diversity: Gender, color, and culture.* Amherst, MA: University of Massachusetts Press.

Essed, P., & Helwig, L. (1992). *Bij voorbeeld: Multicultureel beleid in de praktijk.* Amsterdam, The Netherlands: FNV.

Feagin, J., & Feagin, C. (1993). *Racial and ethnic relations* (4th ed.). Englewood Cliffs, NJ: Prentice Hall.

Finch, J. (1984). "It's great to have someone to talk to": The ethics and politics of interviewing women. In C. Bell & H. Robert (Eds.), *Social researching: Politics, problems, practice* (pp. 70-87). London: Routledge & Kegan Paul.

Gottlieb, R. (1992). Masculine identity and the desire for war. In T. Wartenberg (Ed.), *Rethinking power* (pp. 277-288). Albany: State University of New York Press.

Graham, H. (1984). Surveying through stories. In C. Bell & H. Roberts (Eds.), *Social researching: Politics, problems, practice* (pp. 104-124). London: Routledge & Kegan Paul.

Greenberg, J., Kirkland, S., & Psyszczynski, T. (1988). Some theoretical notes and preliminary research concerning derogatory ethnic labels. In G. Smitherman-Donaldson & T. van Dijk (Eds.), *Discourse and discrimination* (pp. 74-92). Detroit, MI: Wayne State University Press.

Hacker, A. (1992). *Two nations: Black and white, separate, hostile, unequal.* New York: Scribner.

Hall, J. (1974). *Revolt against chivalry: Jesse Daniel Ames and the women's campaign against lynching.* New York: Columbia University Press.

Helmreich, W. (1982). *The things they say behind your back*. New Brunswick, NJ: Transaction.

Hernton, C. (1965). *Sex and racism in America*. New York: Grove.

Jewell, S. (1993). *From mammy to Miss America and beyond: Cultural images and the shaping of U.S. social policy*. London: Routledge.

Kerner Commission. (1968). *Report of the National Advisory Commission on Civil Disorders*. New York: Pantheon.

Labov, W., & Waletzky, J. (1967). Narrative analysis: Oral versions of personal experiences. In J. Helm (Ed.), *Essays on the verbal and visual arts* (pp. 12-44). Seattle: Washington University Press.

Larsen, S. (1988). Remembering without experiencing: Memory for reported events. In U. Neisser & E. Winograd (Eds.), *Remembering reconsidered: Ecological and traditional approaches to the study of memory* (pp. 326-355). Cambridge, England: Cambridge University Press.

Lawrence, E. (1982). In the abundance of water the fool is thirsty: Sociology and black "pathology." In Centre for Contemporary Cultural Studies (Ed.), *The empire strikes back: Race and racism in 70's Britain* (pp. 95-142). London: Hutchinson.

Matsuda, M. (1989). Public response to racist speech: Considering the victim's story. *Michigan Law Review, 87*, 2320-2381.

Mok, I. (1990). *Anti-racisme en schoolboeken*. Amsterdam, The Netherlands: Parel.

Moss, E., & Reed, W. (1990). Stratification and subordination: Change and continuity. In W. Reed (Ed.), *Assessment of the status of African-Americans* (Vol. 1, pp. 1-16). Boston: William Monroe Trotter Institute.

Omi, M., & Winant, H. (1986). *Racial formation in the United States*. New York: Routledge & Kegan Paul.

Perinbanayagam, R. (1991). *Discursive acts*. New York: Aldine de Gruyter.

Razack, S. (1993). Story-telling for social change. *Gender and Education, 5*, 55-70.

Redmond, R. (1980). *Zwarte mensen in kinderboeken*. The Hague, The Netherlands: Nederlands Bibliotheek en Literatuur Centrum.

Reed, W. (1992). Health and medical care of African-Americans. In *Assessment of the status of African-Americans* (Vol. 5). Boston: William Monroe Trotter Institute.

Reinharz, S. (1983). Experiential analysis: A contribution to feminist research. In G. Bowles & R. Klein (Eds.), *Theories of women's studies* (pp. 162-191). London: Routledge & Kegan Paul.

Roelandt, T., Smeets, H., & Veenman, J. (1993). *Jaarboek minderheden 1993*. Houten, The Netherlands: Bohn Stafleu Van Loghum.

Shaw, J., Nordle, P., & Shapiro, R. (Eds.). (1987). *Strategies for improving race relations*. Manchester, England: Manchester University Press.

Smitherman, G. (1977). *Talkin' and testifyin': The language of black America*. Boston: Houghton Mifflin.

Stinton, J. (Ed.). (1979). *Racism and sexism in children's books*. London: Writers & Readers.

Terkel, S. (1992). *Race: How blacks and whites think and feel about the American obsession*. Garden City, NY: Anchor Books.

Tizard, B., & Phoenix, A. (1993). *Black, white or mixed race? Race and racism in the lives of young people of mixed parentage*. London: Routledge and Kegan Paul.

van Beek, K. (1993). *To be hired or not to be hired: The employer decides*. Doctoral Dissertation, University of Amsterdam.

van den Berg, H., & Reinsch, P. (1983). *Racisme in schoolboeken.* Amsterdam, The Netherlands: SUA.

van Dijk, T. A. (1987a). *Communicating racism.* Newbury Park, CA: Sage.

van Dijk, T. A. (1987b). *Schoolvoorbeelden van racisme.* Amsterdam, The Netherlands: SUA.

van Dijk, T. A. (1991). *Racism and the press.* London: Routledge and Kegan Paul.

van Dijk, T. A. (1993). *Elite discourse and racism.* Newbury Park, CA: Sage.

Vickers, J. (1993). *Women and war.* London: Zed Books.

Wellman, D. (1977). *Portraits of white racism.* Cambridge, England: Cambridge University Press.

Wilkinson, D., & Taylor, R. (Eds.). (1977). *The black male in America: Perspectives on his status in contemporary society.* Chicago: Nelson-Hall.

7

The Historical Resilience of Primary Stereotypes: Core Images of the Muslim Other

KARIM H. KARIM

Critical discourse analysis involves the multidisciplinary study of the "intricate relationships between text, talk, social cognition, power, society, and culture," according to van Dijk (1993, p. 253). Apart from studying the microlevel of words, sentences, and sentence connections, this method analyzes the more global levels of texts through semantic macrostructures such as scripts, which contain all that is known in a culture about a specific type of episode. More general than the notion of script is the primary stereotype or *topos* (plural: *topoi*), which operates as the referential basis of interpretation and is essential in making a textual account seem coherent within a particular culture's norms. The term *topos* has been defined as "a 'reservoir' of ideas or core images from which specific rhetoric statements can be generated" (Ivie, 1980, p. 281). Although Ivie looks specifically at the consistency of American characterizations of military enemies, his concept is useful for understanding the endurance of topoi in other contexts.

This chapter seeks to demonstrate that Eurocentric constructions of the Muslim Other are based on a specific set of topoi. It attempts to deconstruct discourses about "Islam" by analyzing the topoi that have generated a seemingly endless series of biased depictions of Muslims for centuries.[1] Preserved in collective cultural memory (Connerton, 1989), they can be traced at least as far back as the descriptions of the prophet Muhammad by Christian polemicists of medieval Europe.[2] These primary stereotypes about "Islam" later were used ideologically in the military and colonial expansion into Muslim societies. Through continual reinforcement of the notion that the Muslim Other was essentially a savage in need of civilization, it was possible to justify the control of his or her land and person. The resilience of age-old notions about "Islam" is evident in the ease with which they still can be used by propagandists. Since the fall of the Communist Other, Muslims seem to be in the process of reemerging as a chief enemy (Huntington, 1993). For the propagandist, Muslims are endowed with historically validated core images that can be efficiently manipulated to influence public opinion, especially when strong action is to be taken against nations whose populations are primarily Muslim.

Although the Orient in popular North American usage refers to East Asia or the Far East, in Edward Said's usage it refers primarily to Muslim lands in Africa and Asia. Said (1978) defines *Orientalism* as:

> the corporate institution for dealing with the Orient—dealing with it by making statements about it, authorizing views of it, describing it, by teaching it, settling it, ruling over it: in short, Orientalism as a Western style for dominating, restructuring, and having authority over the Orient. (p. 3)

Although stereotypes of Europeans and North Americans in Muslim societies obviously exist (A. Ahmed, 1992; Ghanoonparvar, 1993; Mernissi, 1992), their treatment does not correspond to the Orientalist institutionalization of information about "Islam." It should be noted, however, that despite the numerous examples of Orientalist writing that clearly exhibit racist and ethnocentric tendencies, it would be a serious mistake to dismiss all Orientalist scholarship. The value of some Orientalists' contributions to a better understanding of Muslims is acknowledged even by critics such as Said himself (Said, 1978, pp. 266-274; see also A. Ahmed, 1992, pp. 180-182).

Orientalism not only has flourished in Western Europe, North America, Australasia, and Israel but also has been an integral part of the manner in which Eastern Europe has dealt with regions to its south and east (see Poliakov, 1992). For this reason, the term *North* rather than *West* is used here to describe the geographical ambit of Orientalism, except in specific cases such as the Gulf War in which Eastern European countries did not participate. It is recognized that particular Northern and Muslim societies have had distinct historical relationships and that there are Muslim communities within the populations of most Northern countries—all of which have specific "imaginaries" about each other

(Arkoun, 1994, p. 6). But for the purposes of this study, which looks primarily at constructions of the Muslim Other by Eurocentric cultures, the North is treated as a region that is ethnically "white" and has a Judeo-Christian heritage. It is indicated throughout this chapter that the Muslim Other is presented in particular ways by the *dominant* discourses of the North; this acknowledges that there exist other kinds of discourses that coexist and compete with the dominant ones (Karim, 1993, pp. 191-195).

Reducing Islam to Fundamentalism

The Muslim is Europe's " 'Other' *par excellence*" (Hentsch, 1992, p. 1). Before the era of transoceanic travel, it was primarily with the adherents of Islam that European societies fought wars, made peace, traded, and engaged in cultural and intellectual exchange. Due to the large number of military confrontations with the Muslim Other and the religious threat that they were seen as posing, dominant Northern discourses endowed them with certain ignoble traits that have been continually reinforced through history. "Muslim" and "Islamic" in these discourses have largely become what Allport (1958) called "labels of primary potency" that "act like shrieking sirens, deafening us to all finer discriminations that we might otherwise perceive" (p. 175). It has been a general tendency to portray Muslims, whether they be religious figures, caliphs, sultans, community leaders, presidents, prime ministers, dictators, or terrorists, behaving in accordance with dominant scripts that prescribe how they should act; their individual characters have been reduced to fit into the core stereotypes of Muslims.

One central theme emerges from Said's (1978, 1981) seminal work on Northern discourses about Muslims: "Islam" often is manipulated to mean what a particular source wants it to mean. A brief perusal of newspaper and magazine headlines reveals how this is done.[3] The "us and them" theme frequently appears in titles of articles such as "Islam Versus the West" (Woodward, Colton, Liu, & Whitmore, 1985, p. 28) and "Free Speech, Islamic Faith Meet Head-on in Pakistan" (Harvey, 1993, p. D9). Headlines in American magazines across the political spectrum appear to adhere to the dominant Northern discourses on "Islam"; for example, the right-of-center *Atlantic Monthly* has referred to "Muslim rage" (Lewis, 1990, p. 47), the popular newsweekly *Time* to "an angry faith" (Smith, 1989, p. 14) and the "dark side of Islam"

(Nelan, 1993, p. 50), and the left-wing biweekly *Mother Jones* to "the Vatican's dark marriage to Islam" (Hertsgaard, 1993, p. 20). A cover story in *Time* was titled "The Crescent of Crisis" (1979), thus appropriating a symbol of Islam to present the religion as embodying an endemic state of instability.

"Muslim fundamentalist," "Islamic radical," "Islamic terrorist," and so on generally are used in undefined ways by Northern observers, who often portray the approximately one billion Muslims of the world as a monolith. "Muslim" and "Islamic" become synonymous with "fundamentalist" in newspaper headlines such as "Moslems Battle Police in Malaysia Bloodbath" (Reuters, 1985, p. A17), "Egyptian Police, Moslems Clash" (Reuters, 1986, p. A6), "Algerian Muslims Seek Power" (Associated Press [AP] and Reuters, 1990, p. A18), and "Islamic Rioters Demand Freedom for Arrested Activists" (Associated Press, 1994, p. A8). Dailies have also spoken about an "Islamic death threat" (Reuters, 1984, p. D13), an "Islamic suicide mission" (United Press International [UPI], 1984b, p. B1), and an "Islamic powder keg" (Dyer, 1994, p. B3); it seems almost unthinkable that the adjective *Christian* would be used in such ways by mainstream Northern media. "Religious Hardliners Confident Islam Is Just Days Away" (Ibrahim, 1992, p. D7) implies that only "hardliners" adhere to the religion, which in this construct is turned into an event. Another headline, which actually seems to echo 7th-century history when Islam first emerged, declares, "Spread of Islam Likely to Change Arab Countries" (Franklin, 1990, p. G10). With "Islam" repeatedly reduced to fundamentalism, it appears that the dominant cognitive models and scripts treat its name and symbols as essentially signifying a deviant cult, not a worldwide religion.

Although there have been some genuine attempts by certain journalists to cut through stereotypical portrayals, they usually are overwhelmed by the ubiquity of dominant discourses that provide the frames within which public discussions take place (Karim, 1991; 1993, pp. 191-195). Little effort is made to impart an understanding of the considerable degree of diversity in culture, ethnicity, political orientations, and even religious beliefs and practices among those who profess Islam. When the actions of the Muslim Other seem to confirm Northern topoi about him or her, they usually are highlighted at the beginning of news broadcasts and on the front pages of newspapers and newsmagazines. Even though there are significant amounts of coverage about matters "Islamic," they appear in endless streams of episodic "facts" with no cohesive picture ever emerging. This ambiguity, combined with the media consumer's dependence on the macrostructures of previous reportage and on "biased recall" of its details (van Dijk, 1988, p. 23), leaves the propagandist free to manipulate the meaning of "Islam" according to his or her current needs.

Violence, Lust, Greed, and Barbarism

Said found the following "thematic clusters" in media coverage of the Middle East: terrorism as being congenital among Arabs and Muslims; Islamic fundamentalism as being synonymous with "the return of Islam"; contemporary Middle Eastern violence being referred back to "ancient" tribal, religious, or ethnic hatreds; the United States and Israel as representing "our side" in the contested site of the Middle East; Arabs and Muslims as being virulently anti-Semitic; and the Middle East as being "the hatching ground" of Palestinian violence ("The MESA Debate," 1987, pp. 88-89). Although particular aspects of some of these cognitive models have evolved since Said presented them in 1986, they generally reflect the ways in which coverage of the Middle East is framed by Northern journalists.

Shaheen (1984) offers a more concise list of "basic myths" about Arabs perpetuated by television: "They are all fabulously wealthy; they are barbaric and uncultured; they are sex maniacs with a penchant for white slavery; and they revel in acts of terrorism" (p. 4). Such images have framed dominant European perceptions of Arabs and Muslims since the Middle Ages, when, according to Kassis (1992), they were viewed as being "war-mongers," "luxury lovers," and "sex-maniacs" (p. 261). Kabbani (1986) notes in her study of 19th-century depictions of Muslims that:

> among the many themes that emerge from the European narration of the Other, two appear most strikingly. The first is the insistent claim that the East was a place of lascivious sensuality, and the second that it was a realm characterized by inherent violence. (p. 6)

Although differing in emphasis and in relation to the particular Muslim groups to which they have been applied over time, violence, lust, avarice, and barbarism clearly seem to be the primary Northern topoi of "Islam."

Arabs converting by "the sword of Islam" those whom they conquered is a popular myth in the North.[4] (Despite the significant numbers of Arabs who have continued to adhere to Christianity for nearly 2,000 years, dominant Northern discourses usually portray all Arabs as being Muslim.[5]) Out of the scores of Muslim caliphs and sultans under whose rule non-Muslim communities flourished (Hodgson, 1974), the handful of despots who persecuted non-Muslims as well as Muslim sectarians often are presented as being typical. In fact, as Hentsch (1992, pp. 107-113) shows, despotism is portrayed as the characteristically Muslim form of government.

The four Northern topoi of "Islam" often discursively interact with each other. Violence intermingles with avarice in images that imply that the wealth owned by the inherently slothful Muslims is undeserved because it is not the result of labor but rather is obtained through illicit and violent means. Also linked to the greed for material goods is the notion of lust for sexual as well as economic and political power. As we shall see, sexual desire becomes a trope for illegitimate appetite when discussing the involvement of Muslims in business and politics. Technological and cultural differences between contemporary Muslim and Northern societies often are viewed as evidence of barbarism. The latter topos also is seen as manifested in the Muslim's violence and sexual obsessions as well as in his or her implacable opposition to modernity and penchant for superstition and religious fundamentalism. What emerges is a series of paradoxical images of these greedy "lovers of luxury" who, despite being lamebrained and lazy by nature, are nevertheless able to use their wits and energies for nefarious purposes.

Personifications of the four topoi frequently are to be found in figures such as the cruel, barbaric, and lascivious but fabulously wealthy sheik. Inherent in such images is the idea of exoticism. The "mysterious East" invokes simultaneous but contradictory feelings of attraction and revulsion, of fascination and terror; the Orient invites prurient indulgence but is to be kept at a distance. The immense popularity in Europe and North America of the phantasmagoric "Arabian Nights"; the depictions of "exotic" Muslims in alternatively violent or languorous poses by Romantic artists such as Ingres, Delacroix, Deutsch, and Lewis (Kabbani, 1986, pp. 67-85); the numerous Hollywood films in which Muslims are villains (McClintock, 1982); and the portrayal by editorial cartoonists of "oil sheiks" as epitomes of greed (Michalak, 1984) illustrate the contradictory images of "sensuality, promise, terror, sublimity, idyllic pleasure, [and] intense energy" (Said, 1978, p. 118).

Whereas the Muslim Other also appears as a noble savage from time to time, the propagandist can easily strip off his or her nobility—as circumstances require—to display the essentially base nature of the barbarian. The pliability of the Muslim's image is well illustrated in this "final assessment" of the Arab character by the Victorian Orientalist Sir Richard Burton (famous for his travels in the Muslim East and for his translation of *The Arabian Nights*):

> Our Arab at his worst is a mere barbarian who has not forgotten the savage. He is a model mixture of childishness and astuteness, of simplicity and cunning, concealing levity of mind under solemnity of aspect. His stolid instinctive conservatism grovels before the tyrant rule of routine, despite the turbulent and licentious independence which ever suggests revolt against the ruler; his mental torpidity, founded upon physical indolence, renders immediate action and all manner of exertion distasteful; his conscious weakness shows itself in an overweening arrogance and intolerance. His crass and self-satisfied ignorance makes him glorify the most ignoble superstitions, while acts of revolting savagery are the natural results of a malignant fanaticism and a furious hatred of every creed beyond the pale of Al-Islam. (quoted by Tidrick, 1989, p. 83)

The latent Orientalism that Burton had most likely internalized during his upbringing appears to have remained the primary frame for his personal contacts with Arabs. Even after living in the Orient for many years, his "final assessment" amounted to filling in the "terminal nodes" of the scripts that had shaped his views of Muslims before he ever met one.[6] Despite the many Arabs with whom Burton was personally acquainted, he still could proceed to generalize about them as an undifferentiated mass, all sharing the same characteristics. Thus, on the eve of colonial expansion into the Middle East, Arabs were presented as no more than savages whom Europe could place under its suzerainty.

Historical Origins of the Four *Topoi*

There are several views regarding the evolution of Orientalist discourses that may conflict in detail but are basically compatible. Rodinson (1979, pp. 10-11) argues that although Christian polemical attacks on Islam began with the earliest contacts of the two religions, it was not until the 11th century, when Europe began to unite, that its typifications of Muslims began to take a clear shape. The *Reconquista* against Muslims who had occupied Spain, southern Italy, and Sicily, which required making common cause against the infidel Saracen, sharpened the sense of a European identity. The very consolidation of Western Christendom under the Holy Roman Empire and the papacy seems to have contributed to the rise of the Muslim as the primary Other.

Dossa (1987), by contrast, suggests that the differentiation between the Occident and the Orient might be traced back to Aristotle: "To Aristotle, the West is singular, distinctive, inimitable, precisely the respects in which it is rational, just, humanistic, cultured, and free . . . [whereas] *all* Orientals without exception are naturally slavish" (pp. 349-350). According to Dossa, when Aristotle spoke of the Greeks he presaged the notion of the West, and he thought of Asian Orientals as the true barbarians, as most un-Greek.

These views are challenged by Hentsch's (1992, p. 57) assertion that up to the Renaissance the northern Mediterranean region traditionally was included in the notion of the Orient and that the appropriation of ancient Greece into the West is a relatively recent development. He contends that the geopolitical boundary between the Orient and the Occident had been respected by the westernmost continental limits of the Alexandrian empire. The Romans confirmed this border by dividing their eastern and western domains along the same lines, and the western limits of both the Byzantine and the Ottoman empires reinforced them further. Hentsch says that it was not until the dawn of the modern era in the 16th century that Europe began to assume its contemporary shape and identity. "Once historical, the dividing line became, over time, one of 'cultural' demarcation in the deepest sense of opposition between the modern West and the traditional Orient" (p. 57).

Regardless of the differences among Rodinson, Dossa, and Hentsch, they all seem to agree that the definition of the East was carried out in tandem with more clearly defining the Self. They say that the darker lines of the Oriental Other began to emerge at the same time as the crystallization of the idea of the West, whether it happened in the 4th century B.C.E., the 11th century, or the 16th century. Easterners were thought of as everything that the Self was not. Even if derogatory notions of the East predated Islam, European reactions to this religion from the 7th century onward certainly have accentuated the repertoire of negative imagery about the Orient.

Central to the construction of the "Islam" that had to be defeated was the single-minded assault on the character of the religion's founder himself. The image of Muhammad was pitted against the ascetic picture of Christ.

> One of the strategies of this polemic was to ridicule Muhammad in the most virulent manner possible. He was described as an arch-seducer, who wore purple, coloured his lips, and delighted in scented things and coition. He was believed to have brought in God to warrant his own sexual indulgences. (Kabbani, 1986, pp. 14-15)

Such portrayals were meant not only to deny Muhammad's prophethood but also to confirm his sinfulness and the fraudulent nature of his mission. In contrast to the otherworldly Christian perception of Jesus, the Arab prophet not only was married (polygamously) but also was a ruler and led armies into battles. In the eyes of many medieval Christians, he seemed to be the antithesis of Christ; indeed, for some he was the Antichrist (Daniel, 1960, p. 280). One of the more ironic illustrations of this tendency was Dante Alighieri's use of Islamic eschatology. The notion of the various levels of heaven in the Arabo-Spanish narratives of Muhammad's spiritual ascent was borrowed by the 13th- and 14th-century Florentine poet in developing the structure of his *Divine Comedy* (Rozenthal, 1979, pp. 344-346). Despite this literary debt to the Islamic prophet, Dante cast him into the nether extremities of the "inferno."

Even as contact with the relatively advanced Muslim civilization was enabling Europe to emerge out of its Dark Ages (Rodinson, 1979, pp. 14-19), the vituperation against the founder of Islam seemed to increase. Norman Daniel, whose work stands as one of the most detailed studies of this subject, isolates three motifs of Muhammad's life in Christian polemics of the time. These were:

> the violence and force with which he imposed his religion; the salacity and laxness with which he bribed followers whom he did not compel; and finally his evident humanity, which it was constantly believed to be necessary to prove, although no Muslim denied it, or even wished to deny. (Daniel, 1960, p. 107)

We have in these impressions of the Islamic prophet the generative images with which "Mohammedans" were to be characterized in dominant Northern discourses.

In the view of Christian Europe, the greatest threat from Islam seemed to lie not in the differences but rather in the actual similarities with the monotheistic Judeo-Christian worldview (Said, 1978, p. 72). Whereas the Koran repudiates the concept of the godliness of Jesus, it reveres him as a major figure in the series of prophets of which Muhammad is considered the final. Because Muslims believed their faith to be the culmination of the tradition of Abraham, Moses, and Jesus, the Church had reason to see the religion that sprang from Arabia as a dangerous rival. Christendom initially tended to view Islam as one of the many heresies that abounded during the Middle Ages, and its prophet was presented as, among other things, a cardinal who, "thwarted in his ambition to become Pope, revolted, fled to Arabia, and there founded a church of his own" (Hourani, 1974, p. 11). Whereas the Enlightenment produced some less polemical discussions of the life of Muhammad by writers such as Thomas Carlyle, others such as Voltaire continued to attack the prophet of Islam for being violent, salacious, and irrational (Daniel, 1960, pp. 288-294). Even as late as the 20th century, a biography of Muhammad could carry the following summation:

> In spite of everything that can be said in defence of Mohammed's religious integrity and his loyalty to his call, his endurance, his liberality, and his generosity, we are not doing the Prophet of Islam an injustice when we conclude that his moral personality does not stand upon the same level with his other endowments, and indeed, not even upon the same level with his religious endowments. But if we would be fair to him we must not forget that, consciously or unconsciously, we Christians are inclined to compare Mohammed with the unsurpassed and exalted figure whom we meet in the Gospels, and that we cannot avoid seeing his historical personality against the background of the perfect moral ideal to which the faith of his followers tried to exalt him. And when it is measured by such a standard, what personality is not found wanting. (Andrae, 1960, p. 191)

This publication received glowing reviews from the Orientalist establishment. The back cover of the 1960 Harper and Row edition cited the following from a review by Arthur Jeffrey, a leading Islamicist: "As an introductory book on Mohammed, it is by far the best there is. Each year I recommend it strongly, and wish every student had his own copy to read and reread." Initially published in 1932 in German, it later was translated into English, Spanish, and Italian. Texts that conform to dominant models about the Other usually are made accessible to as large an audience as possible.

"Islam" as a Post-Cold War Other

Despite the rise of secularism, the prejudices that developed during the millennium of intermittent conflict between Christian and Muslim societies seem to have remained extant in collective cultural memories. Whereas current opposition against the Muslim Other may not be overtly religious, the perceived threat of being overwhelmed by "Islam" still is very strong. The literary classics that depicted the "Saracen" and the "Moor" as threats to Northern civilization have become part of the lore internalized even by atheist members of technological society (Khalidi, 1957, p. 15). Works such as Shakespeare's *Othello* have helped to link indelibly male jealousy and violent rage against women with the image of the "black Moor." The picture painted in the classics is complemented by that in school textbooks (Hayani, 1994). Operating within dominant Northern discourses, teachers (and adult family members) often present the South as filled with peoples unable to rise above their passions and as needing guidance from the North to become civilized.

And if children are not paying attention in school, they are certain to get the message from toys, comics, video games, and television, which frequently have implicit and explicit negative references to Muslims (as well as to other religious and ethnic minorities). The makers of these cultural products have successfully identified enemy figures that can be exploited for profit. Commercial purposes dovetail neatly with ideological ones in toys that reproduce primary stereotypes of Arabs and Muslims.

> Viciously anti-Arab prejudices are moulded to serve contemporary imperial politics: like the Coleco children's toy Rambo and his enemy "Nomad" with swarthy features, unmistakable head-dress, and Arabic writing on his cloak. The packaging tells us: "The desert is the country of the treacherous soldier Nomad. He is as unreliable as the sand, as cold as the nights, and as dangerous as the deadly scorpions that live there. His family is a gang of assassins and wandering thieves. They are men without honour, who use

> their knowledge of the desert to attack innocent villages." (Briemberg, 1992, pp. 248-249)[7]

Children are socialized in such manner into identifying the Other in the form of an Arab, who almost always is portrayed as a Muslim. References indicating that a significant number of Arabs also are Christian would interfere with their role as villains. Ritual "fights" can be staged with toys between the "good guy," who is the representative of the Northern technological civilization, and the "bad guy," who comes from a backward desert land and adheres to a primitive religion.

Television cartoons frequently have characters with cultural traits that are viewed as being Arab: "Children often see their heroes defeat lame-brained Arabs on magic carpets in cartoons with an Arabian Nights setting. Their knightly actions subdue monstrous genies, crush corrupt rulers, and liberate enslaved maidens" (Shaheen, 1984, p. 24). Even though Muslims sometimes may appear in positive renderings, these alternative images are mere flickers in the blinding floodlight of unfavorable portrayals. By the time children have grown up and are old enough to pay taxes, vote, and enlist in the military as well as publish writings, design toys, and produce films, they have been well socialized into identifying the "enemy." The initiated adults can thus participate in the continual cycle of "educating" yet another generation into recognizing the features of the Muslim Other so that new information about him or her can be interpreted in accordance with dominant models.

A survey of American attitudes toward Arabs elicited the responses "anti-American," "anti-Christian," "cunning," "unfriendly," and "warlike" (Shaheen, 1984, p. 7). Two Canadian studies inquiring about comfort levels with 14 ethnocultural groups (Angus Reid Group, 1992, p. 51) and impressions about eight ethnic and racial groups (Decima Inc., 1993, pp. 39-40) put Muslims near the bottom of both lists. An Australian survey measuring the social distance of respondents to 12 ethnic, racial, and religious groups placed Muslims the most distant (McAllister & Moore, 1988, pp. 7-13). Similar apprehensions were indicated in a French poll asking the question, "Which of the following countries appear to you today to be the most threatening to France?"

> In response, 25 percent said Iran, 21 percent the USSR, and 14 percent the Arab countries in general. More than half the respondents—57 percent to be exact—believed that one or more of the Muslim states are most threat-

> ening to France. Similar opinions can be found in the other countries of Western Europe. (Pipes, 1990, p. 29)

Such attitudes appear to predispose populations to propaganda campaigns such as that carried out by Western powers during the 1991 war between the U.N. Coalition and Iraq. The ease and speed with which the image of a former client state of the West (Friedman, 1993) was turned into one of a diabolical enemy appear remarkable. The journalists who had hitherto been reluctant to condemn the human rights abuses of Saddam Hussein's government suddenly seemed to discover its long-standing brutality (Chomsky, 1992).[8] Latent perceptions about Muslims allowed Northern propagandists to rekindle fear of the jihad that the Middle Eastern "Hitler," Hussein, was waging against civilization. War-mongering propagandists in the former Yugoslavia also have been successful in inciting fear among Serbs against Muslims in Bosnia-Herzegovina by raising the specter of "Islamic fundamentalism" (Reuters, 1992, p. A14). Ellul (1965) notes that:

> propaganda cannot create something out of nothing. It must attach itself to a feeling, an idea; it must build on a foundation already present in the individual. The conditioned reflex or a prior conditioned reflex. The myth does not expand helter-skelter; it must respond to a group of spontaneous beliefs. Action cannot be obtained unless it responds to a group of already established tendencies or attitudes stemming from the schools, the environment, the regime, the churches, and so on. (p. 36)

It is with amazing facility that the cold war frame is being adjusted to accommodate a new global conflict with the Muslim Other. As if to confirm the practical ease with which this can be done, one headline exultantly proclaimed during the Gulf War, "Cold War Battle Plan Transferred to Gulf" (MacKenzie, 1991, p. A9). The terminal node of this script, which previously had been occupied by Eastern Europe, was in this case filled by Iraq. Robert Kaplan, contributing editor to the *Atlantic Monthly,* declared in an article titled "The Cross and the Crescent" that "a cultural curtain is descending in Bosnia to replace the Berlin Wall, a curtain separating the Christian and Islamic worlds" (Kaplan, 1993, p. D3). The global war between "us" and "them," previously scripted as that between capitalism and communism, is being reconstructed by such propagandists as that between the Christian and Muslim societies. Justifications for the continued spending on the military-industrial complex also are made by *Newsweek* writers (Watson, Barry, & Waller, 1993) seeking to demonstrate the need for "A New Kind of Containment" with the subtitle "Stopping a resurgent Iraq—and Iran, too—will require a heavy U.S. military commitment" (p. 30). (Containment had been a key strategy against the Soviet Bloc during the cold war.) An article from the *Congressional Quarterly* on the Central Intelligence Agency, which also was distributed to newspapers by the Scripps Howard News Service, advised both politicians and the mass readership that:

> today, the greater political threat is a long way from Moscow—in newly independent republics like Kazakhstan, where hundreds of former Soviet nuclear weapons are stored, in the streets of Medellin, Colombia, where the drug cartels are based, and in the mosques of Iran, where the seeds of Islamic fundamentalism are sown. (Griffin, 1992, p. B3)

The U.S. Central Intelligence Agency, which had hitherto spent billions of dollars on activities against the Other in the form of the Eastern Bloc, must now shift its sights southward. This is not a difficult case to make to audiences who already adhere to negative cognitive models of the South and "Islam."

Terrorism and Jihad

Dominant Northern discourses on Islam and on violence blend in, creating the notion of "Islamic terrorism." The entrenched image of Muslims as being innately prone to violence and the perception that international violence usually is carried out by Southern countries, either against each other or against Northern interests (Chomsky, 1992), together allow for the construction of Islamic terrorism as a unique phenomenon. The coalescence of these two discourses makes the violence carried out by Muslims the worst kind of terrorism because it is seen as opposing modern civilization with a barbaric irrationality and as being supported by a historical tradition of fanatical violence. Not only does such a view imply that the religion of Islam promotes gratuitous destruction, it completely disregards the structural violence resulting from the North's economic and cultural hegemony over the globe as well as the direct violence supported by Northern powers against Southern interests (George, 1986).[9]

The Muslim terrorist has come to be a major figure in the typology of characters who perform in contemporary "dramas" involving "Islam." It does not require much rescripting to present him or her as a current incarnation of the violent man of Islam. The Muslim terrorist becomes a composite type disassociated from the distinctly different historical and social circumstances in Lebanon, Iran, Egypt, Israel, Afghanistan, India, Algeria, and the United States, where specific groups have attempted to justify their political violence in religious terms. A magazine article titled "Political Terror in the Muslim World" by Elie Kedourie, a well-known Orientalist, supported this mode of thinking: "The fact that political terrorism originating in the Muslim and the Arab world is constantly in the headlines must not obscure the perhaps more significant fact that this terrorism has an old history" (Kedourie, 1987, p. 12).

Because the contemporary actions of Muslims often are attributed to their "ancient" hatreds, it was logical for Kedourie (1987, p. 13) to construct a genealogy of Islamic terrorists. He did this by relating that the "first political assassination" to take place in Muslim history was that of Ali (Muhammad's son-in-law) in 661; that Hasan-i-Sabbah during 11th- and 12th-century Iran "may be considered as a foremost exponent of the theory and practice of terrorism"; that Jamal al-din Afghani (a 19th-century reformer) "certainly believed in assassination"; that during the 1940s and 1950s the Muslim Brethren in Egypt, the Fedayan-i Islam in Iran, and a Communist group in Algeria engaged in terrorism; that President Gamal Abdel Nasser of Egypt had either contemplated or carried out assassinations as a young army officer; that members of a Muslim group attempted to kill President Assad of Syria and another one succeeded in assassinating President Sadat of Egypt; and that "Khomeini's Iran . . . exemplifies the idea of a 'terrorist state.' " Although Kedourie's brief history of Muslim terrorism appears coherent within dominant cognitive models, a similar attempt at linking the murders of the American Presidents Abraham Lincoln, James Garfield, William McKinley, and John Kennedy and of Senator Robert Kennedy to demonstrate that assassination is an inherent characteristic of American presidential politics would be considered ludicrous.

Operating within the parameters of dominant models about "Islam," journalists frequently can get away with making poorly supported statements about Muslims. Because audiences share these models, the obvious bias in journalistic discourse goes undetected. References in news stories about the devotion of Muslim terrorists to Islam often seem to be offered as vague explanations of why they are engaged in illicit activities. For example, an article on the capture of a Lebanese hijacker by the Federal Bureau of Investigation stated, "Fawaz, a devout Muslim and alleged mastermind of a 30-hour airliner hijacking two years ago, was interested in buying a large quantity of drugs for his further sale, the officials said" (United Press International, 1987, p. A18). This person was presented as a "devout Muslim" who carried out hijackings and drug trafficking; it would appear from this that devotion to the Islamic religion includes participation in deviant activities. The writer did not feel it necessary to justify the implicit link because the script for Muslim terrorism renders even such ambiguity coherent.

The "facts" of news merge with fiction in bestselling novelist John Le Carré's depiction of a Palestinian terrorist in his book *The Little Drummer Girl.* In a manner similar to that of the wire service report, the sacred and the profane intertwine as he uses the dominant model of the Muslim terrorist to embellish his work.

> He was picked up again when he arrived by air in Istanbul, where he checked into the Hilton on a Cypriot diplomatic passport and for two days gave himself to the religious and secular pleasures of the town. The followers described him as taking one last good draught of Islam before returning to the Christian commons of Europe. He visited the Mosque of Suleiman the magnificent, where he was seen to pray no less than three times, and afterwards to have his Gucci shoes polished once, on the grassy promenade that runs beside the South Wall. (Le Carré, 1983, p. 58)

It did not seem relevant that during the early 1980s, when Le Carré wrote the book, Palestinian Muslim fundamentalists had not yet become active participants in terrorism or that a significant number of the Palestinians responsible for terrorist acts in Europe had Christian backgrounds (e.g., George Habbash, leader of the Popular Front for the Liberation of Palestine, one of the most active organizations of its kind).

Northern mass media usually link Muslim terrorism to the notion of jihad (literally, righteous struggle), a concept that some Muslims use to justify their military and socioeconomic actions. Those motivated by jihad are not seen as acting according to the logic operative in the "civilized world" and are thus considered deviant and barbaric. The motivations behind jihad and its nature usually are presented as being inexplicable. An editorial in the *Ottawa Citizen* on the ferocity of the war that Iran and Iraq fought during the 1980s stated, "For Iran at least, this is a holy war to which there are seemingly no rational limits" ("Horrifying Crimes," 1988, p. A8). Commenting on the participation of Afghan boys in guerrilla activities, a *Time* magazine article declared, "In a jihad, or holy war, there are no age guidelines for combat. If a commander decides a boy is ready, then he fights" (Stanley, 1990, p. 34). It is ironic that despite the law-bound character of orthodox Islam, it often is described in the North as lacking in formal rules.

During Iraq's war with the U.N. Coalition in 1991, the dominant discourses did not consider the massive force used by the major Western powers as constituting violence; on the other hand, they referred to the former as a "terrorist state." The figure of Hussein as the owner of clandestine weapons of mass destruction and a despot calling Muslims to jihad made him a focal point of such narratives. An editorial in the *Ottawa Sun* declared,

> While *we* may be fighting a war in the Persian Gulf, Saddam Hussein and his followers are fighting a *jihad.* The difference is enormous.
>
> *Jihad* is an Arabic word meaning "holy war," and, indeed, it explains why Saddam's strategies may be unpredictable, even incomprehensible, and will be right until this conflict reaches its inevitable end: the defeat of Saddam Hussein.
>
> The concept of *jihad* has become the wild card in the Gulf War. It makes it impossible to understand fully the goals, aims, and objectives of Saddam Hussein.
>
> Ordinary rules play no role in a *jihad*—only God's law as interpreted by those who believe in *jihad.* ("A Holy War?" 1991, p. 10; emphases in original)

Statements like these that portrayed Hussein in the guise of the Muslim Other rarely were challenged because they seemed valid within dominant models about the ways in which Muslims are supposed to act. The secularist nature of the Ba'athist (Arab Socialist) government and its persecution of Muslim leaders who openly disagreed with it was overshadowed by Hussein's "Islamic" posturing. Also largely unpublicized by the Western media was the fact that Hussein's foreign minister and main spokesperson to the West, Tariq Aziz, is Christian. Western propagandists could use information selectively in this manner to build consensus about a "just war" against Iraq. The focus also was placed on Iraq's Soviet-made long-range (albeit highly inaccurate) SCUD missiles rather than on the billions of dollars worth of Western armaments supplied to Iraq during and after its previous war with Iran (Friedman, 1993). This seemed to create the remarkable consensus for the Western involvement in the Gulf War, much in contrast to the divisiveness engendered by the Vietnam War.

That the "good Muslims" on the side of the U.N. Coalition had also declared a jihad seemed irrelevant to those who used Hussein's "Islamicness" to demonize him. Dominant Western discourses on Islam have systematically tended to make distinctions between those Muslims who are allies of the West and others who are not. This differential treatment is reflected in the semantic techniques that the mass media have adopted in using words such as *jihad* and *mujahidin*. Although the term *jihad* has had an unfavorable connotation in Western media, *mujahidin* (which in Arabic refers to people engaged in jihad) usually was presented within positive frameworks during the 1980s. This appellation generally was restricted to Muslim groups fighting the enemies of the West. Conversely, anti-Western elements who also called themselves *mujahidin* rarely were termed as such; rather, they generally were shown as carrying out a *jihad*. For example, Afghan guerrillas who fought against Soviet troops as well as an Iranian guerrilla organization opposed to the Teheran government usually were referred to as *mujahidin* (see Gerol, 1987, p. A6). On the other hand, *jihad* frequently was emphasized in the coverage of Muslim groups in Egypt and Lebanon fighting their respective national governments—as well as of Afghan groups once the Soviets began retreating from Afghanistan. Therefore, the lack of knowledge among Western audiences about the relations of particular terms used in Muslim discourses allows propagandists to enhance the images of friends and foes in Muslim societies.

Words such as *Shi'ite, ayatollah,* and *jihad,* derived from the terminologies of Muslim peoples, have been appropriated by Northern discourses to connote a planetary war against progress. A cover story in the *Atlantic Monthly* (Barber, 1992) pitted *jihad* and *McWorld* as the "two axial principles of our age," both of which were presented as global threats to democracy. Whereas *McWorld* (derived from the worldwide reach of the fast food restaurant chain McDonald's) indicated the increasing integration of the planet through technology, communications, commerce, and ecological concerns, *jihad* in its interpretation as "Islamic holy war" became the epitome of disorder and a trend toward the "retribalization" of the world. The "two axial principles" were seen as destabilizing the sovereignty of the nation-state within which democracy can properly function. Adhering to the technological myth of the nation, the author did not deal with the frequent failure of the modern state to integrate its component parts.[10] Instead, he glorified it at the expense of "subnational factions," whom he described as being "in permanent rebellion against uniformity and integration—even the kind represented by universal law and justice . . . [and] seeking smaller worlds within borders that will seal them off from modernity" (pp. 59-60). Rebellion against the nation-state was automatically interpreted as opposition to modernity, and what better way to portray such regressive tendencies than through *jihad*—the "Islamic holy war."

The Sultans of Sleaze

Next to the topos of violence, "Islam" is most frequently linked to sexuality. This core image generates secondary portrayals of Muslim men and women as being mainly motivated by lust as well as of males denying females basic human rights, performing genital mutilation of daughters, abducting women, indulging in "white slavery," marrying a large number of wives, confining them to harems, and divorcing them at will. It is certain that some of these injustices are carried out by individuals who profess Islam and who present religious justifications for them. However, although they are by no means practiced uniformly in Muslim societies, dominant Northern discourses traditionally have indicated otherwise. Depiction of Oriental sexuality was a primary preoccupation of many writers, poets, and painters of the Romantic period. Intrigues in the seraglio (i.e., harem), which was forbidden to the outsider, became a major theme of artistic works portraying Muslim societies. Oriental women were presented as spending their lives in sexual preparation and in sexual intrigue. The European painter seemed to become a voyeur, producing a large number of paintings depicting Eastern women bathing or in stages of undress. Jean Auguste Dominique Ingres's famous painting *Le Bain Turc* actually seems constructed to give the impression of looking through a keyhole.

> Such portraits, in wishing to convey the East, described more accurately Europe. They portrayed the repressiveness of its social codes and the heavy hand of its bourgeois morality. The gaze into the Orient had turned, as in a convex mirror, to reflect the Occident that had produced it. (Kabbani, 1986, p. 85)

Depictions of Oriental women differed qualitatively from those of European women because, as will be discussed more fully, discourses on Eastern sexuality generally occur within the context of imperial power. The desires and characteristics that one does not admit having often are projected onto the Other; these features are made out to be exceptions in one's own society and the norm in that of the latter (Ivie, 1980, p. 280).

Although contemporary mores of Northern societies are less restrictive, portrayals of the Muslim East frequently contain references to unrestrained lust. The broader range of media available allow for the proliferation of secondary images in which sex appears as a major motivation for the Muslim's activities.

> Motion pictures of the early 1900s presented Arabia as an exotic land, with harems and seductive belly dancers. Many of today's perceptions can be traced to *the* motion picture of the 1920s, *The Sheik,* starring Rudolph Valentino. The film spurred the practice of lumping Arabs—Egyptians, Iraqis, Bahrainis, and others—as a collective group. The film also spawned the illusion of the romantic sheik who abducts young ladies and confines them in his desert tent. . . .
>
> Television has replaced the movie's seductive sheik of the 1920s with the hedonistic sheik of the 1980s. In today's films and television shows, Arabs do not only pursue women, but a host of things, like American real estate, business, and government officials. (Shaheen, 1984, p. 13)

The primary theme of lust thus merges with that of the Muslim Other's avarice, both appetites being satisfied by immoral, if not illicit, means.

Lust also appears as a key metaphor in explaining Muslims' political activities. The connection between sex and politics seems to occur naturally for some Northern ideologues when discussing Muslim societies. Said (1978, pp. 314-316), in what became a much-debated part of his book *Orientalism,* deconstructed a description of Muslim notions of revolution advanced by Bernard Lewis (a major figure in the Anglo-American Orientalist establishment for more than half a century). Lewis (1972) associated the Arabic term *thawra* (revolution) with the image of a camel rising and with feelings of excitement. Said saw this description as implying that Arabs and Muslims were not capable of serious political action and were ruled by their emotions and their sexuality. According to Said, the systemic linking of Muslims' violence to motives that are less than noble serves to delegitimize it; political activities can readily be interpreted as motivated more by characteristic lust and greed for power than by a sense of social justice. Even if Said can be faulted for overinterpreting Lewis, one would expect the latter to know that in popular Northern culture dromedarian analogies are the common currency of racist insults against Arabs (Michalak, 1984, p. 4). It appears, however, that Said's critical discourse analysis did have an effect. In a later work, *The Political Language of Islam,* Lewis (1988, p. 96) did not reuse the metaphor of excitement for his description of *thawra.*

Journalists often seem to go out of their way to emphasize the sexual when writing about episodes involving Arabs or Muslims. For example, news stories about police raids on upscale bordellos seem to make special efforts to indicate the presence of "Arab sheiks" among the wealthy but otherwise unidentified clients (UPI, 1984a, p. F9). Even the practice of the Islamic religion is at times described with sexual metaphors; festivities surrounding the holy month of Ramadan were related by the Toronto-based *Globe and Mail* with the headline "Egyptians Mark Fast With Orgy of Feasts" (Martin, 1992, p. A6), invoking images of a cult obsessed with satisfying its base appetites. Viewed from the dominantly desexualized worldview of Christianity, the Muslim Other is presented as a foil for the disciplined Self: "The West is social stability; the East pleasure, unrestricted by social dictates" (Kabbani, 1986, p. 21). A feature article titled "The Women of Fundamentalist Islam" by a writer for the U.S.-based Cox News Service stated that "Islamic fundamentalists speak dozens of different languages and come from hundreds of different ethnic groups in more than 30 nations spread across the belly of the world" (Scroggins, 1992, p. B2). Muslim countries were linked to the lower and symbolically unruly part of the body in this critique of male-female relationships in "Islam"; Europe and North America, corresponding to the head, would be the rational and disciplined intellect.

The British newsweekly *The Spectator* ran a lead story in 1991 about the damaging effect on the Bank of England of the collapse of the Arab-owned and Pakistani-operated Bank of Credit and Commerce International (BCCI). The cover page had a cartoon showing a swarthy man with dark glasses attempting to embrace an elderly white woman sitting on a locked trunk marked "Bank of England." She was crying out "Murder!—Murder! Rape!—Murder! O you Villain! what have I kept my Honour untainted so long to have it broke up by you at last? O murder!—Rape! Ravishment! —Ruin! Ruin! Ruin!" ("Political Ravishment," 1991). The caption read "POLITICAL RAVISHMENT or the

Old Lady of Threadneedle Street in danger!" Indignant about the accusations that laid some of the blame for BCCI's collapse on the Bank of England, the magazine portrayed the event as a rape of the "grand old lady" by the Muslim owners and operators of the foreign bank. The publication was able to exploit the scripted images of the Muslim Other's lust, violence, and greed to emphasize the virginal purity of the Self in the guise of the Bank of England.

In a sociological study of Moroccan society, Mernissi (1987) effectively demonstrates the complexity of its male-female dynamics (see also Mule & Barthel, 1992). However, most Northern discourses appear disinterested in looking at the correlations as well as the contradictions between Muslim scripture and history, law and social reality, traditional family structures and modernist aspirations, "Islamic fundamentalism" and current economic dilemmas—all of which shape relationships between contemporary Muslim women and men. Dominant Northern perspectives are insistent in viewing the rest of the world through Eurocentric experiences and expectations. Even Northern liberal, feminist, and leftist analyses of Muslim societies largely remain couched in medieval Christian and colonialist assumptions about Muslims. While criticizing the restriction of women's freedom by the reinstitution of "Islamic law" in certain Muslim countries, L. Ahmed (1992) draws attention to the ideological uses of Northern narratives on Muslim women:

> There can be few people of Arab or Muslim background (including, and perhaps even particularly, the feminists among them) who have not noticed and been disheartened by the way in which Arab and Muslim "oppression" of women is invoked in Western media and sometimes in scholarship in order to justify and even insidiously promote hostility toward Arabs and Muslims. It is disheartening, too, that some feminist scholarly work continues to uncritically reinscribe the old story. (p. 246)

Some Northern feminist discourses appear to be participating—indeed reinforcing—the North's cultural hegemony toward the South. The challenge for those who would seek to develop truly alternative discourses is first to recognize their own deeply embedded biases.

Integral to the topos of lust is the theme of the male Muslim's attempts to control his female counterpart's equally irrepressible sexuality. During the colonial era, European men often thought of themselves as knights in shining armor rescuing Muslim maidens from their oppressive male coreligionists (Kabbani, 1986, pp. 79-81). Contemporary mass media, in various instances, also capitalize on the image of the repressed Muslim female to justify Northern dominance of Muslim societies. When a story confirming this image appears even in a relatively obscure source, the mass media (which usually rely on their own correspondents or major news services) will tend to use it. For example, in its front-page "Spotlight" feature, the *Ottawa Citizen* reprinted a story from the little-known *Dallas Morning News.* Titled "Death or Honor: Ritual Killing Removes Stain," the article attempted to present a West Bank villager's murder of his unmarried pregnant daughter as an event that summed up the character of the entire Arab and Muslim worlds:

> Nura's death—involving family honor and blood revenge—underscores the position of women in traditional Arab society and the struggle by a tribal culture to cope with modernity. It also illustrates the vast cultural differences between Arab and Western societies.
>
> Many Arabs, especially those in urban areas, are well-educated and would be appalled by the thought of a ritual killing. But Arab experts say millions of people have fallen back on the traditional culture and a strict religious code as the answers to economic and social problems.
>
> When Iran's Ayatollah Ruhollah Khomeini sentenced British novelist Salman Rushdie to death for insulting the Muslim prophet Mohammed in the novel *The Satanic Verses,* he briefly lay bare to the West the Arab [*sic*] concept of honor and blood revenge, which is growing in strength with the Islamic fundamentalism.
>
> Many Arab specialists contend that these cultural differences play a major part in the conflict between Israeli Jews and Arabs in the occupied territories and surrounding countries.
>
> "Jewish society, like Western Christian society, is a guilt-oriented society," said Moshe Sharon, a professor of Islam at Hebrew University.
>
> "But Arab society is a shame-oriented society," Sharon said. (Hedges, 1989, pp. A1-A2)

From an incident that occurred in one village in the West Bank, the writer liberally extrapolated in a concentric manner to Palestinian culture, to Arab culture, and then to Muslim culture. The journalist was able to base generalizations about one fifth of humanity on the actions of one man because dominant Northern discourses on "Islam" support such flights of logic. Because Muslim males are viewed as being basically violent, barbaric, and oppressive toward their women, it was possible for him to get away with writing what would be viewed as incoherent in most other contexts. The journalist's bias is largely invisible to the mass readership, which shares his script about how Muslims act.

Only the "well-educated" Arabs—that is, those who are Westernized and who apparently have abandoned traditional cultural and religious values—would be "appalled by the thought of the ritual killing." The barbaric "ritual" is implied as being Islamic in nature and shared by Muslims in Iran; "Islamic fundamentalists" are presented as especially favoring it. Having failed to curb her lust through other forms of "Islamic" repression, Nura's father performed the final sacrificial rite. Ideological closure was drawn from the words of an Israeli Orientalist whom the journalist referred to as an "Arab specialist" and "professor of Islam"; he authoritatively proclaimed what was the essential divergence between Judeo-Christian values and those of Arab-Muslim society—between "us" and "them" (No Palestinian academic sources were cited in the article). It therefore became the burden of Judeo-Christian civilization to introduce modernity and human rights to the Arab Other by forcibly occupying his or her land. The intense level of direct and structural violence against men as well as women and children involved in such colonial ventures is disregarded; instead, as is normal for the mass media, the focus is placed on individual incidents of violence such as Nura's murder. The significance of this article lies not only in its racist content but also in the fact that it was accessed from a little-known source and featured prominently in the newspaper. This was done because it narrated perfectly the part scripted for "Islam." Seeming to validate dominant beliefs about the Muslim Other, it was intellectually comforting and it affirmed the sense of self-superiority. In placing the "spotlight" on barbaric acts in other cultures, we can shift attention from the massive and systemic violence against women in our own culture (Statistics Canada, 1993), assuaging our "guilt-oriented society" that we are not that bad after all.

Conclusion

Stereotypes that people living in the North and those living in Muslim societies have held of each other have inhibited intercultural communication for centuries. This situation does not appear to be improving as propagandists on each side seem intent on mutually portraying the other as the "Great Satan." The North, being vastly more powerful, is in a position to harm Muslim societies militarily, economically, and psychologically. Because it controls international communication networks, its core images of Islam are transmitted across the planet, influencing the way in which hundreds of millions of media consumers perceive Muslims. Viewers of Northern television programs even in countries such as Peru, Lesotho, Samoa, and New Guinea are seeing the followers of the religion as given to violence, lust, greed, and barbarism. On the other hand, Muslim societies, being limited in their access to the means of international mass communication, have a comparatively insignificant effect on global image making.

There are tangible consequences arising from the dominant stereotypes that the North has of "Islam." The motives of Muslims are rendered suspicious because Muslims are viewed as being endemically deceitful, their business dealings become dishonest due to their lust for material possessions, their political activities become illegitimate because they always are motivated by base desires, and their military actions become illicit because they are carried out as "holy wars." "Arab-looking" people are detained by authorities on suspicion of being "Islamic terrorists," and public support for punitive actions against countries with Muslim majorities is mobilized with relative ease, whereas, on the other hand, politicians become indecisive about aiding victimized Muslim groups such as those in Bosnia-Herzegovina and Chechnya. With the rise of the Muslim as the post-cold war Other, the future holds increasing possibilities of clashes with him or her.

The latter is no longer a distant entity that can just be read about in the foreign sections of newspapers; rather, it is increasingly present among us. The Muslim Other is steadily becoming a part of pluralist Northern societies and can no longer be thought of as completely extraneous. He or she is our classmate, coworker, business partner, neighbor, or even spouse. It is inevitable, therefore, that the manner in which the Self approaches the domestic Other will help determine the future of the generational cycle that historically has preserved and perpetuated the core images of the external Other.

The identification of macrostructures, such as the network of primary stereotypes held by one culture about another, allows critical discourse analysts to deconstruct and unveil the discursive strategies that create and sustain structures of power and of inequity. This mode of analysis demonstrates the importance of understanding the role that historical relationships between two cultures play in the construction of contemporary discourses about each other. Discursive material that seems coherent within dominant scripts and models can in this way be shown to be dependent on perceptions developed over time and not on absolute values. By placing a particular depiction of a group within the context of the dominant discourses about the group, this kind of analysis also helps put the lie to the propagandist's ritual explanation that the specific portrayal is an isolated occurrence. An area for further research could be the location and study of specific networks of primary stereotypes that other cultural and social collectivities have developed over time in their discourses about the Other. Apart from helping deconstruct these discourses, such research would be invaluable in enabling members of rival groups to understand and conceivably resolve intergenerational conflicts.

Notes

1. Research on Northern discourses about Muslims usually has concentrated on particular periods or media, for example, Antonius (1988) on mass media and toys, Hayani (1994) on contemporary textbooks, A. Ahmed (1992) on postmodernist culture, Hentsch (1992) on 11th- to 20th-century literature and philosophy, Briemberg (1992) on contemporary literature, Simon (1989) on crime fiction, Dossa (1987) on ancient Greek philosophy, Kabbani (1986) on Romantic art, Shaheen (1984) on television, Michalak (1984) on contemporary popular culture, Said (1978, 1981) on 19th- to 20th-century literature and on 20th-century mass media, and Rodinson (1979) on past and contemporary Orientalist studies. The present inquiry uses the findings of such studies to develop a framework for the discursive analysis of Eurocentric discourses on Muslims.

2. The term "collective cultural memory" is not analogous with the Jungian concept of the collective unconscious. The former is conceptualized as being primarily cultural in nature and the latter as being mainly psychological. See also van Dijk (1988, pp. 25-26).

3. Van Dijk (1988) says that headlines, "together with the activated scripts and models . . . will further guide, facilitate, and sometimes bias understanding of the rest of the news report" (p. 24). For a fuller discussion on the structures and functions of headlines, see van Dijk (1991, pp. 50-70).

4. For example, a documentary produced during the late 1980s by the British television company Granada and a cover story by James Walsh in the June 15, 1992, issue of *Time* magazine both had this phrase as their titles.

5. Arab countries with large Christian communities include Lebanon, Egypt, Syria, and Iraq. A substantial proportion of Palestinians also are Christian. See, for example, Haddad (1970) and McLaurin (1979).

6. "Scripts may be thought of as abstract, schematic, hierarchically organized sets of propositions, of which the final nodes are empty (default values), so that they can be applied to different situations by filling in such terminal nodes with specific information" (van Dijk, 1988, p. 21).

7. Translated and quoted by Briemberg (1992, pp. 248-249) from Antonius (1988).

8. A similar situation has existed in relation to client states of the West such as Egypt, Saudi Arabia, Kuwait, and Indonesia.

9. In distinguishing structural violence from direct physical violence, Galtung (1981) describes it as manifested in the denial of basic material needs, human rights, and "higher needs."

10. Ellul (1965) identifies several myths by which technological society abides: "In our society the great fundamental myths on which all other myths rest are Science and History. And based on them are the collective myths that are man's principal orientations: the myth of Work, the myth of Happiness . . . the myth of the Nation, the myth of Youth, the myth of the Hero. Propaganda is forced to build on these presuppositions and to express these myths, for without them nobody would listen to it" (p. 40). See also Szanto (1978, pp. 47-49).

References

Ahmed, A. (1992). *Postmodernism and Islam: Predicament and promise.* London: Routledge.

Ahmed, L. (1992). *Women and gender in Islam: Historical roots of a modern debate.* New Haven, CT: Yale University Press.

Allport, G. (1958). *The nature of prejudice.* Garden City, NY: Doubleday Anchor Books.

Andrae, T. (1960). *Mohammed: The man and his faith.* New York: Harper & Row.

Angus Reid Group. (1992). *Multiculturalism and Canadians: Attitude study 1991.* Ottawa: Multiculturalism and Citizenship Canada.

Antonius, R. (1988). *Catégories politiques, groupes ethniques et distortion des faits dans le discours sur les Arabes.* Unpublished manuscript, Colloque de Moncton de 1988 de l'ACSALF, New Brunswick.

Arkoun, M. (1994). *Rethinking Islam: Common questions, uncommon answers.* Boulder, CO: Westview.

Associated Press. (1994, October 18). Islamic rioters demand freedom for arrested activists. *Globe and Mail* (Toronto), p. A8.

Associated Press and Reuters. (1990, June 14). Algerian Muslims seek power: Fundamentalists try to capitalize on vote's success. *Toronto Star,* p. A18.

Barber, B. (1992, March). Jihad vs. McWorld. *Atlantic Monthly,* pp. 53-63.

Briemberg, M. (1992). Sand in the snow: Canadian high-brow Orientalism. In M. Briemberg (Ed.), *It was, it was not: Essays and art on the war against Iraq* (pp. 238-251). Vancouver, British Columbia: New Star Books.

Chomsky, N. (1992). *Deterring democracy.* New York: Hill & Wang.

Connerton, P. (1989). *How societies remember.* Cambridge, England: Cambridge University Press.

Crescent of crisis: Troubles beyond Iran. (1979, January 15). *Time,* front cover.

Daniel, N. (1960). *Islam and the West: The making of an image.* Edinburgh, Scotland: Edinburgh University Press.

Decima Inc. (1993). *A report to the Canadian Council of Christians and Jews: Canadians' attitudes toward race and ethnic relations in Canada.* Toronto: Author.

Dossa, S. (1987). Political philosophy and Orientalism: The classical origins of a discourse. *Alternatives, 12,* 343-357.

Dyer, G. (1994, March 16). Islamic powder keg: Coming Algerian explosion could rattle the entire Arab world. *Montreal Gazette,* p. B3.

Ellul, J. (1965). *Propaganda: The formation of men's attitudes.* New York: Knopf.

Franklin, S. (1990, June 30). Spread of Islam likely to change Arab countries. *Ottawa Citizen,* p. G10.

Friedman, A. (1993). *Spider's web: The secret history of how the White House illegally armed Iraq.* New York: Bantam Books.

Galtung, J. (1981). The specific contribution of peace research to the study of violence. In *Violence and its causes* (pp. 83-96). Paris: UNESCO.

George, S. (1986). *How the other half dies: The real reasons for world hunger.* London: Penguin.

Gerol, I. (1987, June 24). West should replace Iran policy with strong support for Mojahedin opposition. *Ottawa Citizen,* p. A6.

Ghanoonparvar, M. (1993). *In a Persian mirror: Images of the West and Westerners in Iranian fiction.* Austin: University of Texas Press.

Griffin, R. (1992, December 26). "The company" seeks a new role. *Ottawa Citizen,* p. B3.

Haddad, R. (1970). *Syrian Christians in Muslim society: An interpretation.* Princeton, NJ: Princeton University Press.

Harvey, B. (1993, January 9). Free speech, Islamic faith meet head-on in Pakistan. *Ottawa Citizen,* p. D9.

Hayani, I. (1994, January 18). Textbooks perpetuate Arab stereotypes. *Toronto Star,* p. A17.

Hedges, C. (1989, March 14). Death or honor: Ritual killing removes stain. *Ottawa Citizen,* pp. A1-A2.

Hentsch, T. (1992). *Imagining the Middle East.* Montreal: Black Rose Books.

Hertsgaard, M. (1993, March/April). The Vatican's dark marriage to Islam has kept birth control off the international agenda. *Mother Jones,* pp. 20-22, 68-69.

Hodgson, M. (1974). *The venture of Islam: Conscience and history in a world civilization.* Chicago: University of Chicago Press.

A holy war? [Editorial] (1991, January 22). *Ottawa Sun,* p. 10.

Horrifying crimes in an atrocious war. (1988, March 28). *Ottawa Citizen,* p. A8.

Hourani, A. (1974). *Western attitudes towards Islam.* Southampton, England: University of Southampton.

Huntington, S. (1993, Summer). The clash of civilizations? *Foreign Affairs, 72,* pp. 22-49.

Ibrahim, Y. (1992, January 7). Religious hardliners confident Islam is just days away. *Ottawa Citizen,* p. D7.

Ivie, R. (1980). Images of savagery in American justifications for war. *Communications Monographs, 47,* 279-291.

Kabbani, R. (1986). *Europe's myths of the Orient.* Bloomington: Indiana University Press.

Kaplan, R. (1993, August 7). The cross and the crescent. *Globe and Mail* (Toronto), p. D3.

Karim, K. (1991). *Images of Arabs and Muslims: A research review.* Ottawa: Multiculturalism and Citizenship Canada.

Karim, K. (1993). Reconstructing the multicultural community in Canada: Discursive strategies of inclusion and exclusion. *International Journal of Politics, Culture, and Society, 7,* 189-207.

Kassis, H. (1992). Christian misconceptions of Islam. In M. Briemberg (Ed.), *It was, it was not: Essays and art on the war against Iraq* (pp. 254-264). Vancouver, British Columbia: New Star Books.

Kedourie, E. (1987). Ideas and anarchy in the Middle East. *Encounter, 69*(2), 58-65.

Keen, S. (1986). *Faces of the enemy: Reflections of the hostile imagination.* New York: Harper & Row.

Khalidi, W. (1957, December). Arabs and the West. *Middle East Forum,* pp. 11-26.

Le Carré, J. (1983). *The little drummer girl.* London: Pan.

Lewis, B. (1972). Islamic concepts of revolution. In P. Vatikiotis (Ed.), *Revolution in the Middle East, and other case studies* (pp. 31-40). London: George Allen and Unwin.

Lewis, B. (1988). *The political language of Islam.* Chicago: University of Chicago Press.

Lewis, B. (1990, September). The roots of Muslim rage. *Atlantic Monthly,* pp. 47-60.

MacKenzie, C. (1991, February 22). Waging of the war: Cold war battle plan transferred to gulf. *Globe and Mail* (Toronto), p. A9.

Martin, P. (1992, March 19). Egyptians mark fast with orgy of feasts. *Globe and Mail* (Toronto), p. A6.

McAllister, I., & Moore, R. (1988). *Ethnic prejudice in Australian society: Patterns, intensity, and explanations.* Unpublished manuscript, University of New South Wales.

McClintock, M. (1982). *The Middle East and North Africa on film: An annotated filmography.* New York: Garland.

McLaurin, R. (Ed.). (1979). *The political role of minority groups in the Middle East.* New York: Praeger.

Mernissi, F. (1987). *Beyond the veil: Male-female dynamics in modern Muslim society.* Bloomington: Indiana University Press.

Mernissi, F. (1992). *Islam and democracy: Fear of the modern world.* Reading, MA: Addison-Wesley.

The MESA debate: The scholars, the media, and the Middle East. (1987). *Journal of Palestine Studies, 16*(2), 85-104.

Michalak, L. (1984). *Cruel and unusual: Negative images of Arabs in popular American culture.* Washington, DC: American-Arab Anti-Discrimination Committee.

Mule, P., & Barthel, D. (1992). The return to the veil: Individual autonomy vs. social esteem. *Sociological Forum, 7,* 323-332.

Nelan, B. (1993, October 4). The dark side of Islam. *Time,* pp. 50-52.

Pipes, D. (1990, November 19). The Muslims are coming! The Muslims are coming! *National Review,* pp. 28-31.

Poliakov, S. (1992). *Everyday Islam: Religion and tradition in rural Central Asia.* Armonk, NY: M. E. Sharpe.

Political ravishment or the Old Lady of Threadneedle Street in danger! (1991, July 27). *The Spectator,* front cover.

Reuters. (1984, March 24). Western envoys get Islamic death threat. *Montreal Gazette,* p. D13.

Reuters. (1985, November 21). Moslems battle police in Malaysia bloodbath: Arrows, torches, bombs. *Montreal Gazette,* p. A17.

Reuters. (1986, December 27). Egyptian police, Moslems clash. *Globe and Mail* (Toronto), p. A6.

Reuters. (1992, August 14). Serbs see selves as "crusaders." *Toronto Star,* p. A14.

Rodinson, M. (1979). The Western image and Western studies of Islam. In J. Schacht & C. Bosworth (Eds.), *The legacy of Islam* (pp. 9-62). Oxford, England: Oxford University Press.

Rozenthal, F. (1979). Literature. In J. Schacht & C. Bosworth (Eds.), *The legacy of Islam* (pp. 318-349). Oxford, England: Oxford University Press.

Said, E. (1978). *Orientalism.* New York: Pantheon.

Said, E. (1981). *Covering Islam: How the media and the experts determine how we see the rest of the world.* New York: Pantheon.

Scroggins, D. (1992, July 11). The women of fundamentalist Islam: Back to a world ruled by men. *Ottawa Citizen,* p. B2.

Shaheen, J. (1984). *The TV Arab.* Bowling Green, OH: Bowling Green State University Popular Press.

Simon, R. (1989). *The Middle East in crime fiction: Mysteries, spy novels, and thrillers from 1916 to the 1980s.* New York: Lilian Barber.

Smith, W. (1989, February 27). Hunted by an angry faith. *Time,* pp. 14-20.

Stanley, A. (1990, June 18). Afghanistan: When Allah beckons. *Time,* pp. 34-37.

Statistics Canada. (1993, November 18). The violence against women survey. *Statistics Canada Daily,* pp. 1-4.

Szanto, G. (1978). *Theater and propaganda.* Austin: University of Texas Press.

Tidrick, K. (1989). *Heart beguiling Araby: The English romance with Arabia.* London: I. B. Taurus.

United Press International. (1984a, October 18). "Ivy League" madam arranged health insurance for call girls. *Montreal Gazette,* p. F9.

United Press International. (1984b, October 22). Islamic suicide mission organizer threatens more violence: Reports. *Montreal Gazette,* p. B1.

United Press International. (1987, September 19). Hijack suspect trapped by FBI with drug sting. *Ottawa Citizen,* p. A18.

van Dijk, T. (1988). *News analysis: Case studies of international and national news in the press.* Hillsdale, NJ: Lawrence Erlbaum.

van Dijk, T. (1991). *Racism and the press: Critical studies in racism and migration.* London: Routledge.

van Dijk, T. (1993). Principles of critical discourse analysis. *Discourse & Society, 4,* 249-283.

Walsh, J. (1992, June 15). The sword of Islam. *Time,* pp. 24-28.

Watson, R., Barry, J., & Waller, D. (1993, July 12). A new kind of containment: Stopping a resurgent Iraq—and Iran, too—will require a heavy U.S. military commitment. *Newsweek,* pp. 30-31.

Woodward, K., Colton, E., Liu, M., & Whitmore, J. (1985, June 24). Islam versus the West: Fundamentalism takes many forms besides terrorism. *Newsweek,* pp. 28-30.

8

Benetton Culture: Marketing Difference to the New Global Consumer

MICHAEL HOECHSMANN

> We felt obliged to get out of the traditional advertising formula. . . . For us, just showing the product at this point is banal.
>
> —Luciano Benetton, founder and managing director of Benetton Group SpA (quoted in Sischy, 1992, p. 69)

> I'd rather be ambiguous than stupid.
>
> —Oliviero Toscani, Benetton advertising creative director (quoted in television interview [Toscani, 1993])

Given the ubiquitous and pervasive role of advertising in the world today—its ability to transcend political, social, cultural, and generational borders—it has become one of the world's most powerful and unifying types of discourse.[1] Naturally, the specific message of advertisers varies according to the context of reception; even universal messages will offer different readings if, for example, they are consumed in the global North or the global South. Nevertheless, although international political bodies such as the United Nations have not supplanted local political discourses, advertising is leading the way in creating the cultural conditions for the so-called global village. The caveat to this argument, however, is that although advertisers have made great inroads in globalizing their message, much of the traditional thematic content of actual advertisements continues to depend on the appeal of the normative white American or European subject.

The clothing company Benetton has set out to change this. Aware of the evolving global political economy, Benetton has taken risks to distance itself from the "stupid" and "banal" tactics of mainstream advertisers. Beginning in 1984 and consolidated in 1985 with the launching of the "United Colors of Benetton" slogan, Benetton has stepped out of the shadows of Italy and France to enter into the global sphere with what I call its "two-tone campaign"—the multicultural, multiracial campaign on which Benetton has built its global empire. Emboldened by its new global prominence and sporting one of the world's best brand-name awareness profiles, Benetton started to take greater risks. This new direction in Benetton advertising, which I call the "small world campaign," began during the years 1989 to 1991 when a number of social and cultural taboos were broken. The campaign really accelerated in the spring of 1992, however, when Benetton began to use real documentary images of human and environmental crises, purportedly to advance the social awareness of issues of global concern.

The rapid success of Benetton is not predicated entirely on its bold initiatives in advertising. In addition to pioneering new directions in advertising, Benetton is a leading proponent of a new model of (post)industrial production, variously termed "post-Fordism," "just-in-time production," or "flexible accumulation." Benetton's initiatives at the site of consumption cannot be fully understood in the absence of some understanding of the broader context of its approaches to production. In fact, it soon becomes readily apparent that Benetton's approach to advertising is not at all enigmatic; rather, it is perfectly congruent with the new cultural politics of post-Fordism.

Benetton Culture

> For almost 10 years, Benetton has used advertising imagery that draws a symbolic parallel between the colorful, casual apparel that we sell and the many "colors" of our customers all over the world. These images have been celebrated internationally for their unique depiction of people of many races—together, united, equal, and in harmony. (Benetton Group SpA, 1992, p. 1)

By pioneering a new global vision aligned to its products, the multicultural two-tone campaign helped to solidify Benetton's current position of considerable prominence in the world clothing market. The two-tone campaign, which continues to characterize all of the company's product-bearing publicity shots, displays beautiful, smiling people of a variety of races and cultures, all decked out in Benetton's colors. To a great extent, Benetton simply reflected the everyday experiences of urban youth in the world's cosmopolitan centers. The underlying idea of the Benetton corporate image, as explained in *Colors* magazine, was simple: "Diversity is good. . . . Your culture (whoever you are) is as important as our culture (whoever we are)" (Benetton Group SpA, 1991-1992, p. 63). Or, as Oliviero Toscani explained to *Advertising Age,* "I tried to show the beauty of human relations that goes beyond the inhibitions of religion and race" (quoted in Levin, 1991, p. 1).

The upbeat shots of smiling, mixed-race models seemed so natural—so normal—compared to the contrived "I want to teach the world to sing" mountaintop utopia of a Coca-Cola advertisement, to mention one competing example. Of course, the success of this early campaign is apparent in the broad range of imitators it has inspired, for example, the Coca-Cola "Foreign Exchange" campaign as well as an "Act Up" gay and lesbian positive poster made by the Gran Fury art collective in New York (Benetton Group SpA, 1991-1992, p. 63). The themes implicit in the two-tone campaign—cultural diversity, world peace, happiness, beauty, and health, among others—were responded to as idealistic but compelling, a sort of pluralistic celebration at the global temple of consumption.

Cultural difference is central to the United Colors of Benetton corporate image—as symbolized by the company logo—and it continues to be signified in all of the company's product-bearing catalog shots. In 1992, Benetton entered the world of publishing with *Colors* magazine, a supplement to the biannual Benetton catalog. *Colors: A Magazine About the Rest of the World* is dedicated to cultural difference, combining interesting feature stories and high-quality images with the Benetton catalog of products. The editors state,

> *Colors* is about people. And music. And food. And sex. And the environment. *Colors* is about the cultural differences that make the world exciting. And how savoring those differences (rather than killing each other over them) could make the world a little less crazy. (Benetton Group SpA, 1992-1993, back cover)

Whereas cultural difference continues to play a crucial role in real-world struggles, the appeal to cultural difference in the united world of *Colors* magazine is a feel-good conviviality of a new global class of consumers who shop at the Benetton franchise outlets in far-flung corners of the world.

The editorial stance of *Colors* magazine mirrors that of the Benetton corporation: "Diversity is good." To maintain the credibility of this position, the editors take great pains to distance themselves from the global homogenizing effects of mass culture:

> While *Colors* is being distributed globally, in five bilingual editions, we feel a little funny about being global. It makes us feel like we're McDonald's, and we're not. We don't want to sell our culture to you. We want you to tell us about your culture. (Benetton Group SpA, 1991-1992, p. 63)

Of course, Benetton is in the business of selling clothes, not culture, and "learning" from other cultures is a necessary strategy for marketing in the growing global economy. This is the new cultural imperialism.

Although traditionally it has been construed as one of the lasting legacies of Coca-Cola, Big Macs, Walt Disney, and low-cost television reruns exported to the global South, cultural imperialism can be seen in retrospect as a misnomer for what has been more appropriately called "coca-colonization." This involves the imposition of the material practices of a dominant culture and its accompanying worldview with the hope of effecting some sort of transformation of everyday life at the receiving end. By contrast, cultural imperialism, as practiced by Benetton, is not so much cultural imposition as it is an opportunistic, branch-plant version of cultural appropriation.

The comparison to McDonald's is instructive of Benetton's new post-Fordist approach to marketing. Rather than fall into step with the coca-colonization approach of the Big Mac, a uniform, universal product so ubiquitous that *The Economist* now uses it as a surrogate global currency, Benetton has chosen to market a constantly shifting kaleidoscope of sweaters that respond to local market conditions. Because product difference is inscribed right into its commercial practices, it is no surprise that the marketing of cultural and racial difference has come to be an indispensable component of Benetton's success. In a nutshell, a simplistic metaphor is being drawn between the models and colors of Benetton sweaters and the world's cultures and races. If we can accept—

indeed embrace—the diverse colors of Benetton's varied sweaters, can we not do the same for the world's peoples?

Although at best the images in *Colors* and the two-tone campaign do normalize a positive vision of community where "diversity" is acknowledged and even celebrated, they gloss over both the troubling reality of racism and the political potential of "difference" as taken up by people of color. This is, of course, an impasse endemic to postmodern theories of social change (Eagleton, 1985, p. 71; Gruneau, 1988, p. 26). At a political level, postmodernism can represent the diverse recuperation of formerly dominant cultural agendas, showing how people respond to and rework cultural artifacts and practices. Seen as such, a bottom-up appropriation of culture rather than a top-down "breakdown of metanarratives," postmodernism is an empowering new concept of agency and the "popular." At best, then, this represents a site for the radical reappropriation by minorities and "marginal" groups of their own cultural realities. At worst, however, postmodernism is nothing more than an eclectic theory of marketing.

In *The Consumerist Manifesto,* Davidson (1992) comments on the broader trend in contemporary advertising of acknowledging and containing cultural difference. Davidson warns that although some critics may see images such as these "as something to be welcomed, it is pretty clear that they don't in themselves represent anything more than shopping getting cosmopolitan—this is not about lending a voice to the globe's dispossessed" (p. 200). Davidson echoes Jonathan Rutherford on the new tendency toward the marketing of difference. Rutherford (1990) states,

> Paradoxically, capital has fallen in love with difference; advertising thrives on selling us things that will enhance our uniqueness and individuality. . . . From World Music to exotic holidays in Third World locations, ethnic TV dinners to Peruvian knitted hats, cultural difference sells. . . . Otherness is sought after for its exchange value, its exoticism and the pleasures, thrills, and adventures it can offer. The power relation is closer to tourism than imperialism, an expropriation of meaning rather than materials. (p. 11)

However, although advertisers are opening up their texts to Other representations, they are actively working to contain and depoliticize the more explosive concept of difference by replacing difference with diversity, its "more manageable" cousin. Meanwhile, the economic interests of those corporations that are on the cutting edge of this new cultural politics of marketing, such as the Benetton Group SpA, are kept on the back burner.

At best, *Colors* is to youth-oriented magazines what World Beat is to popular music—a politicizing, agenda-expanding model. Because the editors of *Colors* believed that "positive change mostly comes from the bottom and percolates upward," they sought new types of heroes—"people who had invented a role for themselves in changing their society"—rather than the usual celebrities and politicians (Benetton Group SpA. 1991-1992, p. 63). However, although *Colors* features many interesting local heroes (from World Beat performers such as the Senegalese Youssou N'Dour to social activists such as the First Nations Canadian Winona Laduke) and many global cultural phenomena (from sushi hip-hop to Polish westerns to toys and food from around the world), the biggest hero seems to be Luciano Benetton and the most important culture seems to be the United Colors of Benetton.

In the first issue of *Colors,* the cast of stars from the Benetton head office is introduced, as is the Benetton compound (capped by a renovated 17th-century villa), much of the world's network of Benetton stores, and Luciano's favorite toy (a Formula I race car that represents Benetton on the Grand Prix circuit). By the time the third issue of *Colors* appeared in 1992, a specific "news" section had been created to house the trivia from *chez* Benetton. On the cover of this "news" supplement is a proud picture of Luciano holding up a "*io voto*" (I vote) United Colors of Benetton campaign T-shirt that sports his smiling visage, a relic from his successful bid to become a senator in Italy.

Benetton Economy

> Currently the largest manufacturer of knitwear in the world, Benetton was founded on a single prodigious idea: Struck by the beauty of his sister Giuliana's homemade sweaters, Luciano decided . . . to test their appeal on the open market. (Moynihan, 1984, p. 104)

The expansion of United Colors of Benetton since 1966 from a small local operation to a global marketing empire is one of those fairy tale success stories that keep entrepreneurial capitalism alive. At last count, there were more than 7,000 franchise stores in more than 110 countries around the world, accounting for gross sales of 2,500 billion lire in 1992, as well as a growing number of product licence agreements and commercial collaborations between Benetton and other producers (Benetton Group SpA, 1993). The commercial success of Benetton is so dramatic that economists and social theorists can even refer to a Benetton model for the production and circulation of goods (Enloe, 1989, p. 155; Murray, 1989, p. 57; Mytelka, 1991, p. 125; Phizacklea, 1990, p. 14), a textbook case of what is more broadly referred to as post-Fordism.

As epitomized by the production methods pioneered by Henry Ford in 1914 for his automated car assembly line, Fordism relied on consistency in both production and consumption. A precise number of cars would roll off the production line daily, and consumers were encouraged to choose from a limited number of models. The regularity of the form of production ensured worker security during a period when unionization was seen as an acceptable alternative to Bolshevism, and the regularity of consumption practices—bolstered by Keynesian social policies on the part of the government—ensured corporate productivity.

The central assumption of post-Fordism is that there has been a major shift in the mode of production in Western countries involving new flexible production techniques, a consolidation of markets, and an internationalization of capital. Although Fordism did not die—and has not died—overnight, the year 1973 is commonly seen as the watershed date of its imminent decline. The Organization of Petroleum Exporting Countries (OPEC) oil crisis of that year did not cause the change; it did, however, accelerate an already existing process. In geopolitical terms, post-Fordism has resulted in the transfer of the mass-production manufacturing industries to the non-Western developing world—and to "sweatshop" ghettos both at home and abroad—and the development at home of an "information society" with an ever-increasing service sector. One of the byproducts of this changing world is the growth of world trading blocks (as can be witnessed in the North American Free Trade Agreement) based in Europe, America, and Asia.

Thanks to computerization, the production and global circulation of goods can be controlled from head offices in New York, in Tokyo, or, in the case of Benetton, in Ponzano Veneto, Italy. The Benetton head office oversees the production of 74 million pieces of clothing each year in 15 factories scattered over two continents and sold through more than 7,000 franchise stores in about 110 countries on all continents. But among economists, Benetton is known not as a producer of goods but as a circulation empire, or, in the words of Harvey (1989), "a powerful marketing machine, which transmits commands to a wide array of independent producers" (p. 157). According to Murray (1989), "Benetton provides the designs, controls material stocks, and orchestrates what is produced according to the computerized daily sales returns which flow back to their Italian headquarters from all parts of Europe [and the world]" (p. 57). In practice, this centralized system of contracting out restricts worker organization or unionization. For example, Murray points out that only 1,500 of the 11,500 Benetton workers in northern Italy are directly employed by the corporation (p. 57). The majority are employed by subcontractors in factories of 30-50 workers each.

In human terms, the salient feature of post-Fordism is the attempt by corporations and social welfare governments alike to delegate social responsibility back to the individual worker. In the name of global competition, corporations have looked for rollbacks in worker wages and benefits as well as cost-cutting options such as contracting out and a part-time labor force. Phizacklea (1990, p. 16) reports that Benetton has been able to reduce its production costs by as much as 40% by contracting out to small, primarily family-run firms. Cash-starved governments have followed suit by trying to privatize public corporations and social services. The Republic of Cyprus, for instance, placed an advertisement in the *New York Times* in 1988 that stated, "The Benetton Approach: A Turning Point for Cyprus" (Enloe, 1989, p. 156). It comes as no surprise that, as a new senator, Luciano Benetton is looking into the "most appropriate way of using my business experience within the parliamentary system" to "promote lesser state presence in the economy" and to hasten "privatization" (quoted in Benetton Group SpA, 1992-1993, p. 2).

In addition to revolutionizing production, post-Fordism is known for a new niche marketing strategy. Instead of mass-producing a uniform style of standardized goods, corporations are attempting to diversify consumer identities into unique market niches. In a postmodern world where cultural identities have come out of the woodwork, niche marketing is an adaptive mechanism for advertisers and producers alike. Although Benetton concentrates on a limited number of products, "about 5,000 new models [are] presented each year, many of which reach as many as 40 colour variants" (Benetton Group SpA, 1991-1992, p. 129). These are designed according to "computer planned production on the basis of the individual shop requests, in order to allow personalized assortments in harmony with local choices" (p. 129). Thus computer inventories from the 7,000 worldwide franchise outlets are consolidated and acted on from Benetton headquarters. Products are subcontracted out as needed.

It should be noted that there is considerable controversy over the extent and scope of the current changes that are represented by flexible accumulation or post-Fordism. Harvey (1989), for one, expresses considerable doubt:

> Is [flexible accumulation] anything more than a jazzed-up version of the same old story of capitalism as usual? That would be too simple a judgment. It treats capitalism ahistorically, as a non-dynamic mode of production, when all the evidence (including that explicitly laid out by Marx) is that capitalism is a constantly revolutionizing force in world history, a force that perpetually re-shapes the world into new and often quite unexpected configurations. (p. 188)

Although post-Fordism appears to constitute a major shift in production and consumption, one of the defining features that distinguishes it from the rigidity of mass production is precisely its flexibility or unevenness. Therefore, Hall (1988) explains, one industry still "just entering its Fordist apogee" is the fast-food industry, which "can guarantee worldwide the standardization of the size, shape, and composition of every hamburger and every potato chip in McDonald's Big Mac from Tokyo to Harare" (p. 24). On the other hand, cars—and Benetton sweaters—have emerged into a post-Fordist era of market niche specialization and multiple variations of single models. As Harvey (1989) remarks, only time will tell whether these changes "betoken the birth of a new regime of accumulation" or merely a "transitional moment of grumbling crisis in the configuration of late twentieth-century capitalism" (p. 189).

Whether post-Fordism represents a significant rupture or not, the emergence of an information-driven economy in the global North has turned on its head the old Marxist base-superstructure metaphor of the relation between the economic sphere and the social and cultural spheres. Hall (1989) cautions that post-Fordism should not be understood as simply an economic phenomenon: " 'Post-Fordism' should also be read in a much broader way. Indeed, it could just as easily be taken in the opposite way—as signalling the constitutive role which social and cultural relations play in relation to any economic system" (p. 119). In stressing the mutually determining nature of the two sides of the old base-superstructure metaphor, Hall underscores the fact that culture cannot be understood simply as a reflection of the economy. Just as post-Fordist economies are marked by unevenness and flexibility, so too are post-Fordist cultural formations.

Concomitant with the new prominence of cultural politics in post-Fordism is the withering of the nation-state, the traditional site of political struggle. Currently, relations of power are being redrawn on a global scale. Whereas citizens are responsive to nationalism, consumers are responsive to brand awareness. In this new context, the ability of advertisers to associate their brand names with marginal or "exotic" cultural formations increases their likelihood of success. The departure of the Benetton Group SpA from traditional advertising formulas acknowledges the rapidly shifting and ever-unpredictable cultural terrain in the global North as well as the necessary inclusion of many new cultural matrices in the new global vision of consumer capitalism occasioned by post-Fordism.

Benetton Pedagogy

> If I was to choose one word for the present state of the world, one quickly comes to mind. Fucked! That's right. Fucked. (Lee, *Rolling Stone,* 1992, p. ii)

> Among the various means available to achieve the brand recognition that every company must have, we at Benetton believe our strategy for communication to be more effective for the company and more useful to society than would be yet another series of ads showing pretty girls wearing pretty clothes. (Benetton Group SpA, 1992, p. 2)

Just as Benetton seemed to have settled into a predictable publicity pattern and an array of imitators struggled to catch up, Benetton really turned heads in the field of advertising with its bold, striking "small world campaign." This is characterized by powerful images that reference social issues that have no apparent correlation to the products sold by Benetton but that prominently display the Benetton corporate logo. These images can be classified into two categories: those that break a variety of social and cultural taboos and those that attempt to promote social and environmental consciousness. The taboo images have included a newly born child still attached by the umbilical cord, a priest and a nun kissing, condoms, and a white child nursing at the breast of a black woman. The consciousness-raising images have ranged from

AIDS to war, from refugees to terrorism, from child poverty to child labor, and from pollution to capital punishment.

The new small world turn in Benetton's advertising has made a blanket condemnation of Benetton's marketing of difference more difficult. Whether these advertisements present images of human or environmental plight to encourage renewed social and environmental consciousness or whether they challenge existing cultural and institutional taboos, they are hard-hitting, arresting images. The impact of these advertisements is twofold. First, their shock value sets the Benetton advertisements apart from the rest, thus ensuring name recognition for Benetton products. Second, despite their shortcomings, they promote discussion of important social issues. Although these purposes overlap considerably, the former is intended primarily to help sell clothes, whereas the latter is an attempt to associate Benetton with progressive causes worldwide.

Although the small world advertisements raise provocative contemporary issues, they are presented in an ahistorical, reified fashion. The criticism that the late Roland Barthes made in *Mythologies* of Edward Steichen's "Family of Man" photography exhibit, first shown in 1955, can be aptly applied to Benetton advertisements:

> Everything here, the content and appeal of the pictures, the discourse which justifies them, aims to suppress the determining weight of History; we are held back at the surface of an identity, prevented precisely by sentimentality from penetrating into this ulterior zone of human behaviour where historical alienation introduces some "differences" which we shall here quite simply call "injustices." (Barthes, 1972, p. 101)

Barthes was tired of "seeing Nature and History confused at every turn." He experienced a "feeling of impatience at the sight of the 'naturalness' with which newspapers, art, and common sense constantly dress up a reality which, even though it is the one we live in, is undoubtedly determined by history" (p. 11). Were it not for one fateful milk truck, Barthes would be here today to level his critique at Benetton's advertising campaigns.

It is the "naturalness" of the Benetton small world advertisements that is particularly troubling. Historical context and human agency are totally missing from these advertisements, as no attempt is made to name the (thematic) subject or the (human) subjects of the images. When asked why the corporation chose to avoid explaining the image of a person dying from AIDS, Luciano Benetton responded that the corporation did not want to overdetermine the meaning of the image:

> Many people have asked why we didn't include a text that would explain the image. But we preferred not to because we think that the image is understandable by itself. You can look at it from many points of view. We become richer this way, because many people give their own versions of what they see, and we are now witnessing that kind of debate. (quoted in Sischy, 1992, p. 69)

Given some knowledge of world events, the general context of several of the small world advertisements, such as the person with AIDS and the Albanian refugees fleeing by boat to Italy, can be read directly from the image. But many of the advertisements present much more ambiguous messages. The companion advertisement of these two (all released during the spring/summer 1992 campaign) showed two trucks full of refugees from somewhere in the African diaspora. Although apparently set in the global South, the range of possible sites for this image includes all of continental Africa as well as the Caribbean and those countries of the Americas with an Atlantic coast. Some deduction surely can reduce this enormous range of sites, but this lack of historical and geographical specificity nonetheless shows the aestheticization of human suffering at its worst.

Another ambiguous image was the oil-slicked duck that appeared on billboards and in magazines and that adorned the cover of the third issue of *Colors*. At the time of its release, the two most recent major oil spills had been caused by the *Exxon Valdez* crash in Alaska and the Gulf War. A partial explanation was given for this image, however:

> Issue 3 of *Colors* is dedicated to the memory of an anonymous duck. May he (or she) rest in peace. Our cover duck swam through an oil slick (which was caused by a war) and came out looking like a whole new species. Maybe it's the duck of the future. We hope not. (Benetton Group SpA, 1992-1993, back cover)

This small concession to context by Benetton gave the duck a history and hence, to the extent that the reader understands something of recent global events, politicized the image. To develop a critique, it is imperative to name the problem. Argument by analogy has its time and place, for example, as a strategy used by writers under authoritarian regimes.

But in the context of Benetton's small world advertisements, where one of the analogical arguments is "buy Benetton," it dilutes and defuses the potential political punch of the message.

Thus, when Benetton ran the image of a person with AIDS taken moments before his death, many AIDS activists reacted in anger. Although this advertisement followed other Benetton advertisements on this subject (one showing condoms and one showing blood vials), the appropriation of the human suffering associated with AIDS by a multinational clothing corporation was too much for many groups committed to this issue, even though some had reacted favorably to the condom advertisement. The outrage extended to a variety of media sources that refused to publish the advertisement, including even the usually sensationalist German magazine *Stern.* Maggie Alderson, the editor of *Elle* magazine, summed up the general mood as follows: "It is an incredibly moving image in the right context, but to use it as an advertisement for a fashion store selling jumpers is incredibly insulting. They have stepped out of the bounds of what is acceptable" (quoted in Benetton Group SpA, 1992-1993, p. 10). Of course, this sort of criticism can be made of all of the Benetton images of human suffering, not just the exceptional ones that reference the global North.

Nonetheless, it is worth noting that the greatest outcry against the Benetton small world advertisements tends to come when it hits too close to home in the global North. When Benetton's computer-retouched image of the queen as a black person was printed on the front page of the British tabloid *Sun* with the caption "Ma'amy," a local furor was touched off. Not only were members of the royal family and ardent monarchists angry, but members of Britain's black community considered the image patronizing and disrespectful (Israelson, 1993, p. A3). In the fall of 1993, Benetton ran yet another campaign on AIDS, this time displaying naked buttocks, a lower abdomen, and a male arm stamped with the words "HIV positive." The French Association for the Fight Against AIDS likened these images to the Nazi practice of tattooing concentration camp prisoners and attempted to sue Benetton under a French law against exploiting the illness and suffering of others for commercial gain (Reuters, 1993, p. C1). The response of Benetton's lawyer to this charge was that the company had long been associated with fighting AIDS, as if sheer repetition could somehow legitimate Benetton's controversial relationship to AIDS. A man dying of AIDS ran his own advertisement in response, a close-up of his face with the slogan "During the agony, the sales continue" (Gumbel, 1994, p. B6).

Seemingly untouched by the criticism generated by so many of his controversial advertisements, Luciano Benetton in the spring of 1994 finally had to issue an apology for an advertisement that threatened to cause substantial negative publicity. The advertisement featuring the blood-soaked clothes of a dead Croatian soldier created such an uproar in Europe that Benetton was forced to concede: "I am very sorry. This is not what a corporate communications campaign should do" (quoted in Gumbel, 1994, p. B1). It should be expected that other Benetton images have sparked similar outrage but that the people represented have not been in a position to launch a significant response. When I gave an early version of this chapter to a group of educators in Mexico City, anger surfaced at Benetton's focus on poverty and human crisis in the global South. To people who live in the global South, Benetton's advertising campaign is at worst intrusive, patronizing, and humiliating. From this perspective, Benetton's version of social and political consciousness is a luxury afforded to young people in the global North, who may be racially heterogeneous but who are in global terms more or less economically homogeneous.

The story that emerged around the advertisement of a man dying of AIDS should be taken as an allegory for the entire small world campaign. Toscani found the controversy that the advertisement caused perplexing given the fact that when *Life* magazine published the same image it had not generated any dissent: "We can't be like ostriches who put their heads in the sand. . . . What is the moral line that divides [*Life* from Benetton]?" (quoted in Sischy, 1992, p. 69). Toscani was so comfortable with the image that he went one step further to aestheticize it into the canon of art history as an authentic version of "La Pieta." Toscani argued,

> The Pieta of Michelangelo during the Renaissance might be fake—Jesus Christ might have never existed. That was real promotion. But we know this death happened. This is the real thing. And the more real the thing is, the less people want to see it. It's always intrigued me why fake has been accepted and reality has been rejected. (quoted in Sischy, 1992, p. 69)

Here, the ethics and responsibility of representation are totally circumvented by the creative director of Benetton's controversial advertising campaign, leaving unacknowledged the ironic representation of pain and poverty in the service of an upscale clothing chain. Rather, the Benetton response to this situation is to further divorce image from reality. Having already commodified this family's tragedy, Toscani distorted the image further by aestheticizing it.

In his criticism of images of people with AIDS, Douglas Crimp registered his surprise that contemporary photographers continue to follow practices that have been roundly criticized. Crimp spoke of the symbolic violence cloaked as charity in documentary representations of people with AIDS. Crimp (1992) argued that these people's privacy is both "brutally invaded and brutally maintained." He explained,

> Invaded in the obvious sense that these people's difficult personal circumstances have been exploited for public spectacle, their most private thoughts and emotions exposed. But at the same time maintained: The portrayal of these people's circumstances never includes an articulation of the public dimension of the crisis, the social conditions that made AIDS a crisis and continue to perpetuate it as a crisis. People with AIDS are kept safely within the boundaries of their private tragedies. (p. 120)

Regardless of creative intent, this now famous image circulates as yet another example of the helplessness of a person dying of AIDS. Crimp quoted Allan Sekula, who argued that the relation of photographer and subject ranges through "seduction, coercion, collaboration, or rip-off." According to Sekula, this relationship involves both a "fetishistic cultivation and promotion of the artist's humanity [and] a certain disdain for the 'ordinary' humanity of those who have been photographed" (p. 125). Of course, this criticism hits home with respect to all of the Benetton small world images that feature human subjects.

Nonetheless, some knowledge of the context of Benetton's person with AIDS advertisement changes and deepens its meaning considerably. In a newspaper article titled "The Man Who Died in an Ad for Benetton," Curry (1992) tells the story of David Kirby of Stafford, Ohio, and his family. The controversial photograph was taken at David's behest by Therese Frare, a graduate student from the University of Ohio, moments before David's death. David had returned to Stafford from California when he feared that he might have AIDS. His final years in Stafford were dedicated to educating people about AIDS by speaking to health care workers, civic groups, and schoolteachers about prevention. He was 32 years old when he died. The grieving relatives in the picture are his father Bill, his sister Susan, and his niece Sarah. As the image shows, David's family was very supportive of him. His mother Kay said,

"What's important is he was a person, and people who are dying need to feel loved. Nobody should have to die alone" (p. D1).

The decision to allow Benetton to publish the image in its advertising campaign did not come easily. Bill Kirby describes his ambivalence toward the image as follows: "I'm not really comfortable with the photo. When I look at that picture, it brings back all the heartache. Until this winter, I couldn't even look at it without crying" (quoted in Curry, 1992, p. D1). Despite their mixed feelings, however, the Kirbys felt a responsibility to allow the photograph to be as broadly disseminated as possible. Kay Kirby stated that "it's what David would have wanted. You can see the family anguish, and people need to know this is reality" (p. D1). Benetton paid the Kirbys a considerable sum of money to use the image in its advertisements, and the Kirbys have spent the money buying a headstone for David's grave, making donations to AIDS charities, and purchasing and renovating a house in Columbus that will be used as an AIDS hospice. As soon as Bill Kirby retires from United Parcel Service, he and Kay plan to work as unpaid managers of the hospice.

Although this information breathes some life into the reified moment of the photograph, it cannot be read directly from the Benetton image. Nor does the Kirbys' permission to use the image exonerate Toscani and Benetton from public debate. While pioneering a new direction in contemporary advertising, both Benetton and Toscani are contemptuous of the critics who question their choices. Although Benetton apologized for the image of the Croat soldier's clothes, in general the company flippantly disregards criticism of its advertisements as the product of individual and social "hang-ups" and "Anglo-Saxon neuroses" (quoted in Back & Quaade, 1993, p. 72). In the case of the person with AIDS advertisement, Luciano Benetton tried to rise above the criticism by lending the issue a personal tone: "It is a grave problem. It is not something that affects only people we don't know. Personally, I have had many friends who have died from this disease" (quoted in Sischy, 1992, pp. 69-70). Given the controversy that this image has created in the global North, Luciano Benetton acknowledged some responsibility by implicating himself in its subject. Of course, if Luciano Benetton had to have friends who had died from every crisis portrayed in Benetton advertisements to legitimate their presence, he would have to be a very busy global human rights activist indeed.

Luciano Benetton wants to establish a position for himself as a benevolent corporate crusader. His company is trying to stake out new moral terrain in the globalizing economy by trying to educate people about the world's problems. Like a good lesson plan, the Benetton advertisements are intended to "encourage thought and discussion about some important issues" while provoking "compassion and hopefully positive action in regard to these issues" (Benetton Group SpA, 1992). According to Giroux (1994),

> Benetton's move away from an appeal to utility to one of social responsibility provides an object lesson in how promotional culture increasingly uses pedagogical practices to shift its emphasis from selling a product to selling an image of corporate responsibility. (pp. 189-190)

Benetton has redefined corporate benevolence as a didactic flourish piggybacked onto its own advertising needs. Toscani has stated that this strategy may be more effective than traditional forms of charity: "By mass communication, by creating awareness, you can sometimes contribute much more than by just giving away money, which can disappear without educating people, and often without even reaching the people it's meant for" (quoted in Sischy, 1992, p. 71). If Benetton and Toscani are to be believed, they are sacrificing their prominent advertising space on billboards and in double-page magazine spreads to create the chalkboards of a new global classroom.

If only things were so easy. It is reported in the *Utne Reader* that the Benetton small world campaign was inspired by a survey that found that a new generation of young consumers was more "socially aware" than its predecessors (Ouellette, 1993, p. 32). But it gets more complex than that. Squiers (1992) argues in *Artforum* that the small world campaign "can be seen as an ingenious attempt symbolically to appropriate, tame, and control the alarming contemporary political events that are disrupting the psychic drives carefully nurtured for decades by public relations and advertising" (p. 19). Again, we see an example of recuperation and containment, this time of the same unjust world that large corporations such as Benetton have helped to create. In a world where "denial in the service of upbeat consumerism is no longer a workable strategy" (p. 19), Benetton again is leading the way, now demonstrating how to sustain "business as usual" in the meantime.

By pioneering new frontiers in socially responsible advertising, Benetton has issued a strong challenge to the advertising industry and to corporate image makers worldwide. As consumer activism gathers steam in the global North and the corporate dream of limitless growth and expansion comes to an inglorious end, corporations are increasingly under pressure to legitimate their activities by being perceived as exercising some sort of social justice. The purpose of the small world campaign, according to Benetton promotional literature, is "to generate discussions of serious social issues while creating brand awareness." Or, in the words of Spike Lee, "Benetton wants to make a buck like any other company . . . [but] the imagery involved in the Benetton ads stands head and shoulders above the rest" in trying to get everyone involved "to ensure that this planet does not self-destruct" (Lee, 1992, p. iii). Coming from the lips of a film director cum mass merchandiser whose "Spike's Joints" are featured in the first issue of *Colors,* this is an injunction to Benetton's youthful clientele to think globally while shopping locally.

Whereas the two-tone advertisements soothed the psyche, the new advertisements are a jarring indictment of the "fucked" (to borrow a description from Lee) "small world" in which we live. Many of these images depict human suffering—primarily in the global South—and most reference Others to the norm of the privileged jumper-clad Benetton consumer. Although these images are purported by Benetton to advance global consciousness of issues of social and environmental concern, they also reinforce the prevalent stereotypes of Others as victims whose pathos requires the benevolence of enlightened consumers in the global North. Just as Benetton's two-tone campaign was about the containment of difference, the small world campaign also is about the channeling and containment of the incipient consciousness and activism of young people, primarily in the global North.

On the one hand, Benetton is a world leader in the cybernetic circulation of inventory and purchase information; on the other, it is gaining prominence through a hypocritical campaign of global concern. While presiding over a cutthroat, ever-expanding economic empire based on the circulation of information and goods, Benetton is developing environmentally and socially relevant advertising. With a new globally oriented economy comes the need to turn a new breed of consumers into a new global (upper-)middle class. By marketing cultural difference, Benetton is again showing its pioneering corporate spirit by opening up the texts of advertising to include a broader range of potential consumers. And by simultaneously promoting social and environmental consciousness on a global scale, Benetton is providing a communication-based model of corporate ethics that operates through images but allows business to continue to take place as usual in these tumultuous times.

Note

1. I acknowledge the financial aid of the Social Sciences and Humanities Research Council of Canada in carrying out the research for this chapter.

References

Back, L., & Quaade, V. (1993, Spring). Dream utopias, nightmare realities: Imaging race and culture within the world of Benetton advertising. *Third Text,* pp. 65-80.

Barthes, R. (1972). *Mythologies* (A. Lavers, Trans.). New York: Hill & Wang.

Benetton Group SpA. (1991-1992, Fall/Winter). *Colors,* issue 1.

Benetton Group SpA. (1992). Fall/winter 1992 advertising campaign. In *United Colors of Benetton.* New York: Author.

Benetton Group SpA. (1992-1993, Fall/Winter). *Colors,* issue 3.

Benetton Group SpA. (1993). [Promotional material]. New York: Author.

Crimp, D. (1992). Portraits of people with AIDS. In L. Grossberg, C. Nelson, & P. Treichler (Eds.), *Cultural studies* (pp. 117-133). New York: Routledge.

Curry, C. (1992, April 26). The man who died in an ad for Benetton. *Toronto Star,* pp. D1, D5.

Davidson, M. (1992). *The consumerist manifesto: Advertising in postmodern times.* New York: Routledge.

Eagleton, T. (1985, July/August). Capitalism, modernism, and postmodernism. *New Left Review,* pp. 60-73.

Enloe, C. (1989). *Bananas, beaches and bases: Making feminist sense of international politics.* Berkeley: University of California Press.

Giroux, H. (1994). Benetton's "world without borders": Buying social change. In C. Becker (Ed.), *The subversive imagination: Artists, society and social responsibility* (pp. 187-207). New York: Routledge.

Gruneau, R. (1988). Introduction: Notes on popular culture and political practice. In R. Gruneau (Ed.), *Popular cultures and political practices* (pp. 11-32). Toronto: Garamond.

Gumbel, P. (1994, March 8). Benetton suffers backlash as lurid ad backfires. *Globe and Mail* (Toronto), pp. B1, B6.

Hall, S. (1988, October). Brave new world. *Marxism Today,* pp. 24-29.

Hall, S. (1989). The meaning of new times. In S. Hall & M. Jacques (Eds.), *New times: The changing face of politics in the 1990s* (pp. 116-134). London: Lawrence & Wishart.

Harvey, D. (1989). *The condition of postmodernity.* Oxford, England: Basil Blackwell.

Israelson, D. (1993, March 28). Britain's brassy press joins in controversy. *Toronto Star,* p. A3.

Lee, S. (1992, November 12). United colors of Benetton. *Rolling Stone,* pp. i-iv.

Levin, G. (1991, July 22). Benetton gets the kiss-off. *Advertising Age,* p. 1.

Moynihan, M. (1984, April). Luciano Benetton. *Andy Warhol's Interview,* p. 104.

Murray, R. (1989). Benetton Britain. In S. Hall & M. Jacques (Eds.), *New times: The changing face of politics in the 1990s* (pp. 54-64). London: Lawrence & Wishart.

Mytelka, L. (1991). Global shifts in the textile and clothing industries. *Studies in Political Economy, 36,* 109-144.

Ouellette, L. (1993, March/April). Smells like the subversive spirit. *Utne Reader,* pp. 32-34.

Phizacklea, A. (1990). *Unpacking the fashion industry: Gender, racism and class in production.* New York: Routledge.

Reuters. (1993, October 9). AIDS group seeks ban on Benetton posters. *Globe and Mail* (Toronto), p. C1.

Rutherford, J. (1990). A place called home: Identity and the cultural politics of difference. In J. Rutherford (Ed.), *Identity: Community, culture, difference* (pp. 9-27). London: Lawrence & Wishart.

Sischy, I. (1992, April). Advertising taboos. *Interview,* pp. 69-71.

Squiers, C. (1992, May). Violence at Benetton. *Artforum,* pp. 18-19.

Toscani, O. (1993, March 20). [Interview on fashion television]. Toronto: CityTV.

9

Afrocentricity and Inclusive Curriculum: Is There a Connection or a Contradiction?

GEORGE J. SEFA DEI

Schooling as a culturally and politically mediated experience requires an approach to education that centers all human experiences in the student's learning. There is a need for transformative ways of thinking about schooling and education in multiracial and multiethnic contexts, especially an approach to educational change that avoids the empty talk of bland pluralism and the "add-and-stir" approach to incorporating difference and diversity (Tice, 1990).[1]

The task of achieving an equitable schooling outcome for all Canadian youths continues to occupy the minds of many school administrators, educators, parents, students, and teachers. There is some recognition from Canadian educators and parents that current debates about educational equity and academic excellence must be conducted within a critical framework for examining the structures of schooling and the delivery of education in the Euro-Canadian context (Braithwaite, 1989; Braithwaite & James, 1996; James, 1990; Solomon, 1992). It is argued that structural processes of schooling and education provide unequal opportunities and create differential outcomes for students according to race, ethnicity, gender, sexuality, and class (McCarthy & Crichlow, 1993). A critical examination of these factors within our educational institutions reveals disturbing information as to how schools function to engage some students while disengaging others. Educators, in particular, need to comprehend fully why schools fail some youths and, conversely, why some of our students are failing school.

As May (1994) points out, in trying to understand the issues of the educational experiences of students, liberal-democratic theories of education have tended to focus on family-school relations, conceptualizing schools and homes as sites and sources of students' educational problems and pathologies. Reproduction theories of schooling, on the other hand, have focused on how the structural processes of schooling create unequal outcomes, particularly for racial minority students and those from low socioeconomic family backgrounds. However, what is never adequately examined by such theories is how the structural processes of schooling are mediated by students' individual and collective forms of resistance and oppositional cultures that challenge the normativity of whiteness in the curriculum (Apple, 1986, 1989; Giroux, 1983a, 1983b; McCarthy, 1990; Willis, 1977, 1983).

Conflict theories, in the examination of the school's role in the unequal distribution of rewards, resources, and opportunities in society, accord primacy to the dictates of capital (Bowles & Gintis, 1976). Conflict theorists fail to explore how the labor demands of the economy shape schools and the processes of schooling, and vice versa. Critical/radical educational theorists (Apple, 1986; Giroux, 1983b; McCarthy, 1990) have drawn attention to how schools function to reproduce dominant ideologies of society. The focus on the examination of differential power relations within society and how they implicate the processes of delivering education has provided us with an understanding of how the ideology of public schooling works to maintain the status quo. But schools are not only agencies of cultural, political, and economic reproduction; they are also sites of conflict between groups differentially situated in terms of power relations. The critical ethnography of schools reveals instances of resistance from both students and educators, challenging the prevailing culture of dominance.

A contemporary educational and pedagogic challenge is to understand the nature of minority student/educator resistance to the power of schools to dominate subordinate groups through definitions of what is acceptable and what is not acceptable, what is valid knowledge and what is not knowledge. Within Euro-Canadian schools, there is a constant "ordering of knowledge" (Giroux, 1984) through the process of giving recognition and validation to the experiences and knowledge of some groups while denying those of others. Through the school curriculum, we are provided with academic definitions of what counts as valid knowledge and how such knowledge should be produced and disseminated. For marginal voices, the school curriculum and pedagogic practices have become sites and sources for contesting their marginality as well as opposition to the traditional roles of schools. By "curriculum," I refer to the written and stipulated rules, codes of conduct, norms, and values of the school as well as to the manner in which issues are taken up in academic texts and classroom discussions (Apple & Taxel, 1982). I also refer to the "unwritten practices and procedures that influence student activities, behaviours, perceptions, and outcomes" (Mukherjee & Thomas, n.d., p. 7), and that serve to give schools their character (Bhyat, 1993, p. 12).

Conceptualizing the school as a site for student conformity as well as student resistance allows us to understand how alternative knowledges and pedagogies can be developed from everyday school practices and interactions. Current calls for "alternative pedagogies," "inclusive curriculum," and "representative school environments" must be understood as a challenge to the hegemony of Eurocentered norms, values, and ideas that characterize the organizational life of schools. Educators and school administrators have to lead the way by opening up spaces for alternative, non-hegemonic viewpoints to flourish in the schools. Educators must interrogate (rather than cursorily dismiss) alternative ideas and viewpoints on schooling, particularly those emanating from subordinated groups in society, for the sources of students' cultural, political, and intellectual empowerment and disempowerment. The interrogation, validation, and incorporation of multiple and alternative ways of knowing should not be seen as a call to replace one hegemonic form of knowledge with another or to denigrate Euro-Canadian scholarship in a bid to foster an oppositional discourse. Rather, it must be viewed as a call for Euro-Canadian schools to be more inclusive and to inform students about the variety of ideas and events that have shaped, and continue to shape, human growth and development. Schools require a new curriculum that is inclusive and caring and that fosters respect, encouragement, and self-worth among *all* students. The new curriculum must develop students' commitment to learning. It must ground students' learning in their cultural heritage and ancestry.

A Case Study

It may now be a cliché to say that Canada is a multiracial and multiethnic society. In fact, in 1991 the total estimated "visible minority" population of Canada was 2,488,100 (including nonpermanent residents). Classified in the visible minority groups are blacks, Indo-Pakistanis, Chinese, West Asians and Arabs, other Asians, Filipinos and other Pacific Islanders, and Latin Americans (Kalbach, Verma, George,

& Dai, 1993). The figure reflects a 58% increase over the 1,577,710 total for 1986 compared to the 9% increase for Canada's population as a whole during the 1986-1991 period. The province of Ontario, with 37% of the total Canadian population, had 49.1% of the visible minorities in Canada.[2]

Between May 1992 and April 1995, I had the privilege of interviewing more than 200 black and non-black youths (including some school "dropouts"), as well as more than 55 black/African Canadian parents, as part of a 3-year study of the Ontario public school system. This project examined black/African Canadian youth experiences from the students' own perspectives.[3] With the assistance of graduate students from the Ontario Institute for Studies in Education, the research project asked students what they liked and disliked about school, who their favorite teachers were and why, and to pinpoint some of the factors they believed impinged on their schooling and educational outcomes. We also asked students for the specific changes they wanted to see effected in the public school system to help maximize their opportunities in society.[4]

Elsewhere (Dei, Holmes, Mazzuca, McIsaac, & Campbell, 1995; Dei, Mazzuca, McIsaac, & Zine, 1997), black students' and parents' concerns about the Canadian public school system were presented. It is argued that students' narrative accounts reflect the influence of race/ ethnicity, class, gender, and school culture on "dropping out." The complex personal stories of many students point to the fact that our understanding of the school dropout dilemma must be grounded in the institutionalized policies and practices of exclusion and marginalization that organize public schooling and structure the home environment of many youths.

There is no doubt that some of the youths are succeeding in school. Many students speak about the good intentions of their teachers. But it is also very apparent that many black youths are struggling to deal with the "low expectations" that some teachers have of them. Male students, in particular, are struggling to deal with the labeling and negative stereotyping of the African male in society in general. These students talk of the need for black and other racial minority teachers in the schools, although a few students are quick to add that having black teachers would not necessarily make a major difference in itself. In fact, these few talk about "black teachers who are not really black." But students feel it is important to have teachers who have the interests of black and minority students at heart and who would encourage them to do well in school. Many see black teachers as important role models and/or authority figures, and a few speak about the likelihood of black teachers having a social perspective with which they could identify.

Many youths feel that they are not being heard and see themselves as existing on the margins of their schools, despite the relatively recent and well-intentioned attempts at their "inclusion." It is obvious to a critical researcher that educators, administrators, and parents have a long way to go in addressing the emotional, spiritual, and psychological aspects of schooling and education of youths living in multiethnic communities. Many of the students appear to be at school in body but not in spirit and mind.

Many students have wondered about the separation and disconnection between the school and the wider community. They yearn for schools to reflect the communities in which they live by teaching about their ancestral histories and cultural heritage. They want to "bring the school into the community," and vice versa, and are very frustrated because they do not see this happening. Adding to these pressures and frustrations are black students' constant struggles to maintain their individual self-identities and group cultural identities at school. Students attribute this struggle to a very narrow school curriculum that, until very recently, failed to emphasize their cultural and ancestral backgrounds. They speak about the importance of knowing about African history in its own right and of learning about the contributions of peoples of African descent to Canadian society and world civilization.

Students' Voices

Jane is a school "dropout" who later enrolled in a community college and now works as a receptionist with an industrial firm in Toronto.[5] We discussed a variety of issues about her experiences in high school, touching on the absence of black scholars in academic texts and the absence of representation of black peoples in important aspects and segments of the school curriculum. In our conversations, I was made acutely aware of her worries about the fact that, as she put it, "All those who have done something worth mentioning in the schoolbooks are white men" (November 15, 1992).

What is worth emphasizing here is that Jane's views are widely shared by many black students (Dei et al., 1995). For example, Michael, a 19-year-old general-level student, came to Canada from Jamaica nearly

9 years ago.[6] The frustrations and emotions with which he speaks about the deprivileging of black people's history and contributions to society throughout his public schooling cannot be lost on the astute listener.

> I only know about Canadian history, which is white history. I did not learn anything about black people. And then, probably in the past 2 years, I would say we have improved in our geography, but we don't really learn about the cultural background. We just learned about the . . . not even the people, but just the city or the country. Basics, nothing deep. Is it tough? I mean, I would like to know more about my history, yes. A lot more. I think I need to know a lot more than I know. (November 15, 1992)

Then there is Maxine, who dropped out of school when she became pregnant. Her views about the formal curriculum support Michael's contention. She also shares Jane's sentiments:

> The curriculum, I don't like it. I found it very one-sided, especially when it came down to history. There was never a mention of any black people that have contributed to society, what they have done. Everything was just white. . . . I mean, everything, it's the white man that did it. (June 22, 1992)

Marlo, 21, was a participant in a summer jobs training program when he was interviewed. From him, one learns how the official school curriculum can be very disempowering to minority students, leading to the point of being disengaged from the classroom:

> When I was going to school, the teachers focused on European history. European this . . . Alexander Graham Bell discovered this, and when you sit in a classroom full of 12 white people and all you hear is white this, white that, you think, "So what am I here for?" Right! A lot of times you think it's a lot of shit, you know, a lot of bullshit. So you don't find that interesting, you just sit down and you, OK, Alexander this and George Washington this. But at the same time, the teacher could always say, well this came from the Caribbean and this came from Africa and just—or this came from Germany and kind of add everyone's input. (June 8, 1992)

These narratives imply the absence of an inclusive school environment in the definition of the youths themselves (Board of Education, Toronto, 1988; Braithwaite, 1989; James, 1990; Solomon, 1992). On an analytical level, students' narratives speak to concerns about representation in school texts, academic discourse, and societal curriculum as well as to the impact on schooling outcomes for the youths.[7] For educators, the question is, how do we address black youths' lack of a sense of identification with, and connectedness to, the schools? What sorts of changes are required in the schools? Asante (1992, p. 30), writing in a related context, has pointed out that what schools have to contend with is the historical, social, cultural, and psychological dislocation of all youths in general and black/African youths in particular. Educators need to work toward a truly inclusive school environment. We can start with a shared understanding of what an inclusive curriculum really means (Banks, 1988; Nieto, 1992).

Dealing with our social differences is at the core of the concern for an inclusive curriculum in the schools. Despite pretensions to the contrary, there is some social harm committed when we ignore our differences and simply proceed to accentuate our basic humanness. As argued elsewhere (Dei, 1996), developing a culture of inclusiveness within the school system means dealing foremost with *equity,* that is, the qualitative value of justice. Inclusivity also means addressing the question of *representation,* that is, having a multiplicity of perspectives entrenched as part of academic discourse, knowledge, and texts. Furthermore, inclusivity means that school pedagogies must respond to the challenges of *diversity,* that is, the social construction and structuralization of difference within the context of schools and in the wider society (e.g., understanding the relational aspects of race, class, gender, and sex differences). In effect, *inclusive curriculum* means developing a broad-based curriculum that promotes diverse teaching strategies and nurtures support systems in the schools to enhance school success for all students regardless of race, ethnicity, class, gender, sexual orientation, and physical ability. A theoretical stance, which argues that schools must reinforce, not devalue, diversity as part of the challenge for inclusivity, allows educators to link concerns for an inclusive curriculum to the academic and political project of antiracism education in Euro-Canadian schools.

Responding to the Challenge of Inclusivity

The question is, how do educators, administrators, and parents respond to the challenge of schooling and education in multiethnic communities? Responding to the challenge will require multiple, overlapping, and nonexclusive educational strategies. Hilliard (1992) calls for the "meaningful rendition of the whole human experience" (p. 13) in the education of the young. In the Canadian context, many educators are pushing for antiracism education as part of a broader strategy of inclusive education (Coehlo, 1991; Dei, 1994; Lee, 1985; Ontario Institute for Studies in Education, 1994; Roman, 1993; Thomas, 1984; Walcott, 1990). However, designing one model of antiracism education for all Canadian people ultimately will fail because this would disallow the particular histories of various groups of people. In other words, an antiracist education for whites must indeed be different from that for blacks because both groups historically have been placed in vastly different positions through the mechanics of social oppression (Dei, 1993, p. 37). Therefore, what ought to be promoted is an inclusive form of education that recognizes the validity of all non-hegemonic perspectives (Oyebade, 1990, p. 234).

Canadian educators who have written specifically on the education of black children have called for a critical interrogation of what Afrocentric education and African-centered schools can do for the young (Calliste, 1994; Collins, 1994; Dei, 1994; Farrell, 1994; Henry, 1992, 1993).[8] Indeed, I believe the cause of African-centered education is properly served by a recognition of the validity of knowledge centered on the historical cultural experiences of all groups in Euro-Canadian society. The task for Canadian educators is to critically interrogate and validate the histories and cultures of all peoples and to allow students to learn from these experiences. The educational premise is that "human culture is the product of the struggles of all humanity" (Hilliard, 1992, p. 13).

Afrocentricity

Following from the pioneering works of Asante (1987, 1988), Karenga (1986), Keto (1990), and many others, I see Afrocentricity as an educational tool for understanding society. In epistemological thought, Afrocentric discourse is a paradigm shift that argues that the contextual basis for knowledge is practice and experience. The Afrocentric pedagogic method seeks to ground the teaching and learning of black youths in their cultural heritage. To engage in Afrocentric education (curriculum and pedagogy) is to teach and learn about a way of knowing, informed by the histories of peoples of African descent. As a pedagogic and communicative tool, Afrocentric education is about the investigation and understanding of phenomena from a perspective grounded in African-centered values, epistemological constructs, and philosophies (Asante, 1991; Karenga, 1986). Specifically, Afrocentric education calls on Euro-Canadian educators to conduct their investigation and analysis of African and black issues from a perspective grounded in African ways of knowing. The challenge, as Asante (1991) puts it, is to move or bring all peoples of African descent from the margins to the center of post-modern history. For the educator, the challenge is to allow the African child to interpret the world from his or her own eyes rather than through those of the Other.

As an intellectual paradigm, Afrocentric knowledge problematizes the structural impediments to the education of black and minority students. Afrocentricity is not just a concern for culture-centered educational issues; it deals with other dimensions of power and oppression. It has been argued that the ideology of public schooling, represented in official school curriculum and in the authority structures of schooling, supports the dominating power relations (Apple, 1989; Giroux, 1983b) that alienate many students from the school system. The Euro-Canadian public school system thus far has failed to respond adequately to the needs and concerns of many black and minority students (e.g., the need for more minority teachers and a curriculum that reflects students' realities).

Arguably, one of the paramount goals of transformative education is to make visible those marginal cultures and voices that traditionally have been suppressed in the school system (Giroux, 1992, p. 206). A related goal is to have educators in the school system who are a reflection of the diverse student population. A related question is, how can African-centered knowledge be used as a transformative pedagogy to answer practical questions in education and bring about social change? As I have argued elsewhere (Dei, 1994), an African-centered discourse is forged in the dialectic of a critique of existing practices of exclusion and marginalization in dominant Euro-Canadian schooling as well as in the possibility of reforming the school system for the transformation of society. To teach African-centered values in the school system is to make a commitment to a pedagogy that is political education and that works toward the transformation of the structural conditions that provide an unequal educational outcome for black and minority youths.

The ideology of individualism within the Euro-Canadian public school system undermines group solidarity and the collective struggle for social justice. If education is to transform society, then learners and educators must be encouraged to work in collaboration and to "think critically, struggle against social injustices, and develop relations of community, based on the principles of equality, freedom, and justice" (Giroux, 1992, p. 200). African-centered pedagogy calls for making a critical linkage with other progressive forms of education (antiracist, feminist, liberatory pedagogy) as a pedagogic tool of liberation and as counterknowledge to fight Euro-Canadian ideological domination in the schools. In the context of promoting African youth education, I find Afrocentric pedagogy an appropriate tool for educational change because it seeks to ground and center the African child in the schooling process. But African-centered education must be more than "emancipatory" or "liberatory" pedagogy (Freire & Shor, 1987), imbued with self-reflection, social critique, and action (Gordon, 1990, p. 102).

Writing in a different context, Giroux (1992) suggests an educational perspective that makes "visible the social problems and conditions that affect those students who are at risk in our society, while recognizing that such problems need to be addressed in both pedagogical and political terms inside and outside the schools" (p. 200). It is in this regard that I believe African-centered education can make a contribution, particularly in the education of African Canadian youths. For African youths, the understanding of Afrocentric teachings means opportunities not only to reclaim new forms of knowledge but also to "provide new ways of reading history through the reconstruction of suppressed memories that offer an identity with which to challenge and contest the very conditions through which history, desire, voice, and place are experienced and lived" (Giroux, 1992, p. 204). The pursuit of an Afrocentric pedagogy, hopefully, should allow black students to become actively engaged in the production of their own knowledge.

Basic Principles of African-Centered Knowledge

In conceptualizing Afrocentric education, I have looked to the system of thought of indigenous African communities for their commonsense knowledge of the social and natural worlds.[9] This knowledge forms part of the cultural heritage of all African peoples. I refer specifically to the cultural traditions, values, belief systems, and worldviews of society imparted to the younger generation by community elders. Such knowledge is a worldview that shapes the community's relationship with its environment. It is the product of the direct experience of nature and its relationship with the social world. It is knowledge that is relevant for the survival of society. This is not to refute the idea that other cosmologies and cosmographies might be relevant as well.

Among the major themes emphasized in indigenous African ways of knowing are the ideas of community membership, social responsibility, social cohesiveness, and the commonality of all peoples. Such ideas and knowledge are expressed in local traditions, cultural beliefs, traditional songs, fables, and proverbs. These principles are not necessarily unique to African cultures. In fact, they are shared by other groups in varying forms. In discussing these ideas as principles of Afrocentric knowledge, it is important to acknowledge the ethnic diversity of African peoples. However, I share the sentiment of others that beyond the fragmentation of culture along ethnic, religious, ideological, class, and gender lines lie some common themes.

It is also important to recognize that indigenous knowledge systems do contain sources of cultural disempowerment for certain groups in society, for example, women and ethnic/cultural minorities. Hilliard (1992, p. 13) points out that no cultural tradition is immune to criticism. I am aware that "tradition" has been used by the most powerful in society (when it is expedient) to perpetuate domination and oppression and to silence Other voices. Furthermore, I acknowledge that the past is not fossilized; no tradition is static or frozen. Modernity has altered (if not corrupted) African value systems. However, it does not mean that educators cannot engage traditional values and systems of thought as a pedagogic and communicative project for educational change.

Therefore, following the pioneering work of Mbiti (1982) and Gyekye (1987), among many others (see also Die, 1995), I would put forward the following as 12 of the basic principles of Afrocentric knowledge.

1. All knowledge is accumulated knowledge, based on observing and experiencing the social and natural worlds. Consequently, there is no marketplace for ideas in the sense of knowledge that can be bought or sold in the Eurocentric sense.

2. We all are learners of the social and natural world, and social learning has to be personalized to develop the intuitive and analytical aspects of the human mind. In other words, every way of knowing is subjective.

3. All knowledge is socially and collectively created through the interactive processes among individuals, groups, and the natural world.

4. Humans are part of the natural world. We do not stand apart from, nor are we above, the natural world.

5. Our basic humanness is a value system that speaks to the importance of relating to, rather than of mastery over, nature and the environment. This humanness stresses points of conciliation rather than of presenting the universe as a world to be studied and dominated.

6. To understand social reality is to have a holistic view of reality. The acquisition of knowledge is a process of interactions among the body, the mind, and the human spirit. The action of thought itself is a causal factor in social action.

7. Both our social and natural worlds are full of uncertainties. There is no certainty in knowledge. Humans do not need to strive to explain away everything about their worlds. Knowledge is continually evolving or transforming itself.

8. We do not possess the earth. As living humans, we have borrowed the earth from our ancestors, and the living would incur the wrath of the ancestors if they destroyed nature to satisfy societal and individual material needs.

9. The concept of the individual only makes sense in relation to the community of which he or she is part. The collective spirit is stronger than the individual mind. Consequently, there are implications of accountability, responsibility, and self-reflexiveness in the act of knowledge production and use.

10. To every individual or group right in society is married some individual and social responsibility.

11. Humans need a nondualistic mode of thought that balances all relationships and precludes any binaryisms or dichotomizations of social categories.

12. Knowledge and survival go hand in hand. Daily routine social practices constitute a body of knowledge that has ensured human survival. We cannot separate theory from practice. Practical experience is the contextual basis of knowledge.

Many of these principles are important for education in Euro-Canadian contexts. By teaching about these aspects, which are least emphasized in the Euro-Canadian school system (e.g., values of human coexistence with one another and with nature [not control over nature], group solidarity, mutuality, collective work, and responsibility), students may be able to perceive the interest of their group as more important than individual self-interest (Oliver, 1986, p. 29).

Afrocentricity and the Challenge of Curriculum Reform

Incorporating some of these principles in Euro-Canadian education requires that educators critically reflect on some pertinent questions about the current public school system. For example, whose interests are being served by current school policies? How do the relations of power and knowledge within schools hegemonize the norms and values of mainstream Canadians? Do all students have equal access to available resources and materials in the school setting? Who are presented (or not presented) as "ethnics" in classroom discourses and in academic texts? How do teachers and students negotiate and play out their respective roles and responsibilities as well as rights and privileges in the school system? What is taught in the schools? What is not taught? What should be taught? By whom and how? Who wields the ultimate power to make these and other school decisions? What interpretations do we, as educators, attach to the background characteristics of the student population?

Canadian educators should further be guided by other, more focused concerns such as the following. What is the political project for engaging in an inclusive pedagogy? Do current teaching styles and practices successfully equip students with critical thinking skills to question both the official and hidden curricula of the school? Do teaching strategies assist students in critically reviewing classroom discourses with the implications for the dynamics of social difference (race, class, gender, and sexuality)? How does the school's official curriculum prepare students to deal with stereotypes and the false sense of superiority that some share in society. How does the curriculum prepare students to deal with the contradictions and hardships of living in a multiethnic, diversified society?

This last question demands some attention because of its relevance for the politics of inclusion. On the one hand, difference and diversity have long been associated with negativity, yet school culture promotes a cult of individualism that contradicts the negative evaluation of difference. It is equally difficult to talk about cooperation as a practical philosophy when much of school culture is based on competitiveness in examinations, sports, and entertainment. The educational challenge, then, is to prepare students to think and act beyond the individual by valuing difference at the same time as communality is privileged. The curriculum must be able to speak about differences and assist students to work across these differences. The education must be able to pitch inclusive education to an audience with different interests and stakes but wedded to some common goals.

Deconstructivist and critical pedagogues have called for teaching as a participatory process with students. Such a process provides students with a critical and powerful voice to question some of the assumptions about teaching, research, and schooling and to reaffirm the voices of the oppressed in society (Giroux, 1986; Moore, 1988). Minority students' voices are likely to be heard in the classrooms if students can identify with the teaching and resource materials and if educators can provide them with some sense of control over the learning process.

One of the pressing issues in the developing of an inclusive curriculum is resource materials. The issue goes beyond legitimate questions of relevancy to availability and knowing how to access and use resource materials. There also are questions about educators' responses and approaches to oppressively biased materials/texts as well as about the appropriate models and/or approaches for developing an inclusive curriculum. If an inclusive education is to assist in transforming society, then the answer to what is an appropriate model for an inclusive curriculum lies in how an inclusive school environment best enables the school system to deal with structural inequities in society (Sleeter & Grant, 1987, pp. 434-436).

In transforming an existing school curriculum, educators must know what differences are important in adapting a curriculum (Carlson, 1976). However, a hierarchy of social differences and social oppression must not be constructed in an inclusive curriculum. For example, inclusive educators must guard against the tendency to prioritize racial issues while overlooking the embedded inequalities that arise from class, ethnicity, culture, gender, sexual orientation, religious, and language disparities. Educators cannot talk about an inclusive curriculum without a reform of existing teaching practices to create new alternative teaching and learning practices in the schools. Strategies for cooperative learning that emphasize collaboration and bonding between students and teachers are required in a diverse school environment. Teachers, administrators, and students would have to network together and develop a community of scholars. To address critical questions of what should be taught in the schools and how, educators need to devise a curriculum aimed at providing students with group learning and survival skills as well as the requisite educational capital to be able to identify and solve basic human problems. The curriculum would allow students to set priorities for their own learning. It could be adaptable to the local environment as well as the interests and activities of the students. Teaching an inclusive curriculum as praxis would allow students to examine their own educational histories and the experiences of living in their communities.

Inclusive education (curriculum and pedagogy) means teaching students to follow through on what is learned. Educators lead the way by setting appropriate examples. Students do not have to feel any dissonance in terms of what their teachers speak about theoretically in the classroom and what they actually do outside the school walls.[10] Inclusive educators ensure that the subjugated and situated knowledge of students is resurrected in the classroom. Inclusive educators ensure that particularly minority students' voices and experiences are brought from the "margin to the center" of mainstream academic discussions. Inclusive educators assist students in exploring alternative and oppositional forms of knowledge, informed by the students' histories and experiences. As Estrada and McLaren (1993, p. 32) have argued, an affirmation of the voices of students and the oppressed in classroom discourse allows students to undertake a critical and oppositional reading of school texts and to create their own alternative and oppositional forms of knowledge. Classroom pedagogical practices of inclusive educators must assist students in developing a critical understanding of the causes of oppression and social inequality.

The pursuit of an Afrocentric education presents many challenges for inclusive educators, for example, how can Afrocentric education be pursued as an alternative pedagogy to equip black and minority students with what Senese (1991) refers to as "intellectual power?" (p. 15). How can educators teach Afrocentric knowledge in a nonexclusionary way and work toward the inclusion of other perspectives and experiences in understanding contemporary society? Can educators talk about an inclusive curriculum and at the same time highlight the importance of Afrocentric knowledge? How would educators address the disjuncture between the assertion of inclusionary education (which addresses race, gender, class, and sexual differences) and a focus on Afrocentric perspectives? Is there a seeming contradiction in speaking about a nonexclusionary Afrocentric pedagogy when this (like all pedagogies) is bound to be partial and exclusionary about some experiences and some knowledge? Do all black students share a sense of a common ancestral heritage? If they do not, how can it be ensured that teaching about black heritage does not merely feed on black students' sense of alienation?

What are the implications of an Afrocentric curriculum for the education of nonblack students in the Euro-Canadian school system?

These are important questions for Afrocentric educators. These questions should serve to guide the interrogation of what Afrocentric education and Afrocentric educators can and cannot accomplish in Euro-Canadian schools. I believe Afrocentric education can address some of these questions by proceeding, foremost but not exclusively, with the political agenda of enhancing black students' self-worth and social power through knowledge creation (see also Henry, 1992). Educators, while operating from an Afrocentric perspective, can conduct teaching in a manner that recognizes the multiplicity of ways of knowing and the importance of holding up each perspective to scrutiny, interrogation, and criticism. In this way, Afrocentric education is presented as just one model or strategy of ensuring inclusivity to deal with the asymmetrical power relations between and among social groups within the conventional school system. As a model of inclusivity, Afrocentric curriculum equips particularly black and minority students with the knowledge and skills to confront their marginalization by the dominant culture of schooling by legitimizing their subjugated voices, experiences, and histories in classroom instruction and school culture.

An Afrocentric curriculum is not synonymous with an inclusive curriculum, but it is related to the task of achieving inclusivity. Similarly, Afrocentric education cannot mean one thing to all people. There can be multiple strands of Afrocentricity that would dwell on questions of gender, class, sexual, and ethnic differences among people. Whichever strand of Afrocentricity one takes, depending on personal and subject locations, it requires the recognition of the partiality of all forms of knowledge. The implications of an Afrocentric curriculum for whites and other nonblack minority students is cultivating the knowledge that the interrogation of multiple ways of knowing contribute to enrich learning. It is not simply a question of a dichotomy between Afrocentric teachings and Eurocentric teachings but rather how each knowledge form can and does borrow from the other.

Wright (1994) has correctly pointed to a possible marginalization of Afrocentric knowledge in the academy if the Afrocentric discourse is strictly self-referential. He argues that a self-referential Afrocentrism can be self-defeating. Thus Afrocentrists must seek to construct an alliance with other critical theorists and pedagogues and to articulate an emancipatory pedagogy relevant to *all* students. Afrocentric educators have to avoid the pitfalls of romanticizing and overmythicizing African cultures and historical experiences. It is insidiously problematic for Afrocentric educators to glorify African culture and history in response to Euro-Canadian negation and denigration of the African past. The strength of Afrocentric education lies in its liberatory potential while at the same time recognizing that teaching Afrocentric education does not call for the negation of European influence on African peoples (scholarship and culture), nor does it call for African peoples to separate from nonblack cultures.

There is a place for Afrocentric knowledge in the Canadian school system, and the challenge is to incorporate such knowledge as part of a broader strategy for developing an inclusive curriculum. Knowledge of indigenous African cultural values is important for the personal development and schooling of *all* students. Educational approaches to addressing problems of exclusion in the school system should target *all* students. Curriculum design, reform, and management should have input from *all* stakeholders in the educational system. A primary objective of curriculum reform and structural change of the current school system is to let students develop their self-concept and self-worth and to recognize their responsibility to a larger citizenry. The creation of an inclusive learning environment, in which every student (black or nonblack) sees himself or herself in the school's curriculum and in classroom pedagogical practices, would assist students in making a connection between their individual self-worth and their wider social responsibilities.

Conclusion

I conclude this chapter by highlighting the basic themes around which Afrocentric knowledge connects with an inclusive educational agenda (Dei, 1995). First and foremost, education in the Euro-Canadian context never can truly rid itself of a Eurocentric frame of reference. This is because of the dominance of Eurocentric knowledge in which most educators have been schooled and are likely to pass this on to their students. But what progressive forms of education and transformative learning through oppositional discourses like Afrocentric pedagogy can do is to challenge Eurocentric knowledge as the only legitimate way of knowing about our world.

Second, alternative and oppositional discourses like Afrocentric education are needed in the schools to help black youths "reinvent their

Africanness within a Diasporic context" and create a way of being and thinking that is congruent with positive African traditions and values (Lee-Ferdinand, 1994). The success of Euro-Canadian schools in developing an inclusive school environment will depend largely on how *all* students are allowed to learn about the values, beliefs, and traditions of their various community cultures. This learning is crucial to strengthen students' social, emotional, and psychological well-being at school. Afrocentric education can assist particularly students of African descent to understand and affirm their "home and community cultures" (Banks, 1992, p. 32) and the interconnections with other cultures.

Third, conventional education has long defined non-European communities as ahistorical. Alternative pedagogies, such as Afrocentric knowledge, should be promoted to emphasize the rich and diverse histories of the various constituents of the school body. Such knowledge would reflect power sharing in the reformulation of the curriculum to speak to and about the "experiences, histories, struggles, and victories . . . [as well as] voices, visions, and perspectives" of marginalized groups (Banks, 1992, p. 33).

Fourth, conventional schools require alternative pedagogies, such as African-centered education, that emphasize cooperation rather than competition as the ultimate good in society. Schools should promote moral and holistic education and should teach students to associate themselves spiritually with their cultures, languages, and communities. Afrocentric pedagogy seeks to connect the individual student to a spiritual and moral foundation so that he or she can cultivate self-respect and respect for others.

Finally, knowledge creation, self-identity, and identifications are linked. The promotion of an inclusive school environment requires retraining teachers and hiring new teachers to reflect the diversity of our population. Some of the educators should necessarily be Afrocentric in the sense of looking to what the critical interrogation of Africa's past, culture, and traditions has to offer the rest of our humanity in general and peoples of African descent in particular.

There is a long history of Euro-Canadian dominance of what constitutes valid knowledge and how such knowledge should be produced and disseminated nationally and globally. Such dominance ought to be challenged if we truly want to develop an inclusive school environment. This is the challenge for contemporary inclusive educators living in an epoch that is radically different in its celebration of difference, cultural fragmentation, and pluralism. The emphasis in this chapter on an Afrocentric curriculum should be seen as a challenge for educators to teach other ways of knowing and understanding our world. The goal of an inclusive curriculum is worth pursuing if it helps provide the means for the subjugated and the powerless to share in the social power accorded to dominant groups in the school system and the wider society.

Notes

1. I acknowledge the sharing of knowledge with the many students who have worked over the years on my research projects, particularly Deborah Elva, Gabrielle Zachariah, Thato Bereng, Bobby Blanford, Elizabeth McIssac, Josephine Mazzuca, Jasmine Zine, Lianne Carley, Maria Castagna, Marcia James, Paul Broomfield, Bethlehem Kidane, and Rachel Campbell. Elva and Domenic Bellissimo of the Ontario Institute for Studies in Education, University of Toronto, provided valuable comments on the initial manuscript.

2. In the 1991 Canadian census data, nearly half of all people in Canada who reported origins other than British or French resided in the province of Ontario, which had a total population of 10,079,442 (Statistics Canada, 1993). The province is home to some of the largest racial communities in Canada. It is reported that "over half of all persons in Canada reporting West Asian, South Asian, African, Caribbean, and black single ethnic origins lived in Ontario" (p. 1). For example, 228,955 (66%) of the total 345,445 peoples of African descent (African, black, or Caribbean) in Canada were living in Ontario in 1991. Similarly, 723,395 (49%) of the total 1,463,180 peoples of Asian descent (South Asian, West Asian, East Asian, or Southeast Asian) in Canada resided in Ontario (p. 1). Kalbach et al. (1993, p. 33) projected that Canada's total black population could reach 1,381,500 by the year 2016. In the province of Ontario, the racial and ethnic diversity of Canadian society is indeed reflected in the student population (Board of Education, Toronto, 1993).

3. I use the term *black* synonymously with *African* to refer to all peoples who trace some ancestral affinity to continental Africa, that is, peoples of African descent and all those who define themselves as Africans or blacks.

4. The project was extended to cover interviews with parents and community groups, teachers and school administrators, and a small sample of non-black students in part to cross-reference black students' narratives of their school and home experiences.

5. "Jane" and other student references are pseudonyms.

6. In the Ontario public school system, until 1993, students entering Grade 9 were placed into one of three different course levels based on their "academic ability": the *basic* or *vocational* level, the *general* level, or the *advanced* level, the latter of which included courses leading to university entrance. This is a process referred to in the Canadian context as "streaming." Many black/African Canadian parents, community workers, and educators complained about the practice, which was seen as limiting the opportunities for some students to pursue higher education. Studies also have revealed that students placed in basic- and general-level classes were disproportionately black and from working-class backgrounds (Radwanski, 1987). In 1993, the Ontario Ministry of Education and Training abolished the practice and Grade 9 classes were "destreamed."

7. As ponted out elsewhere (Dei, 1996), my own educational experiences make it possible for me to identify with these concerns and to share the frustrations of students,

parents, and colleagues at the misrepresentations, negation, deprivileging, and devaluing of some experiences, while privileging others, in both academic discourse and classroom texts (see also Board of Education, Toronto, 1988). I can recall the colonial education I received growing up in my birthplace, Ghana. My frustrations were not so much about what the colonial curriculum taught me; even to this day, I am angry about what was *not* taught. I have wondered in my later years, for example, why learning about Niagara Falls in Canada was more important than being taught about the local rivers in my village. After all, these were rivers in which I swam, bathed, caught fish, and fetched water for household use.

8. As recently as November 1992, a multilevel government task force, the African-Canadian Community Working Group, proposed that one predominantly black junior high school should be set up in each of the six metropolitan Toronto municipalities. In a report, titled "Towards a New Beginning" and issued in November 1992, a 15-member working group suggested a 5-year pilot scheme establishing "black-focused" schools at which black history and culture would be taught. Such a school would have more black teachers and administrators on staff. The agenda is to provide black students with the choice of an alternative learning environment and to develop their sense of identity and belonging to a school. The hope is that, by teaching about black students' heritages, such a school will deal appropriately with the problems of isolation and frustration that many black youths have in society.

9. Like Muteshi (1996), I use the term *indigenous* to refer to the African past that offers a means of staking out a position as "African" that is outside the identity that has been, and continues to be, constructed in Euro-Canadian ideology.

10. I am referring to the tendency of many educators not to practise what they teach despite their theoretical exhortations against oppression, cultural criticism of social injustice, and political affirmation of social difference.

References

Apple, M. (1986). *Teachers and texts: A political economy of class and gender relations in education.* New York: Routledge & Kegan Paul.

Apple, M. (1989). American realities: Poverty, economy, and education. In L. Weis, E. Farrar, & H. Petrie (Eds.), *Dropouts from school: Issues, dilemmas, and solutions* (pp. 205-223). Albany: State University of New York Press.

Apple, M., & Taxel, J. (1982). Ideology and the curriculum. In A. Hartnett (Ed.), *Educational studies and social science* (pp. 166-178). London: Heinemann.

Asante, M. (1987). *The Afrocentric idea.* Philadelphia: Temple University Press.

Asante, M. (1988). *Afrocentricity.* Trenton, NJ: Africa World Press.

Asante, M. (1991). The Afrocentric idea in education. *Journal of Negro Education, 60*(2), 170-180.

Asante, M. (1992). The Afrocentric curriculum. *Educational Leadership, 49*(2), 28-31.

Banks, J. (1988). *Multiethnic education: Theory and practice* (2nd ed.). Boston: Allyn & Bacon.

Banks, J. (1992). Multicultural education: For freedom's sake. *Educational Leadership, 49*(4), 32-36.

Bhyat, A. (1993). *Bias in the curriculum: A comparative look at two boards of education.* Unpublished major research manuscript, Department of Sociology in Education, Ontario Institute for Studies in Education.

Board of Education, Toronto. (1988). *Education of black students in Toronto: Final report of the consultative committee.* Toronto: Author.

Board of Education, Toronto. (1993). *The Every Secondary Student Survey, Part II: Detailed profiles of Toronto's secondary school students* (Research Services, Publication No. 204). Toronto: Author.

Bowles, S., & Gintis, H. (1976). *Schooling in capitalist America: Educational reform and the contradictions of economic life.* New York: Basic Books.

Braithwaite, K. (1989). The black student and the school: A Canadian dilemma. In S. Chilingu & S. Niang (Eds.), *African continuities/L'heritage Africain* (pp. 195-216). Toronto: Terebi.

Braithwaite, K., & James, C. (Eds.). (1996). *Educating African-Canadians.* Toronto: James Lorimer.

Calliste, A. (1994, February). *African-Canadian experiences: The need for inclusion in the university curriculum.* Paper presented at the forum on Diversity in the Curriculum, Toronto.

Carlson, P. (1976). Toward a definition of local-level multicultural education. *Anthropology and Education Quarterly, 7,* 26-30.

Coehlo, E. (1991). *Caribbean students in Canadian schools.* Markham, Ontario: Pippin.

Collins, E. (1994, February). Black focused schools: An examination. *Pride Magazine.* Toronto, 3: 23-24.

Dei, G. (1993). The challenges of anti-racist education in Canada. *Canadian Ethnic Studies, 25*(2), 36-51.

Dei, G. (1994). Afrocentricity: A cornerstone of pedagogy. *Anthropology and Education Quarterly, 25*(1), 3-28.

Dei, G. (1995). The emperor is wearing clothes: Exploring the connections between anti-racist education and Afrocentricity. *International Journal of Comparative Race and Ethnic Studies, 2*(1), 86-101.

Dei, G. (1996). *Anti-racism education: Theory and practice.* Halifax, Nova Scotia: Fernwood.

Dei, G., Holmes, L., Mazzuca, J., McIsaac, E., & Campbell, R. (1995). *Push out or drop out? The dynamics of black/African-Canadian students' disengagement from school.* Final report submitted to the Ontario Ministry of Education and Training, Toronto.

Dei, G., Mazzuca, J., McIsaac, E., & Zine, J. (1997). *Reconstructing "dropouts": A critical ethnography of black students' disengagement from school.* Toronto: University of Toronto Press.

Estrada, K., & McLaren, P. (1993). A dialogue on multiculturalism and democratic culture. *Educational Researcher, 22*(3), 27-33.

Farrell, V. (1994, January 6). Support for black focused schools. *Share,* p. 8.

Freire, P., & Shor, I. (1987). *A pedagogy for liberation: Dialogue on transforming education.* South Hadley, MA: Bergin & Harvey.

Giroux, H. (1983a). Theories of reproduction and resistance in the new sociology of education. *Harvard Educational Review, 53,* 257-293.

Giroux, H. (1983b). *A theory of resistance in education: A pedagogy for the opposition.* South Hadley, MA: Bergin & Harvey.

Giroux, H. (1984). The paradox of power in educational theory and practice. *Language Arts, 61,* 462-465.

Giroux, H. (1986). Radical pedagogy and the politics of student voice. *Interchange, 17,* 48-69.

Giroux, H. (1992). Resisting difference: Cultural studies and the discourse of critical pedagogy. In L. Grossberg, C. Nelson, & P. Treichler (Eds.), *Cultural studies* (pp. 199-212). New York: Routledge & Kegan Paul.

Gordon, B. (1990). The necessity of African-American epistemology for educational theory and practice. *Journal of Education, 172*(3), 88-106.

Gyekye, K. (1987). *An essay in African philosophical thought.* London: Cambridge University Press.

Henry, A. (1992). *Taking back control: Toward an Afrocentric womanist standpoint on the education of black children.* Unpublished doctoral dissertation, Department of Curriculum, Ontario Institute for Studies in Education.

Henry, A. (1993). Missing: Black self-representations in Canadian educational research. *Canadian Journal of Education, 18,* 206-224.

Hilliard, A. (1992). Why we must pluralize the curriculum. *Educational Leadership, 49*(4), 12-15.

James, C. (1990). *Making it: Black youth, racism, and career aspirations in a big city.* Oakville, Ontario: Mosaic.

Kalbach, W., Verma, R., George, M., & Dai, S. (1993). *Population projections of visible minority groups, Canada, provinces and regions, 1991-2016.* Unpublished manuscript prepared for the Interdepartmental Working Group on Employment Equity Data. Toronto, Ontario.

Karenga, M. (1986). *Introduction to black studies.* Los Angeles: University of Sankore Press.

Keto, T. (1990). *The Africa-centered perspective of history.* Blackwood, NJ: C. A. Associates.

Lee, E. (1985). *Letters to Marcia: A teacher's guide to anti-racist education.* Toronto: Cross-Cultural Communication Centre.

Lee-Ferdinand, J. (1994). *Reinventing the self: The new postcolonial intellectual.* Unpublished manuscript, Ontario Institute for Studies in Education.

May, S. (1994). *Making multicultural education work.* Clevedon, England: Multilingual Matters.

Mbiti, J. (1982). African views of the universe. In R. Olaniyan (Ed.), *African history and culture* (pp. 193-199). Lagos: Longman.

McCarthy, C. (1990). *Race and curriculum: Social inequality and the theory and politics of difference in contemporary research on schooling.* Basingstoke, England: Falmer.

McCarthy, C., & Crichlow, W. (Eds.). (1993). *Race, identity, and representation in education.* New York: Routledge & Kegan Paul.

Moore, R. (1988). *Racism in the curriculum: The role of the reader in the curriculum—The third report.* North York, Ontario: North York Board of Education.

Mukherjee, A., & Thomas, B. (n.d.). *A glossary of terms.* Toronto: Toronto Board of Education.

Muteshi, J. (1996). *Women, law and engendering resistance: A pedagogical project.* Unpublished doctoral dissertation, Department of Curriculum, Ontario Institute for Studies in Education.

Nieto, S. (1992). *Affirming diversity: The sociopolitical context of multicultural education.* New York: Longman.

Oliver, W. (1986). Black males and social problems: Prevention through Afrocentric socialization. *Journal of Black Studies, 20,* 15-39.

Ontario Institute for Studies in Education. (1994, September). Anti-racist education: Working across differences [Special issue]. *Orbit* (Ontario Institute for Studies in Education Press).

Oyebade, B. (1990). African studies and the Afrocentric paradigm: A critique. *Journal of Black Studies, 21,* 233-238.

Radwanski, G. (1987). *Ontario study of the relevance of education, and the issue of dropouts.* Toronto: Ontario Ministry of Education.

Roman, L. (1993). White is colour! White defensiveness, postmodernism and anti-racist pedagogy. In C. McCarthy & W. Crichlow (Eds.), *Race, identity, and representation in education* (pp. 71-88). New York: Routledge & Kegan Paul.

Senese, G. (1991). Warnings on resistance and the language of possibility: Gramsci and a pedagogy from the surreal. *Education Theory, 41,* 13-22.

Sleeter, C., & Grant, C. (1987). An analysis of multicultural education in the United States. *Harvard Educational Review, 57,* 421-444.

Solomon, P. (1992). *Black resistance in high school: Forging a separatist culture.* Albany: State University of New York Press.

Statistics Canada. (1993). *Ethnic origin: 1991 census update.* Ottawa: Author.

Thomas, B. (1984). Principles of anti-racist education. *Currents, 2*(3), 20-24.

Tice, K. (1990). Gender and social work education: Directions for the 1990s. *Journal of Social Work Education, 26*(2), 134-144.

Walcott, R. (1990). Theorizing anti-racist education. *Western Canadian Anthropologist, 7*(2), 109-120.

Willis, P. (1977). *Learning to labour.* Farnborough, England: Saxon House.

Willis, P. (1983). Cultural production and theories of reproduction. In L. Barton & S. Walker (Eds.), *Race, class, and education* (pp. 197-238). London: Croom Helm.

Wright, H. (1994). Multiculturalism, anti-racism, Afrocentrism: The politics of race in educational praxis. *International Journal of Comparative Race and Ethnic Studies, 1*(2), 155-161.

10

The Assimilation of the Other Within a Master Discourse

WILLIAM E. CONKLIN

Racism and sexism generally are considered to be exclusionary phenomena. Excluded groups are considered as existing outside the norm. Thus texts, interpretive practices, and social conduct differentiate among persons to render benefits to some persons and to exclude others. Even well-intentioned discursive practices may isolate a group with the intent of benefiting it; the privileging of the group has the effect of excluding it from the dominant discourse. The statutory treatment of Amerindians during the 19th century exemplifies such a well-intentioned exclusionary practice.

There is another less considered phenomenon, however. Even in the effort to erase ethnic origin, gender, or race from the vocabulary of legal discourse, there remains an Other to the discourse. Legislators sometimes instruct public servants to review statutes and regulations to erase derogatory or paternalistic terms from the vocabulary. More commonly, legislatures enact human rights codes and constitutional bills of rights to have offensively worded texts rendered invalid. Human rights codes, for example, proscribe landlords and employers from differentiating tenants and employees on the basis of their gender, ethnic origin, or race. The appearance of an objective, neutral, impartial, and sanitized vocabulary makes the possibility even more difficult to appreciate.

Notwithstanding the erasure of ethnic origin, gender, and race from the vocabulary of legal discourse, a problem remains. The neutral language in the human rights legislation and the constitutional bills of rights remains to be interpreted. Shortly after their enactment, a cadre of experts takes hold of the interpretation of the texts. These experts read the texts through terms that represent doctrines long familiar to their profession. They profess the doctrines. Someone who feels excluded by a public official, a landlord, or an employer must retain an expert to represent his or her experienced harm. The expert represents the harm through special configurations of signs whose doctrines enclothe the experience of harm. The more scientized the configurations and the more intricate the differentiations among the signs, the more distant the legal discourse becomes to the person who has felt harmed, for the legal discourse becomes embodied with the meanings that the experts have lived at the same time that the discourse becomes a dead object for the person harmed. An aggrieved becomes an aggrieved to the legal discourse as well as to the same identifiable agent who had explicitly or tacitly excluded him or her on the grounds of race, gender, or ethnic origin.

The problem is that each word gives cause for interpretation. And, with the exception of the U.S. Bill of Rights, each human rights code and constitutional bill of rights in Western European and Commonwealth states provides exceptions to general proscriptions against exclusion. In the American discursive practices, courts have implied such exceptions into the absolute character of the Bill of Rights. Each word gains a color of meaning as lawyers usher forth evidence, collate the evidence, make their arguments, and interpret past decisions. The words are read with such issues in mind as the following. Who has the onus of establishing a claim, the aggrieved or the state? Which institution—court or legislature—possesses the authority to determine whether a group or an individual has been excluded from the legal discourse? Does the human rights text proscribe the exclusion of individuals per se or, alternatively, individuals as members of a group? What characterizes membership in the group, a racial or sexual characteristic with which one was born, a historically disadvantaged condition of the group itself, or a historically disadvantaged condition that an individual has experienced? Is a decision of a human rights tribunal final, or may one appeal to a common law court? Does the term "equality before the law" entertain social conditions, economic conditions, or merely a formal procedural equality?

Each neutral term in a human rights code is read through special chains of signs that are related to such crucial legal issues. Over a period of time, the cadre of experts elaborates wave on wave of signs to represent different ways in which to approach each issue. The experts are enchained to the signs. The aggrieved is situated into such chains of signs. To the nonexpert, a term in a human rights code may seem clear and straightforward. But to the expert, the term raises complex legal issues because of the indeterminate character of the word. This indeterminacy takes its character from the transposition of context-specific meanings that an aggrieved has experienced into universal abstract conceptions of the legal discourse. The nonexpert does not "know" what conceptions to associate with the configurations of signs in which the expert is immersed. Nor does the nonexpert "know" how to configure signs in different ways to produce different signifying effects in the legal discourse. This special knowledge privileges the lawyer as the expert knower of legal discourse. The lawyer professes the knowledge of the signs as a member of a legally protected profession. The monopoly position of that profession is enforced in the very legal discourse that the lawyer professes. That monopoly control of legal knowledge permits the lawyer to charge special fees for the privilege of one's gaining access to the lawyer's knowledge of the special terms in the human rights codes. Although corporations generally fare better than individual litigants precisely because they can afford the expensive proprietors of legal knowledge, the crucial point here is that the language of expert knowers displaces the embodied meanings that an aggrieved has experienced. Without access to the lawyer's monopoly control of legal knowledge, the neutralized verbiage in human rights texts remains emptied of an enforceable and authoritative signifying context.

Unfortunately, the legal discourse of a modern state simply cannot address the aggrieved through the language of the aggrieved. The aggrieved's language is an Other to the legal language. The legal discourse of a modern state inevitably is violent against the language of the aggrieved, for even well-intentioned human rights legislation invites interpretive acts that displace the everyday language through which one experiences a harm of exclusion. One who has been harmed by an exclusionary practice becomes an aggrieved to the legal discourse itself. The harm is doubled, although the harm done to the language of the Other is of a different character of harm from the indigenously experienced harm of being excluded. Because the legal discourse cannot address the aggrieved in the aggrieved's language, the authoritative chains of legal signs cannot be just, for justice is the language of an Other.

Examples

Let me give some examples. From June 1974 to May 1978, Ms. Bhadauria applied for 10 openings on the teaching staff at Seneca College.[1] A court reported that she was "a highly educated East Indian woman" holding a bachelor of arts, master of arts, and doctorate of philosophy in mathematics. She was qualified to teach in the province of Ontario and had 7 years teaching experience. All positions had been publicly advertised. She was not granted an interview for any of the openings. All of us can appreciate the feeling of emptiness and worthlessness when we receive a rejection letter in the mail for a job that we believed we were qualified to obtain. Indeed, it is difficult to put the felt experience on paper. After the initial feeling of inferiority, one might become angry at oneself or deny the experience by rejecting the employer as unworthy of one's professional or work experience and qualifications. Ms. Bhadauria surmounted these initial feelings of pain and applied 10 times to 10 different advertised openings at Seneca. Finally, she decided to go to a lawyer, who launched a civil action alleging that she had experienced discrimination on the grounds of her ethnic origin.

The trial judge granted the lawyer's application as disclosing a reasonable cause of action, although he dismissed the action with a brief endorsement that Ms. Bhadauria's situation was covered by the typification in another case. That is, Ms. Bhadauria was not alone. She shared certain characteristics with others. She retained a biography, but her concrete experiences were enclosed inside the boundaries of the categories, doctrines, rules, and principles that the legal signs represented. Ms. Bhadauria was a juridically defined person whose rights and duties were drawn from a human rights code rather than from a common law court. Whether situated in a chain of signs labeled "human rights law" or another categorized as "common law tort law," the expert knowers would read her pain through the chains of signs peculiar to the respective institutions. For later judges, lawyers, and human rights administrators, her name represented a special legal doctrine, namely, that one who feels aggrieved should go to the human rights tribunal rather than sue in the common law courts. The Ontario Court of Appeal held that the trial judge had wrongly typified Ms. Bhadauria's circumstances as an "Ontario human rights" case rather than as a matter of common law for the common law courts. According to the Supreme Court of Canada, Ms. Bhadauria should have proceeded with a complaint under the

Ontario human rights code even though the code allowed for substantially less damages and the code's administrators alone, rather than the complainant, would decide whether to proceed against the community college. In the latter circumstance, the human rights administrators would guide the administrative treatment of the alleged harm while Ms. Bhadauria slid between the differentiating signs of the universalist legal language. The Supreme Court of Canada held that the Ontario Court of Appeal had wrongly typified Ms. Bhadauria's situation, returning to the view of the trial court judge that she fell under the Ontario human rights situation rather than a civil law typification.

Now, what is striking about the reported reasons offered by the Ontario Court of Appeal and the Supreme Court of Canada in Ms. Bhadauria's situation is that the pain of being rejected for a job interview was coded in a chain of signs that lawyers and judges would easily recognize. The judges took Ms. Bhadauria's experiences as a "given": "This court must assume that the facts alleged by the plaintiff can be established." The discrimination was taken as a fact. The judges perceived that their whole project was to typify her "facts" correctly. To that end, the judges set out magic code words such as *Christie v. York* (1940), *In re Wren* (1945), *Ashby v. White* (1703), *Prosser,* and the *Human Rights Code.*[2] Did these magic words share a common principle? Or did the names represent competing doctrines as to the authority of a human rights tribunal and the tort of racial discrimination?

In searching for a shared principle in the discourse in which Ms. Bhadauria was reconfigured, Ms. Bhadauria was transformed into a juridical person. She became a plaintiff whose harm became displaced in favor of issues of "jurisdiction," "civil wrong," and authority. She had experienced the pain of being rejected for employment again and again. But her pain was lifted from context-specific experiences into the universal rights and duties of a juridical person. The judges ruled *about* the signs that made sense to the expert knowers of human rights law. They ruled about such signs as *Prosser, In re Wren, Christie v. York,* and the like.

When one rereads the Court of Appeal and Supreme Court judgments *about* her alleged harm, one finds no reference to her felt experiences in the college's initial rejections of her applications. Nothing is written about her initial felt experiences of humiliation, indignity, loss of self, bitterness, or anger. It seems as if Ms. Bhadauria even lacked a historically contingent biography. Nor is any mention made of the workings of the hiring process at institutions of higher learning in Ontario—the networking, the perceived hierarchy of graduate schools, the contacts that members of recruitment committees have with the referees of some applicants, the loyalties that faculty members retain for their own alma mater, their unconscious projection of their own self-images or idealized self-images in the differentiating process, the desire of some committee members to hire more people in their own fields or to perceive a faculty weakness in their own fields, or the fears and speculations that faculty members have even before a decision is made whether or not to invite the applicant for an interview. It was decided that such factors need not be examined because the important issues drew from chains of signs that may have represented some special doctrine or institutional context for lawyers but little for the aggrieved's former experience of pain.

Let me offer a second example. The complaint has been made that the common law legal system fails to recognize the customs of Amerindians. Whereas the common law draws from authored texts, such as statutes, and the trace of precedents that represent cognitive principles, the customs of Amerindians were gestural in character and without an identified promulgation from an author. Canadian officials have faced this problem by advocating a constitutional amendment that recognized the "inherent right of self-government within Canada" of the Aboriginal peoples. Aboriginal governments were to be recognized as "one of three orders of government in Canada." Such a proposed amendment was placed before the Canadian electorate in a referendum in October 1992. Even if the electorate and public officials had supported such an amendment, however, judges who were duly appointed by the Canadian state would have had to interpret the phrases "inherent right" and "self-determination." When would an Aboriginal law be made pursuant to the right of self-determination? Would an "unwritten" custom be subordinate to a legislated rule of a tribal council? What does self-determination mean? Does it mean that Aboriginal communities will be like sovereign states with the authority to enact their own criminal and civil laws and to be recognized as sovereign states in the international community?

This basic guarantee was to be subject to the authority of the legislatures and governments of the provinces and the federal agents if the enactment of Aboriginal laws conflicted with the "peace, order, and good government of Canada." Of course, the phrase "peace, order, and good government" was not some new phrase in Canadian or Commonwealth constitutional discourse. Section 91 of the basic text of the Canadian Constitution, formerly called the "British North America Act, 1867-present" and recently renamed the "Constitutional Acts, 1867-present," provided that the federal Parliament had the authority to enact laws generally for the "peace, order, and good government of Canada." Over the decades, the Canadian judiciary has held that the phrase represented diverse and complicated doctrines. One such doctrine, called the "emergency doctrine," restricted the application of the phrase to conditions that the federal government considered to be "emergencies." When transferred to the context of the Aboriginal right to self-government, however, the onus would be for the juridical agent of the Aboriginal peoples to establish why certain provincial or federal laws were not enacted in emergency conditions. A second doctrine, elaborated by the Canadian judiciary, has interpreted "peace, order, and good government" even more widely to reach matters that carried a "national dimension." A third doctrine has restricted "peace, order, and good government" to a residuary of laws that remain unclassified by the basic text that delineates the jurisdiction of levels of government. A fourth doctrine has provided that the phrase represents "new matters" such as nuclear power, aeronautics, radio communications, or other technological "advances" that did not exist at the time when the phrase "peace, order, and good government" was first enacted.

Each of the four doctrines carries a further series of rules, principles, and other doctrines that magic case names represent. Although an Amerindian community might consider its customs as its own, the juridical agents of the Canadian state would have to interpret the subordinate phrase "peace, order, and good government" and ultimately would have to determine the right of self-government of the Aboriginal peoples. The irony is that by recognizing the "inherent right" of "self-government" of the Aboriginal peoples, the customs of the latter would be assimilated into the master discourse of the state of Canada. However narrowly the courts interpreted "peace, order, and good government," the legal discourse of the Canadian state, not the discourses of the Amerindian peoples, would have remained the master.

Let me give a third example of the phenomenon of assimilation into a modern legal discourse. During the 1950s, 1960s, and 1970s, the Canadian political elite believed that if only the written constitution entrenched what they considered to be fundamental rights and freedoms, there would be no Other to the Canadian political system. Government pamphlets, distributed through the post offices of the country, more or less made this claim (Conklin, 1979). The final text that guaranteed the rights (including the right to equality before and under the law and the equal benefit of the law without discrimination on the grounds of race) set out one simple exception, namely, that the fundamental rights could be restricted if the restriction were a "reasonable limit" that could be "demonstrably justified in a free and democratic society." If a citizen read the text on its own, he or she no doubt would read the text of the Canadian Charter of Rights and Freedoms much as the government claimed in its pamphlets. The basic text stated in Section 52 that the text itself was supreme over all legislative and regulatory enactments. Freedom and democracy were "guaranteed," according to the text. The guarantee, however, lay only in the legal discourse itself.

However, since the entrenchment of the rights in 1981, judges have interpreted the limitations clause through extraordinarily complex legal tests. Moreover, the tests delineated the constitutional rights and duties of juridical persons, not human participants with embodied experiences. Indeed, corporations launched the majority of Charter cases before the Supreme Court of Canada even though they could hardly be said to have had the felt experiences of embodied aggrieved persons. The juridification of the Charter world occurred through the special terms that represented special doctrines that highly specialized lawyers claimed to "know." For example, lawyers, judges, and law professors understood the phrase "reasonable limits" by reading a series of "tests" or other magic names into "reasonable limits." So, an aggrieved was required to seek a specialist who would typify his or her felt experience in terms of the category "reasonable limits," which, in turn, was represented by such legal tests as "objective tests of validity," "the reasonable member of the public," "balancing of values," "the fair-minded member of the public," and "comparative legislation of other acknowledged free and democratic societies."

The United States and Great Britain were recognized as the main source of laws in a "free and democratic society." Canadian lawyers searched American constitutional discourse to find more precise magic terms. Lawyers came to understand just one magic term—the "balancing of values," for example—as "permissible limits of a government," "legislative means which are carefully designed to achieve legislative purposes," "values," "a living tree," "teleological," "goals," "the interests," "interest balancing," "significant interests," "government interests," "substantial interests," and the like. Even the name of a litigant, such as *Big M Drug Mart* or *Oakes,* represented special doctrines that competent lawyers alone "knew." An aggrieved, once resituated as a juridical person in a specialized language, was enclosed within one of the doctrines. The aggrieved was disembodied of particular experiences. His or her context-specific meanings were transformed into signifying relations that carried the universal character of rights and duties. The aggrieved, as a juridical person, became "alive" with lawyers' meanings. The aggrieved, as an embodied participant, was forgotten.

In sum, the more complex and scientific the special cognate doctrines of legal discourse, the more estranged the master discourse becomes vis-à-vis the meant objects that an aggrieved has experienced. At the same time, the citizen becomes dependent on legally trained personnel whose "knowledge" of the magic names and categories bring social status and national marketability within the legal profession. The lawyer pictures the world and the place of the aggrieved's harm in it. The lawyer's images of the world constitute the juridical person (Conklin, 1989).

The Interpretive Act of the Expert Knower

More to the point, when confronted with the report of racial or sexually constructed harm in a concrete circumstance, a lawyer (or judge) himself or herself undergoes a sequence of experiences that transforms the report into terms that the lawyer can understand. The lawyer typifies the reported circumstances under a category with metaphysical boundaries. The lawyer names the typification. Such a name gains its signification by being differentiated from other names that the lawyer recognizes as authoritative. So, for example, the name "Bhadauria" represents a "human rights case" as opposed to a "civil action." And the "right of self-government" in the constitutional referendum discussed earlier gains its signification by being opposed to "peace, order, and good government." So too, a "freedom of speech" as "guaranteed" in the Charter is differentiated from a "reasonable limit." The act of typification may occur in a few moments, or it may require substantive research into the chains of terms accepted in judicial decisions and legal scholarship.

Drawing from one of Husserl's metaphors, the lawyer's category enclothes the reported circumstance with a sign "like a garment." That is, in assigning a sign to social circumstances so as to "understand" it, "consciousness reaches out beyond what it actually experiences" to the thing referred (Husserl, 1970b, p. 701). The referent is absent from the interpretive experience. The lawyer *re*presents an aggrieved's harm by associating the harm with a recognizable sign. The sign represents a special category with boundaries that the lawyer claims to know and also claims to know how to apply to all hypothetical social facts. In the *Bhadauria* case, for example, the appellate judges accepted the alleged discrimination on grounds of ethnic origin as a social fact. The event of Ms. Bhadauria's pain, however, slipped from the vision of the judges as they situated Ms. Bhadauria into the chains of signs going to the jurisdiction of "human rights" tribunals and of civil courts. However, the latter chains of signs are not dead letters. The posited fact evokes an interpretation from within the lawyer's own experiential horizons of understanding. These horizons take form in a professional law school. They are shared horizons, notwithstanding the diverse social and ethnic experiential past of each law student before he or she enters his or her first day of law school. When a lawyer interprets a witness's report of a felt experience, he or she does so against *the lawyer's* professional experiences with similar reports. The lawyer situates the reported experience in the typification that his or her training has induced. Gadamer (1985, pp. 235-274) would call these typifications "prejudice" or "forestructures of meaning."

If one of the victims that Essed discusses in this volume decided to report his or her experience to a lawyer, the lawyer would not and could not perceive the victim's felt experience as if it were the lawyer's own. The lawyer's typifications *would not attach* to the initial circumstances. The lawyer would only possess an intuitive idea of the suffering. The intuition is what Husserl describes as an "unmediated seeing" rather than as a feeling or an occult power (Husserl, 1970b, pp. 682-683; see also Natanson, 1970). The lawyer would place the harm into *his or her own* intuitive idea of such harm. The lawyer's immersion within the legal discourse shapes his or her intuition. But the intuition is that of the lawyer.

The gap widens between the lawyer's intuition and that of the aggrieved. If a victim reported an event also interpreted by the lawyer, then the victim would re-present the event through signs that represented something special to the aggrieved's forestructures of meaning. He or she would do so through the horizons of his or her prior ego experiences. But those experiences might well have little connection to the experiences of a professional knower as a professional knower. Indeed, the aggrieved might well perceive the lawyer's magic names to be meaningless in that the aggrieved, unfamiliar with the lawyer's discourse, would not recognize the lawyer's representation of his or her pain. The aggrieved becomes victimized by the lawyer's language itself.

In sum, the lawyer reinterprets an aggrieved's story. The lawyer's reinterpretation parasitically "lives" from the story. But the story is transformed into chains of signs that a lawyer will recognize. A disjuncture erupts into an unsignified "chiasmus" (Merleau-Ponty, 1968). Lyotard (1988) calls this disjuncture a "differend." As the aggrieved reads a lawyer's letter, he or she may be destabilized—indeed terrorized—although the formal letter, authored by a juridical agent, may be considered harmless within the legal discourse. If anything, the lawyer's magic names and formalism may awaken experiences in a client that go in a very different direction from the lawyer's intended trace of precedents to some inaccessible origins.

The Assimilation of the Other Into Legal Discourse

The more ingrained the shared experiences of lawyers, the more predictable the intuitional responses of lawyers to each other. But from the viewpoint of the aggrieved excluded from the master discourse, the lawyer lives through an idealized world in the sense that the lawyer's discourse transforms context-specific meant objects into signs whose typifications the lawyer alone claims to know. That is, the context shifts from an unmediated felt experience of the aggrieved to mediating signs that the lawyer claims to know. Signs signify other authoritative signs. The unmediated felt experience slips into the chiasmus between the signs. This trace of signs conceals the aggrieved's bodily experiences by transforming the latter into signs that signify cognate objects for the lawyer.

From the viewpoint of the lawyer, the aggrieved who has been subject to racial or gender discrimination is a juridical person. He or she is pictured in terms of his or her rights and the duties of others. Even when the trial lawyer or judge claims to be dealing with "facts," the lawyer interprets those "facts" through the categories that only the expert knower claims to know.

Even if the victims of exclusion, described in such rich and varied contexts in this volume, could articulate their suffering, lawyers would take the words from the victims, reorder the words into a different chain of magic names associated with the *lawyers'* experiences *as lawyers,* and then re-present the new typifying sentences as the "facts." A victim's pain is without a voice. The victim of racial discrimination becomes an aggrieved to the legal discourse in that he or she cannot speak to his or her pain except through a foreign language. He or she finds it necessary to retain a special knower of this language to represent his or her story about the pain through terms that other experts will recognize. The embodied participant becomes a victim at the very moment when he or she attempts to gain access into the legal discourse. He or she suffers twice over. Using Lyotard's (1988, para. 12) understanding of the term *victim,* the nonlawyer is divested of the means to argue through his or her own idiom. The lawyer's interpretive act decapitates the victim's interpretive world.

What the *Bhadauria* courts took as social fact, then, was from the viewpoint of the client/nonlawyer an idealized construction into which lawyers alone had gained access. An optical illusion results. The lawyer's whole life virtually takes place within prescientific, experiential meanings that the lawyer brings into the client's reported stories. But the lawyer's meanings are signified through magic names shared with other lawyers. The mere citation of the name carries magic among the expert knowers. The lawyer's discourse masters other discourses, the discourses of the Other to the legal discourse. And yet, the lawyer's discourse cannot "exist" without parasitically "living" from the other discourses through which Others live. The closest that the lawyer can reach to the aggrieved's meaningful experiences is a *representation* of the aggrieved's report of such experiences through a secondary chain of magic names whose cognate objects—rules, principles, doctrines, policies—the lawyer claims to know. The experiencing meaning-forming process of the client, as a pained living participant, is left untouched and concealed.

Because the legal method merely *re*presents the experiential world through the invisible classifications associated with the magic names "known" to lawyers, the lawyer's resulting worldview is naive. Not surprisingly, the lawyer who interprets social events through his or her own *prejudice* as a professional knower would find it very difficult to understand *how* this naïveté became possible. The lawyer is open to the same charges that Husserl (1970a, pp. 50-52, 82, 88, 95-96) makes against Galileo, Descartes, Locke, Hume, and Kant. The problem is that the lawyer who "lives" within the modern legal genre simply cannot acknowledge the role of his or her own prior experiences without betraying the very genre that excludes such experiences as external to legalism itself. By enclothing the client's utterances with his or her own prior experiences within the genre (and all the while denying such is happening), the lawyer excludes the client's meanings, as embodied, from the "facts" to which the lawyer refers. The lawyer re-presents the client's experiences prior to the experiences. The client is an Other to the lawyer's own living acts of interpretation. As a consequence, the client's lived meanings die as the lawyer begins the project of resignifying events. The client is disembodied at the very moment that he or she is assimilated into the master discourse.

The Juridical Person and Embodied Persons

This assimilation occurs through the phenomenon of *reported speech* or what Bakhtin describes as "a speech within a speech" (Volosinov, 1973, pp. 115-117). A lawyer/interpreter regards the reported "speech within a speech" as an utterance belonging to someone else: "the witness stated that . . .," "it was provided in section 91 that . . .," and so on. The utterance becomes a sentence. The sentence is integrated into one unified narrative, initially projected by a lawyer and then by a judge. This relationship between the lawyer's unifying speech and the speech of the aggrieved is not a dialogue because the reported speech is continuous with the lawyer's present speech, whereas in a dialogue the two are discontinuous. The narrative unity is of one single consciousness. This single consciousness of the reported experience excludes parts of the aggrieved's report as inadmissible, irrelevant, of little credibility, or of little weight.

The unity of legal consciousness is reconciled with the independence of the reported speech through an almost imperceptible reconstruction of the embodied participant by the interpreter/lawyer. Reported speeches take on a hierarchical "existence," first, concerning the evidence of witnesses in terms of their closeness to the issues that the lawyers recognize as relevant to the authorized typifications and, second, concerning the weight of texts in terms of their place in the hierarchy of sources of the master discourse's magic names. The more rigidly and sharply defined the boundaries between the different reported speeches, the less accessible they are to penetration from an outside retort or critique.

I recounted earlier how the *Bhadauria* judges broke through the alien horizon of felt experiences of Ms. Bhadauria only to construct the judges' own magic terms in an alien world. The "I" of Ms. Bhadauria became a juridical person, a complainant who, in turn, was assimilated into the "we" of the court. She no longer had a biography. The court appropriated her discourse. In representing her harm to the court, her legal representative would have gestured and spoken to the mastery of the legal discourse. In this subtle process, her experiences of humiliation and indignity did not even have to be reported. They were accepted as social facts. As facts, they were assimilated into hidden typifications that lawyers had hitherto taken for granted. Her pain was frozen and then transformed. Even the "I" of her lawyer and of each judge was lost in the values, assumptions, style, and images of a mystical law that they presupposed to have been previously authored. They presupposed a law that narrated as an impersonal third person (an "it"). All this was done in the name of "the court," "the law," "justice," and/or "his honor." It was a product—an object—in whose "name" painful experiences were transformed into the typifications represented by names such as *In re Wren* and *Prosser.* The judges consumed these names, just as future lawyers will consume the name "Bhadauria" as signifying an old, although possibly new, typification. "Bhadauria" becomes one name in a linear evolution of a transcendent impersonal law. Jauss (1989, p. 208) describes this process as the objectification into an external world of what has been experienced. The identity of this law is gained through an identity with its own self. The architecture, furnishings, costumes, seriousness, and all other gestural components of the rhetoric of juridical agents institutionalized a distance between Ms. Bhadauria and the agents. Ms. Bhadauria, as an Other to the legal language, was displaced. A single law spoke through a collective memory in the name of the whole. As Bakhtin (1981) writes, "The authoritative word is located in a distanced zone, organically connected with a past that is felt to be hierarchically higher. . . . It is a prior discourse" (p. 342). The judge is believed to sit above and apart from the characters of social struggle.

Although the judge considers himself or herself above the social struggle, he or she feels constrained by the gaze of some outside inaccessible justice (Conklin, 1996). As the agent of this justice, the judge considers all juridical persons equal before and under the law. But the judge/interpreter tells a story within a monologue vis-à-vis an aggrieved who does not understand the legal language. The judge seeks the legal signification of different terms in the human rights codes and precedents. It is the lawyer's ordering of the *report* of the aggrieved's words, not the latter's utterance itself, that matters. In "fact," it is the lawyer's forms that constitute matter, even though the lawyer associates his or her forms with the preexisting signs of legislatures and courts. The aggrieved's utterances become anonymous. The language of the particular Other is lost in the web of a monologue.

The experiential body of the living participant who had experienced pain in a concrete situation is deconstructed. His or her effort to voice pain shifts into the third person of the lawyer's language: "he or she said," "they said," "it was said," and so on. The lawyer simply does not say "I believe . . ." or "I am arguing . . . ." Rather, the lawyer utters "It is submitted to the court that . . ." or "Paragraph 37 of the plaintiff's statement of claim provides that . . . ." The lawyer's language does carry the color of a dialogue with the aggrieved. As Benveniste (1971, pp. 218, 220) argued, "the reality of discourse" involves a unique I/thou relationship in which each speaker sets himself or herself up as the "subject." Each "subject" refers only to the instance of his or her own discourse. But when an utterance refers to the third person (as do the pleadings and arguments of a lawyer or judge), the utterance appeals to an objective situation. The aggrieved's utterance is produced as a resignified sentence. The formal pronouns (third person) function as abbreviated substitutes. The third person *represents* "the unmarked member" of the objective reference. The member is "disembodied."

The master discourse is so successful in deconstructing the embodied meanings of an aggrieved that the participant cannot actively respond to the lawyer's language except through the latter. The participant is a victim (Lyotard, 1988, pp. 9-14), for the court's categories preexist the witness in such a manner that an unbridgeable gulf lies between their two sets of signifying relations. The human participant as plaintiff or defendant cannot respond, nor is he or she allowed to respond through his or her own idiom. The legal discourse's reconstructed juridical "person" represents an abstract unity without being determined by the aggrieved. In the process of reconstructing the events surrounding the indigenous suffering of an embodied participant, the latter is demarcated, abstracted, concealed, and ordered within the judge's second-level story. That act of concealment returns the participant to the realm of the voiceless.

The aggrieved can "participate" in the monologue. But he or she can do so only if he or she accepts the legal genre's boundaries. As in the case of Ms. Bhadauria, the aggrieved initially enters into the genre by becoming a plaintiff or a defendant in a legal proceeding. Indeed, nowhere do the appellate law reports of Ms. Bhadauria's plight indicate her bodily experience, such as her felt experience on being rejected for interviews on 10 occasions at the same institution. If Ms. Bhadauria had merely visited a lawyer who chose not to litigate (of course, the lawyer, true to his or her own representative status, would state that the decision whether to litigate was the client's choice), an aggrieved may be transformed into a juridical person without even becoming a litigant. He or she need only visit a lawyer; the visit would awaken a series of questions from the lawyer, questions that other expert knowers would consider as relevant and appropriate however viewed by the new client. The *Bhadauria* court of appeal, like any court of appeal, aimed to sort out whether the pained participant was recognizable as a juridical person with an acceptable juridically defined "pain" within the secondary language. If a court of appeal finds that one is not a juridical person, then the claimant does not possess standing before the representers of the secondary language. Such a nonperson lacks standing before "the eyes of the law." Ms. Bhadauria was treated as nonexistent.

The Violence of the Displacing Discourse

Sometimes a group of participants will "take the law into their own hands." That is, they will insist on retaining the integrity of their experiencing bodies and refuse to be assimilated into the master language. Robert Redford recounted such events in the film *Incident at Oglala.* Similarly, Canadian Indians with firearms occupied property near Oka, Quebec, during the summer of 1991 to prevent the commercial development of their ancestral lands. Here the ultimate violence of legal interpretation was visible for all to observe. The "rule of law" had been challenged, and a crisis of authority invariably ensued. The armed participants, whose persistent experiences of pain had led them to stand fast, were perceived as challenging the master discourse. The juridical agents labeled the insurgents as outlaws, as outside the master discourse. The representers of the master discourse offered to negotiate or even to hear the grievances of the aggrieved. They would do so, however, only on the condition that the insurgents lay down their arms and recognize the ultimate legitimacy of the master discourse. Deference to the master discourse must come first, before negotiation.

My point in raising the Oka case is not to suggest that an aggrieved who takes up arms against the legal discourse ought to be protected under the guarantee of freedom of speech. Guns are, indeed, a rather more advanced form of speech than that in which Ms. Bhadauria was engaged. Guns are likely to produce a different response than the appeal to legal argument by Ms. Bhadauria's representer. My point, however, is that violence inheres in the most technical interpretation of a statute, regulation, or judicial precedent. The violence inheres because of the "natural" assimilation of the aggrieved's everyday meanings into the legal discourse as the expert knowers of the signs of the legal discourse begin to typify the aggrieved's representation of his or her meanings. This violence remains invariably hidden behind the appearance of an impartial elaboration of objective legal tests and doctrines. The violence remains hidden until, as occurred at Oka, an aggrieved refuses to bow down to the web of representers of the legal discourse.

Of course, one may consider such challenges to the master discourse as aberrations in a generally deferential populace who invariably accepts the "rule of law." However, the contemporaneous events in the former Yugoslavia demonstrate that challenges to a master discourse sometimes may succeed, although the authority of the new master discourse may be quickly challenged by a formerly concealed Other. The veneer of civility, identified as the "rule of law," depends on a monopoly of violence for the cadre of expert knowers. The discourses of those in power struggle to master, to dominate, and to assimilate all competing discourses. If the assimilation remains unsuccessful, then the master discourse may (re)define the outlaw as nonexistent, as a nonjuridical person in "the eyes of the law." And if the outlaw's experiential body still emerges from the night, then the representers of the master discourse will *enforce* their categories on the outlaw's body; the body will be imprisoned, raped, beaten, tortured, disciplined, or, more commonly, exterminated as in the case of Kuwait, Iraq, Yugoslavia, Guatemala, Indonesia, and Waco, Texas. As President Slobodan Milosevic put it, "I think we are on the threshold of the final solution" (quoted in Jackson, 1993). Even the master discourse of international law, in turn, cannot allow for outside discourses that refuse to recognize its mastery; Iraq, Serbia, Croatia, and Somalian military lords exemplify such Others during recent years. The representers of the master discourse *picture* or *imagine* the Other as an enemy to the all-inclusive juridical discourse of the state. The representers of this discourse will typify representers of competing discourses as contemptuous, seditious, treasonous, traitorous, mad, inhuman, savage, and/or evil. And all this is done in *the name* of a *rule of law.*[3] Anyone who lives through a discourse outside of the master spectacle threatens mastery and invariably poses potential political/juridical instability. To mend the possible opening, the Other is redefined. The Other must acknowledge such retypification. A bourgeois peace will ensue upon such acknowledgment.

In "fact," contemporary legal reasoning in common law discourses thrives on a distinguishing of one category from another. What concrete experience is excluded from one category is included in another, just as Laskin stated of Ms. Bhadauria's predicament. Legal categories colonize the concrete. As Hegel (1977, para. 158; see also Gadamer, 1985, p. 317) argued in his "inverted world" analyses, by making the very distinction between an inside and an outside, consciousness must venture beyond its former limits within the inside. To make a boundary between the inside and the outside, a master discourse always must claim to know what is the other side of the boundary. The representers of the master discourse do not have to recognize the other side to include (by excluding) it within the master's totality.

The Phenomenon of Concealment

The Other's language is not always displaced. The aggrieved's meanings may remain *concealed,* however, within the play of signs that excite the cadre of expert knowers. Professionally trained knowers of the names claim the monopolistic privilege of interpreting the names. Educational certificates awarded from professional schools support the recognition of this privilege, just as do the high costs of gaining the certificates, the examinations, the expert training, the admission into a society by a governing body, and all the other indicia of a bureaucracy described by Weber (1970, pp. 196-209, 224-235, 240-244; 1971, pp. 240-250). Preoccupied with discovering the intent of some historical author such as a legislature (Conklin, 1996), the lawyer's enterprise and motives are enclothed with authority. A professionalized discourse emerges. The addressee of the written codes is the professional knower, not the citizen. To this end, law reform in a modern state aims to render the categories associated with the legal signs intellectually coherent, consistent, ordered, clear, and logical, much as do the yellow pages of a telephone directory. *Recht* is *Gesetz* for the lawyers/interpreters; the master discourse is posited in the consciousness of the professional knowers.

But for the victim, the master discourse risks becoming estranged from the concrete, context-specific meanings that the victim experienced in moments of indignity and exclusion. Franz Kafka (1964) demonstrates in *The Trial,* for example, how confused and estranged from the master discourse the victim can become. The "developed" language of a modern state is someone else's language whose signs I, as a victim and nonlawyer, find it difficult to understand. My experience with the master discourse remains separated from my meant objects of my everyday discourses. The master discourse cannot share the initial experiences of humiliation that I *mean* when Others excluded me in the situations that Essed, for example, describes in this volume. A lawyer "lives the law," one is reminded again and again. But that law, true to its character as a master discourse in a modern bureaucratic state, is embedded within a monologue far removed from any recognition of the lived experience of an Other *before* its categories begin to envelop my experiences. As a client/witness, I must passively accept the narration of my story by the professionally trained representers of the master discourse. I may cry to be recognized. I may protest in an outburst. But just as Foucault's (1975) students showed in *I, Pierre Riviere,* the representers will likely typify me as unruly or even as mad; my body may even be enchained in a cell while the representers of the master discourse dialogue about the fate of my body. The representers narrate my story in their language. Their narration is final, self-sufficient, and a "given" for any subsequent typification.

Suffering Through the Phenomenon of Displacement

Several of the essayists in this volume raise examples of "things they say to your face" when one is openly excluded from a juridical discourse. The phenomenon that I have been describing, however, involves a concealed exclusion when one's pain is assimilated into a dominant discourse. The reader may no doubt insist that I could hardly be describing his or her own legal discourses, the discourses of liberal societies with rich heritages of respect for individual rights; surely, I must be describing the legal discourse of some newly independent state. Why does legal language conceal the victim's suffering, of necessity, in every modern state?

This concealment occurs in part because a law, to be authoritative in a modern state, must generalize between or among contingently situated living participants. The generalization abstracts from contingent circumstances to form a category. The category is disembodied unless and until a representer applies it to a circumstance. Precisely at that moment, however, the legal category, being an intellectualization and idealization, encloses the experiential body inside a mental picture of it. The category typifies the experience. In this manner, the body of the particular Other is assimilated *into* the typification without being destroyed. The latter occurs at the point where, after representers attempt to assimilate the body into their categories, the particular Other refuses to recognize the authority of the typification. I have recounted incidents earlier where this has occurred. At such a moment, the representers of the master discourse must use violence against the Other's body to retain the self-identity of the master discourse. The former act of concealment erupts into the open.

The master discourse conceals the production of suffering, second, because the legal genre is *unilingual.* Although the professional experts may well be recruited from a diversity of backgrounds, the juridical language of the state cannot allow indigenous discourses to compete with it for authority. The categories of an indigenous discourse cannot be considered on an equal plane with the typifications of the legal discourse without compromising the latter's self-identity and authoritativeness. Such competition among different discourses existed in the early Greek tribal life before the rise of the city-state. Such discourses were lived at the very moment that they were authoritative. But the language of the modern state excludes the possibility of a multiplicity of voices beyond, before, and under the typifications of that language. No other discourses can prevail over the legal monologue.

A third factor works to conceal the production of suffering within the master discourse. The representers and victims alike perceive the professional knowers as involved in a *practice.* "How is your practice coming along," one lawyer will be heard to say to the other. The professional "teachers" of the legal language will be evaluated by students and peers alike according to their success at inculcating typifications that can be "practiced." And yet, notwithstanding its practice as a practice, the typification project of the lawyer is an intellectual exercise. The professional knowers intellectualize the world through signs—such as *In re Wren, Christie,* and "equality before the law"—that represent cognitive pictures of absent objects. The expert knowers typify social events and aggrieved persons. What could be more theoretical than a general, socially contextless metaphysics of typifications?

The Lawyer King

Contrary to Plato's vision, the lawyer—not the philosopher—has become the king of the bureaucratic state. It is the lawyer's lived experiences that are brought into legal discourse. The lawyer dialogues with other lawyers about which cognitive typifications to associate with each sign or configuration of signs. The lawyer's special knowledge of the doctrines that legal signs represent privileges the lawyer as the indispensable figure in the modern state. The vocabulary of human rights codes may well seem neutral and objective and straightforward to the person who has been harmed by racially or gender-motivated conduct. The gestures of the lawyer in the courtroom, the style of writing in a letter, the lawyer's clothes and automobile, and all the other genre-like elements of legal language may well seem technical. The juridical agent will declare that the agent merely applies the intent and words of the human rights code.

But as the legal language becomes increasingly more technical and complex, the interconnected chains of signs become distanced from the everyday meanings that the aggrieved brings *into* his or her own experiences. The technical web of signs loses the aggrieved's embodiment of meaning. Legal language becomes a distant object whose enforcement the aggrieved must accept to his or her chagrin or whose assimilative project the aggrieved must trust. The lawyer's discourse counts because, ultimately, the typifications of such a discourse can be *enforced* against the lived meanings of an aggrieved. The "good" legal practitioner is the ultimate metaphysician in that the lawyer is privileged to know what typifications to assign with authoritative signs. Such a metaphysics dominates at the very moment that civil society understands the lawyer as a practitioner. The professional expert becomes unattackable in the enforcement of the master discourse. The assimilation of the life-world of the aggrieved into the master discourse of the modern state is complete.

Notes

1. See *Bhadauria v. Seneca College* (1981).

2. *Christie v. York,* (1940) S. C. R. 139. *Re Drummond Wren,* (1945) O. R. 778. *Ashby v. White* (1703), 2Ld. Raym. 938. Prosser, *The law of torts* (4d), 1971. Ontario Human Rights Code, R. S. O. 1970, c. 318.

3. Lyotard (1988) links this totalizing character of Recht to Nazism:

> That is why savages make war. They endlessly carry out, and thus endlessly hear and tell, the narrative of their we. They merit their name. Who the adversaries are is of no importance. They are not adversaries. Nothing will happen through them that has not already happened.
>
> Nazism restores this genre of discourse, which modernity has brought to ruin. . . . The parody consists in the deployment of the means to persuade the people of its exceptional nature. What is foreign to the people [the representatives of Recht] gives rise to a policing by extermination (Auschwitz) or to a sacrificial "beautiful death" (Stalingrad). (p. 105)

A close study of the speeches of President George Bush during the conduct of the recent war in Iraq reflects the interrelationship of the rule of international law and its enforcement when the Other refuses to succumb to its monologue, just as the Iraqi state is seeking to destroy the Kurds as an Other today.

References

Bakhtin, M. (1981). *The dialogic imagination: Four essays.* Austin: University of Texas Press.

Benveniste, E. (1971). *Problems in general linguistics.* Coral Gables, FL: University of Miami Press.

Bhadauria v. Seneca College. (1981). 37 N.R. 455 (S.C.C. per Laskin, C.J.C.) overrulling (1979), 11 C.C.L.T. 121 (Ont. C.A. per Wilson, J.A.) overrulling Callaghan (unreported).

Conklin, W. (1979). *In defence of fundamental rights.* Alphen aan den Rijn, The Netherlands: Sijthoff & Noordhoff.

Conklin, W. (1993). Teaching critically within a modern legal queue. *Canadian Journal of Law and Society, 8*(2), 33-57.

Conklin, W. (1996). The invisible author of legal authority. *Law and Critique, 6.*

Conklin, W. (in press). Hegel, the author and authority in Sophocles' *Antigone.* In L. Rubin (Ed.), *Justice vs. law in early Greek philosophy.* New York: Longman.

Foucault, M. (Ed.). (1975). *I, Pierre Riviere, having slaughtered my mother, my sister, and my brother: A case of parricide in the 19th century.* Lincoln: University of Nebraska Press.

Gadamer, G. (1985). *Truth and method.* New York: Crossroad.

Hegel, G. (1977). *Phenomenology of spirit.* Oxford, England: Oxford University Press.

Husserl, E. (1970a). *The crisis of European sciences and transcendental phenomenology.* Evanston, IL: Northwestern University Press.

Husserl, E. (1970b). *Logical investigations* (Vol. 2). New York: Humanities Press.

Jackson, J. O. (1993, July 26). The lessons of Bosnia. *Time,* pp. 20-22.

Jauss, H. (1989). *Question and answer: Forms of dialogic understanding.* Minneapolis: University of Minnesota Press.

Kafka, F. (1964). *The trial* (W. Muir & E. Muir, Trans.). New York: Modern Library.

Lyotard, J.-F. (1988). *The differend: Phrases in dispute.* Minneapolis: University of Minnesota Press.

Merleau-Ponty, M. (1968). *The visible and the invisible.* Evanston, IL: Northwestern University Press.

Natanson, M. (1970). Phenomenology and typification: A study in the philosophy of Alfred Schutz. *Social Research, 37,* 1-22.

Volosinov, V. (1973). *Marxism and the philosophy of language.* New York: Seminar Press.

Weber, M. (1970). *Max Weber: The interpretation of social reality* (J. Eldridge, Ed.). New York: Scribner.

Weber, M. (1971). *From Max Weber: Essays in sociology* (H. Gerth & C. W. Mills, Eds.). London: Routledge & Kegan Paul.

11

Subverting Poor Me: Negative Constructions of Identity in Poor and Working-Class Women's Autobiographies

ROXANNE RIMSTEAD

> To dare an adventure I cannot afford is the tension I experience in realizing myself as a writer. A question of identity. To step out of my heritage as a member of the working class to attempt to say something of importance is the adventure. I was not meant to do this. As a woman. As a working-class woman. Writing is an act of defiance, rebellion . . . arrogance.
>
> —Cy-Thea Sand (1987, p. 61)

Self-representations by poor and working-class women are an adventure for writers and readers alike because they often raise previously unspoken questions of identity. They defy the class and gender imperatives that would otherwise keep these women invisible or contained within representative images and, in many cases, expose the social mechanisms of exclusion. But the act of self-representation for working-class and poor subject often is, paradoxically, shameful as well as defiant in that it so often is accompanied by the shame of being made visible and of admitting powerlessness. In the opening quotation, Sand (1987) represents writing as a life choice that requires daring and represents it through the appropriately economic image of an "adventure [she] cannot *afford.*" This image draws attention not only to the heightened economic stress of a writer's existence for a working-class woman who already occupies an economically precarious position, but also to the psychosocial danger of stepping beyond the place of a silenced subject.

More than the angel-in-the-house mechanism of feminine self-censorship, which Virginia Woolf and other feminist critics have identified, we see in poor and working-class women's autobiographical writings (such as those to be discussed in this chapter, Sand's [1987] "A Question of Identity" and Campbell's [1973] *Halfbreed*) class- and race-based negative constructions of identity functioning as compelling sources of cultural muting. For example, one such negative construction of how Sand experiences herself as a writer turns "rebellion" into "arrogance" in her formulation quoted earlier. In *Halfbreed,* the subject reflects less on the act of narrating or self-censorship than she does on the events and family members in a long life of struggle. As both survivor and witness, Campbell testifies in a seemingly transparent style to the material consequences of racism and poverty and to the despair and self-destruction triggered by internalized negative constructions of her people as "halfbreeds." Both writers venture the risk and shame of self-representation to defy the dominant definitions of the Self. Moreover, it is through the unfolding of a shamed Self that is fixed and partially constructed by negative definitions that their oppositional voices can emerge.

In this chapter, I use the term *constructions* of identity in opposition to "strategies" of identity to imply the palpable and received nature of negative images (despite complicity on the part of marginalized subjects). I use the term *negative* when constructions of identity reflect exclusionary practices by people at the center against those on the periphery—such as stereotyping, blaming, disbelieving, misrepresenting, or silencing—or when these constructions of identity result in feelings of shame, self-blaming, passivity, or powerlessness on the part of poor women. These references to received negative constructions of identity are tentative working labels that are subjectively unfolded in the narratives themselves rather than rigorously theorized here. What is central to my exploration, at this point, is not how to isolate or categorize these discursive events or to present a taxonomy of them; rather, it is how autobiographical subjects report them as complex lived experiences of exclusionary discourse and how we may interpret them as readers.

If writing is for poor and working-class women, as Zandy (1990) suggests in *Calling Home* ("a way of locating oneself, a way of finding a home in an inhospitable universe" [p. 1]), then one of the crucial processes in that search for a sense of cultural belonging is navigation through exclusionary discourses and negative definitions of the Self. As autobiographical subjects, poor and working-class women frequently call on negative constructions of identity as markers of past selves to position themselves as participants even when they report conversion to more self-affirming or more oppositional discourses on their own marginalization. To position themselves in this way, subjects may testify directly to the lived consequences of a rhetoric of exclusion, they may unfold a shameful "I" who experiences powerlessness and muting in the face of internalized negative definitions, or they may subvert the negative identity through defiance or the use of a collective "we." Shortly, I discuss in some detail how negative constructions of poor and working-class women are generated culturally in both simple and complex ways, for example, through popular myths about the poor, through a liberal discourse that is covertly exclusionary (especially toward poor women), and through representative narrative forms that often misrepresent lived experiences of poverty. I then focus on how Sand and Campbell report experiencing insults and stereotypes, internalizing such constructions, and defying them—but not necessarily in a linear progression whereby the subject's relationship with negative constructions of identity resolves itself in any definitive way. These readings of Sand's and Campbell's subjective experiences are exploratory. I want to suggest that it is not enough to study the genealogy and dissemination of negative definitions of the poor; we must also examine how these definitions are lived by concrete subjects themselves as a significant part of their life histories.

The Poor as Colonized Subjects

The sociologist John Porter began his cornerstone study of the correspondence among class, racial, and ethnic stratification in Canada, *The Vertical Mosaic,* with the statement, "The most persistent image that Canadians have of their society is that it has no classes" (Porter, 1965, p. 3). In general, the lived context of poor and working-class women's self-representations is subordination to such popular myths that erase or misrepresent the lived experiences of the poor in an affluent society.

In *Women and Poverty,* for example, Daly (1989, pp. 6-7) notes the power of popular myths to discredit claims of the poor on society; such myths circulate the misconceptions that there is no poverty now like there was during the 1930s and 1940s, that no one needs to be poor anymore because of welfare, and that people are poor due to some fault or failing of their own. Harrington (1962), in his pioneering work *The Other America: Poverty in the United States,* identifies the most familiar form of social blindness about the poor as the myth that the poor do not work and that they cheat on welfare. The poor:

> are dispossessed in terms of what the rest of the nation enjoys, in terms of what the society could provide if it had the will. They live on the fringe, the margin. They watch the movies and read the magazines of affluent America, and these tell them that they are internal exiles. (p. 178)

The long genealogy of moral judgments against the poor in Anglo-Saxon society is summarized in *The Stigma of Poverty: A Critique of Poverty Theories and Policies* by Waxman (1983) along with corresponding genealogies of legislative controls, charitable movements, social work, and their discourses. Popular myths have been shifting over the centuries, Waxman explains, first constructing the poor as morally righteous under early Christianity; then as a negative status group with a collective and morally suspect identity during 14th-century Europe; then as increasingly immoral but more and more individualized after the 16th century; and finally, from the 19th century on (with the advent of social Darwinism), as naturally deviant and deficient, more than simply morally culpable. Characterizing the stigma of poverty in North America during the 20th century are the inherited labels and categories of "deserving" and "undeserving" poor, the further individualization and psychologizing of poverty, and a close association between welfare and the poor (pp. 72-92). Waxman argues that the popular myths representing the poor as prolific breeders, welfare cheats, unemployable, lazy, dishonest, criminal, and so on spill over into scientific concepts and social programs and function as the rationalization for the dominant group's material exclusion of the poor. In the following passage, he adapts Goffman's (1963) theory of stigma to expose the social logic of exclusionary discourse:

> The effect of all these labels is to stereotype the poor, to isolate and distort their position by concealing their roles in terms of their interaction with

> both themselves and the non-poor. These legitimations and ra
> serve what Goffman calls "stigma-theories," or ideologies w
> his (the stigmatized's) inferiority and account for the dan
> represents," and thus justify our "exercise [of] varieties of disc
> through which effectively, if not unthinkingly, [we] reduce his li ...ces.
> (Waxman, 1983, p. 75)

A striking dramatization of how popular myths, stereotypes, and labels become nuanced and personalized as they are internalized by the poor is the following passage that appeared in the introduction to *The Real Poverty Report.* Written by four men who resigned from Canada's Special Senate Committee on Poverty during the early 1970s because they could not agree with the censorship imposed on their findings, *The Real Poverty Report* survives as an important historical document in the construction of the poor in Canada. The following passage gains imaginative power by dramatizing the colonization of the subject as a series of acts of discursive violence:

> From the very beginning, when you are still a child, you must learn to undervalue yourself. You are told that you are poor because your father is too stupid or too shiftless to find a decent job, or that he is a good-for-nothing who has abandoned you to a mother who cannot cope. And as you grow up on the streets, you are told that your mother is dirty and lazy and that is why she has to take money from the welfare department. Because you are poor, the lady from the welfare office is always coming around asking questions. She wants to know if your mother is living with a man, and why she is pregnant again.
>
> If as a child you are going to survive, you must close these violences out of your mind and retreat into a smaller world that you can handle. . . . If your parents are Indian, black, or Eskimo [*sic*], then all these strikes against you are multiplied. (Adams, Cameron, Hill, & Penz, 1971, p. xi)

The passage goes on to describe more of these discursive "violences," the myths of failure and personal responsibility for poverty, intruding on the subject's consciousness at each new stage in life. On the one hand, this dramatization of the poor person's psyche stresses the unrelenting quality and pervasiveness of popular myths. The oft-repeated quality and taken-for-grantedness give discursive power to negative constructions of identity, making them intrusive and capable of flattening the psychosocial space that houses our sense of identity. On the other hand, the dramatization may oversimplify the process of colonization in that the subject shows no complicity with, or resistance against, the messages she receives about herself but seems, rather, to internalize them passively.

Yet the complicity of poor people, their passivity and resistance, and their recycling of hegemonic representations has been at the core of theoretical discussions about how class inequality gets reproduced as culturally acceptable, generation after generation. Among the leading theorists of cultural reproduction such as Pierre Bourdieu, Louis Althusser, Antonio Gramsci, Paulo Freire, Theodor Adorno, Raymond Williams, and Stuart Hall, the discussion has focused on how able cultural actors are to extricate themselves from entrapment by culturally disseminated ideology and what the role of intellectuals can and should be in mediating popular discursive fields outside the traditional bounds of academic discourse. There has been fundamental disagreement about the degree to which education and the media maintain structures of class domination over the poor. For the more populist theorists such as Freire, Gramsci, Williams, and Hall, the power to resist socialization belongs to the the poor themselves as well as to intellectuals and political theorists, largely because their models of class oppression and cultural reproduction are agent centered. They are constructed in such a way that the participants' complicity and resistance must be factored in. According to agent-centered models of cultural reproduction, emergent forms of art, popular culture, and radical pedagogy may help poor people contest popular myths and stereotypical identities and thus decolonize themselves. Such complex accounts of cultural reproduction depend on models of interaction that show that popular myths and stereotypes construct participants but that participants, as agents and readers, may also participate in shaping their own relationship to dominant myths.

In addition to the complicity and resistance of poor people to misrepresentation, a further complexity of their colonization as subjects is multiple stigmatization, whereby an individual may be constructed by exclusionary discourses based not only on poverty but also on racial, ethnic, and/or religious stigma; on physical differences; on gender; and so on (Waxman, 1983, pp. 71-73). In reading Sand (1987) and Campbell (1973) later, I focus on how the psychosocial space of poor women may be shaped by gender-based and racial prejudices. The double stigmatization of poverty and gender has only recently been brought into the field of academic discourse through the paradigm of the feminization of poverty (Gelpi & Hartsock, 1986; Goldberg & Kremen, 1990; Gunderson, Muszynski, & Keck, 1990; Pearce, 1978; Sidel, 1986). This expert discourse has not trickled down to offer masses of poor women the means to redefine themselves more positively, nor has it increased the cultural access and visibility of poor women as agents and participants of their own oppositional discourse, speaking among themselves or on behalf of themselves oppositionally. Besides the occasional collection of these voices in ethnographic oral histories, there has been limited attention to the details of poor women's position of multiple oppression and stigmatization as well as limited attention to how to read these voices. One reason why the academy has been slow to recognize this position of double stigmatization is because of the blind spot around the subject of gender in Marxist discourse. Marxist paradigms of class identity never were adequate to make visible or coherent working-class women's gendered experiences, as we are increasingly being made aware by feminists critiquing and adapting Marxist paradigms of culture (e.g., Barrett, 1988; Delphy, 1984; Hansen & Philipson, 1990; Kaplan, 1990; Robinson & Vogel, 1978). A lack of class identification among working-class and poor women has come about partly because women could not see their experiences of oppression being illuminated by a political discourse based on market relations and wage labor. This silence on the subject of the gendered specificity of women's experiences of poverty and class has reinforced the naturalized link between the stigmas of class and gender in the popular imagination.

Smith (1989-1990) links the construction of poverty and female identity in liberal humanist discourse, showing how language itself tends to construct both on the outside of civil society. She discusses the projection of disorder and deficiency onto the poor by capitalist society, and onto poor women in particular. Smith traces the workings of an inside/outside paradigm in liberal discourse about the poor that functions on the covert exclusionary logic that the poor and women are on the outside of civil society:

> not as a result of external order and rule but as a result of their own nature. . . . Within the logic of this ideology, the "natural" extends into the interior of the person erasing essential signs of order, control, and rule. (p. 222)[1]

As objects of this exclusionary liberal discourse, working-class women see themselves not as members of a market-based class of workers or poor but as somehow inherently and individually deficient and disorderly. This naturalization of poverty explains in part why it is so difficult for poor women to make demands on society and speak out collectively, why even academic studies of the working class often will overlook the poor and their lived experiences as naturally outside the bounds of civil society, and why civil society can rationalize interventionist policies into the lives of poor women via a welfare machine that polices the poor.

Social scripts and judgments may serve the interests of dominant groups by discrediting and belittling the testimonies of the poor (evidence of the way in which they experience themselves), whereas the narrative form of self-representation itself may exercise a form of distortion or misrepresentation on the participants' stories. With respect to British popular autobiography, Bromley (1988) emphasizes the importance of a reading practice that challenges iconic perceptions of poverty. He maintains that cultural images of interwar poverty have become "sepia-tinted," fixed in icons of "four in a bed, bugs, tuberculosis, poor relief, raggedness, stylized forms of the unemployed" (p. 7) and, further, that these extreme versions of poverty now are considered as "authenticating data" for contemporary claims of poverty. Bromley's thesis is that retrieving the history of the period through literary versions can be achieved by showing how authentic versions have been "lost" through a cultural process of "organized forgetting." According to Bromley's thesis, conventions for representing poverty in popular forms mediate history in such a way as to mediate the present also. Instead of seeing current experiences of poverty in terms of what they mean historically, collectively, and politically, he argues, we see them uncritically in the shadow of icons from a remote and discontinuous past and in the form of representative figures such as hard-working, upwardly mobile individuals who travel through poverty and are represented apart from their class.

Exclusion of the poor from society is naturalized not only in discourse and narrative form but also through the absence of widely disseminated counternarratives that could convincingly contradict exclusionary attitudes. Although the poor have been described as having their own culture or subculture, it is both muted and isolated, having less access to public discursive space than the discourses on the poor generated by the nonpoor. In North America, the poor and the working class often experience themselves as alien and powerless in the context of an affluent society in which working-class identity and organized solidarity have been sufficiently eroded to be replaced by what Harrington (1962) and Lewis (1961) conceptualized, during the early 1960s, as a "culture of poverty." Harrington (1962) observed that the poor in "developed" countries have become another nation: "alien citizens . . . the invisible land . . . the underdeveloped nation within a nation . . . the internally exiled" (pp. 10, 17, 158-159, 178-179). But behind this invisibility, Harrington maintained, there lay a different culture, one that was both alien and effectively colonized:

> There is, in short, a language of the poor, a psychology of the poor, a worldview of the poor. To be impoverished is to be an internal alien, to grow up in a culture that is radically different from the one that dominates the society. The poor can be described statistically; they can be analyzed as a group. But they need a novelist as well as a sociologist if we are to see them. They need an American Dickens to record the smell and texture and quality of their lives. The cycles and trends, the massive forces, must be seen as affecting persons who talk and think differently. (p. 17)

Criticized for locating the cause of poverty internally in the participants themselves rather than situationally in the external market forces or attitudes of the nonpoor (Waxman, 1983, pp. 27-68), Harrington's view of the Other culture was largely negative in that he saw it as reproductive of poverty and "immune to progress." Hence he assumed that the "internally exiled" could best become visible through representations by experts—sociologists, novelists, and the like—rather than through their own cultural interventions. This view of a wholly negative content to the culture of poverty was different from Lewis's (1961) fuller conceptualization, which attributed both positive and negative content to the culture of poverty as he observed it in several countries. Lewis, one of the first anthropologists to experiment with transcribing the taped voices of the poor as oral histories, also described the culture of poverty as a subculture, that is, a creative response to the destruction of a traditional community by capitalist and imperialist society and a means of coping and surviving in hostile circumstances. Noting its counterculture potential, Lewis allowed that it could be acted on, if not eliminated, by revolutionary or nationalist movements with an alteration of its ideological basis—without, necessarily, having first to alter the objective state of poverty. At the same time, however, Lewis claimed that a mere change in material circumstances would not undo the cultural isolation of the poor, for it was generational in scope.

Harvey and Reed (1992), examining a wide range of academic paradigms for studying poverty, endorse Lewis's (1961) concept of an adaptive "subculture of the poor" rather than Harrington's (1962) view of negative content because Lewis's concept is

> sensitive to the survival enhancing immediacies which the culture of poverty has for everyday life while, at the same time, acknowledging the role which such a culture plays in reproducing the overall structure of capitalist social relations. . . . Like all cultures, the subculture of poverty has simultaneously creative, oppositional elements, as well as constraints which in the larger picture reinforce existing class relations. (Harvey & Reed, 1992, p. 278)

This larger relational view of the subculture of poverty situates the participant's reactions to negative constructions of identity within a more complex schema that explains resistance and complicity as more than matters of solely individual choice.

Waxman (1983) also favors the relational theories that focus on the connections between the nonpoor and the poor, especially on the level of discourse and attitudes. Once again adapting Goffman's (1963) theory of stigmatized identity, Waxman writes,

> Just as the reaction of normals to stigma must be understood within "a language of relationships," within the societally established "means of categorizing persons and the complement of attributes felt to be ordinary and natural for members of each of these categories" (Goffman, 1963, p. 2), so too must the reactions of the stigmatized individuals be understood within the context of culturally derived techniques of adjustment to situations where the stigmatized individual is interacting under a disadvantage. (Waxman, 1983, p. 93)

Seeing the subculture of poverty as a variety of responses to the stress of stigma within a relational view of the poor and the nonpoor, according to Waxman, facilitates a deeper understanding of those responses as strategies arising both from social practices carried out in the interest of dominant groups and from individual and collective identity construction among the poor. He explains that strategies for coping with stigma on the part of the poor may entail isolating oneself from "normals" and forming solidarity with other stigmatized members, hiding one's identity through acculturation, or "managing" the stigma itself in an adaptive way by appropriating its power for other uses (Waxman, 1983, p. 93). According to this theory of strategies within a relational context, negative constructions of identity are not internalized directly but entail a number of choices on the part of the poor (both conscious and unconscious as well as both collective and individual). Waxman also notes that the relational context of the construction of poverty allows us to see identity itself more profoundly. In respect to positive constructions that might counter stigma (e.g., the "American dream"), Waxman notes studies that show that poor participants, due to cultural isolation, may not internalize the "goal of success" fundamental to capitalism and affluent society:

> One of the harshest effects of the stigma of poverty is that it results in the isolation of the poor from not only the material provisions of the society, but also, and perhaps equally important, from the cultural provisions as well. It is from the society and its culture that each member receives his social self, his sense of identity and self-identification, and it is only when the individual is part of the society and identifies with it that he internalizes its normative system, its values, and its definitions of reality. . . . Unless [the poor] have a different cultural system with which they identify . . . , their "me" is quite different in nature from that of the real members of society. They do not completely internalize the normative system of society. This does not mean that they are unaware of the norms and values of society. They are very much aware of them, but these have not become part of their subjective consciences to the extent that they adhere to them because they really believe in them. (pp. 97-98)

Although Waxman's reference to "real members of society" is misleading and his representation of "the poor" seems unnecessarily homogenizing, he does at least strain for the words to explain how the identity of the poor and hence their cultural participation are shaped by stigma, taking care to establish relational connections between cultural differences and situational causes. But I would like to posit further that the complex phenomena of marginalized subjectivities resulting from stigma may rest with the participants themselves to articulate rather than with theorists. In the details of individual and subjective testimonies, we can find hitherto silenced knowledge about marginal experience, and such insider knowledge may inform our reading practices further than may any single theory of socialization or discourse analysis.

Decolonizing Poor Subjects Through Autobiography

For the remainder of this chapter, I discuss the ways in which life-writing may offer poor and working-class women discursive strategies of subverting negative constructions of identity. The motif of colonized subjects and the oppositional cultural project of decolonizing these marginalized subjects have appeared in culture-of-poverty theories, in feminist theories of women as colonized subjects in patriarchal society, and in postcolonial theories. For example, Smith and Watson (1992, pp. xiii-xvii) discuss, at some length, the extended use of the term "colonial subject" with respect to internally marginalized groups. Smith and Watson borrow from Abdul JanMohamed and David Lloyd the notion that colonial subjects speak from a shared position and employ this notion as a possible clarification of the shared circumstances of oppression experienced by externally and internally colonized groups that experience widely varying degrees of physical violence and restrictions of movement,

> a position of damage, one in which "the cultural formations, languages, the diverse modes of identity of the minoritized peoples are irreversibly affected, if not eradicated, by the effects of their material deracination from the historically developed social and economic structures in terms of which alone they 'made sense.' " (quoted in Smith & Watson, 1992, pp. xvi-xvii)

No matter what we call it, the effect of this shared "position of damage" usually is, according to Chandra Moohanty, the suppression of the heterogeneity of the subjects (cited in Smith & Watson, 1992, p. xvi). Hence the oppositional potential of autobiography to decolonize the subject lies partly in its power to demystify the experience of cultural Others and to reconstruct the identity of those Others according to their own sensibilities. In other words, the autobiographical utterance holds out the possibility of repairing cultural damage by enabling marginal subjects to represent identities closer to their experiences, hence decolonizing them as the objects of others' definitions.

Smith and Watson (1992, pp. xvii-xviii) also observe, conversely, that the genre of autobiography itself may function imperialistically to reassert meaning over the subject by making "meaning stick" through the genre's own discursive imperatives, through its resonant ideology, and through a particular genealogy of privilege. The colonized subject always will have a troubled relationship to the genre, they claim, because the generic conventions are based on patriarchal and Eurocentric assumptions about the "I" including a cult of selfhood, rationality, and uniqueness that ultimately erases or filters difference and collective resistance by prioritizing individual consciousness. The colonized Other who steps into the politics of the "I" to represent herself is therefore, according to Smith and Watson, unwittingly collapsed into an essentialized Other. Rather than gaining access to this privatized and privileged participant position, Others remain outside because they cannot be accommodated by such a position in all of their heterogeneity.

Although the ideological implications of genre are important to consider, I am wary that theorizing about ideal forms of oppositional autobiography leads to prescriptions, for example, that new self-reflexive modes of autobiography are necessary to combat the imperialism of the old genre. Recent prescriptions for postmodernist forms of autobiography that are self-reflexive and demand a knowledge of the textual mechanisms of representation rarely reflect concern for whether or not marginalized people actually have access to knowledge of these esoteric forms of expression or whether or not their stories and traditional relation to language is best reflected by these forms. For example, Smith's (1991) implicit prescription for postmodernist expression and *jouissance* (pleasure) and Denith and Dodd's (1988) prescription for "complex ways of seeing" assume that the autobiographer is an educated subject. Both are pioneering essays in their own right and show a strong spirit of resistance to hegemonic imperatives on the subject. But neither can claim to democratize the subject because each prescribes a form of resistance writing that is too esoteric for most people. Such theorizing rarely considers texts by uneducated or materially disadvantaged participants and thus fails to show how these prescriptive forms of utterance challenge dominant discourse by democratizing the subject.

On the one hand, prescription of mediated forms of autobiography whereby educated writers transcribe the words of marginal Others, as in oral histories and "testimonial literature,"[2] sometimes fail to allow that marginalized subjects—even uneducated subjects—can subvert and appropriate traditional author positions through their own innovative styles and their own languages. Such theories about testimony often suggest that mediated forms such as *testimonio* and oral histories are somehow inherently more oppositional because they eschew the author positions (Beverley, 1989; Sommer, 1988). Rather than debate which forms of autobiography best challenge hegemonic values discursively, I feel we should turn to a variety of individual life stories and discover the uses to which autobiography has been put by marginalized people given the details of their concrete lives and the subtleties of their own lived relations to language. We might ask, for example, how in each life story the fact of telling that life subverts or reproduces the specific negative constructions of identity experienced by the participant from her own standpoint.

According to Steedman (1986), we cannot hope to restore a complete picture of excluded lives simply by writing and reading working-class women's personal stories, but we can hope to make the fragments more meaningful by restoring fullness to the landscape of this subculture through the specificities of history and place and through a more receptive attitude to the psychological differences created by material distress and social exclusion. Steedman proposes that working-class women as autobiographical participants can make sense of their deracinated and culturally muted lives by reusing the past and interpreting it through social information, that is, "what people know of a social world and their place within it" (p. 5). She suggests, for example, that we look at the development of class consciousness as a process that may occur, especially for women and children, in relative isolation and in private rather than through organized public struggle and may also involve the formation of a class-marked unconscious that would be discernible by looking at loss and desire in terms of social exclusion.

Steedman (1986) goes on to say that the adventure of making women's working-class experience visible does not end with the writing; rather, it also is present in the reading. The muted meaning of the text and the class-marked "I" at its center often elude the "central interpretive devices" of a culture designed to receive and decode bourgeois subjectivity, so that even working-class women have difficulty seeing or decoding the meaning in autobiographies of other women in their class, including their own mothers' stories, although they may experience them on an empathic level (pp. 284-285). What Steedman seems to be arguing here is that working-class women's life stories cannot be decoded through available categories of collective symbolization; instead, they must be studied in terms of their own internal logic and personalized metaphors and signposts. Moreover, she suggests that we can better come to terms with the fragmentary nature of our own knowledge and of the lives represented by reading these stories in tension with master forms or master narratives rather than by trying to absorb them into these categories for forced coherence. In the two texts that I discuss in this chapter, personal stories emerge in tension with at least two forms of master narratives: the negative constructions of marginal identities circulated through popular myths, insults, stereotypes, and so on and the master form of autobiography itself.

Sand's Cultural Smuggling

In her personal essay, "A Question of Identity," Sand (1987) testifies to class experiences that fixed her sense of identity, and she contests these limiting definitions by speaking out about how it feels to be fixed in this way. The essay begins with a number of tropes representing limited physical and psychosocial space: "narrow-halled Verdun flat," "crowded flat," "close city quarters," "squeezing me into a psychic corner," "[my] father's irritability marked the boundaries of my childhood like the fence of our tiny backyard" (p. 55). The sensation of physical restriction quickly passes to one of linguistic restriction as Sand describes her fear of publicly occupying the author position to tell her own story: "I cannot call myself a writer without hesitating" (p. 59). She also relates her frustration with the limitations of a muted class language: "I want the garbled and hesitant language of my life to become intelligible" (p. 62).

Sand's most formidable barrier to sharing fully in the dominant culture is not her lack of social opportunity or leisure, as in many stories by poor and working-class women; rather, it was her learned fear of partaking publicly in a culture that she had learned was not rightfully hers. Her family members' greatest fear, she explains, was to be laughed at, and their lives consequently were "choreographed" by shame and fear. Her first and often repeated lesson is that "You are nothing without money . . . impressed upon [her] memory as regularly as rent-collection day" (Sand, 1987, p. 55). This negative construction of identity is always in the narrator's memory, telling her that despite publishing successes, she is never safe from complete nervous collapse—as though speaking out of place and with a sense of self-importance as a working-class subject would project her immediately into a place of contradiction whose only response could be madness.

If read on the level of social allegory, Sand's marginalized Self seems to confront the dominant culture in a somber struggle over language, culture, and identity. When read on the level of personal history, the details are just as somber. Sand grew up in Verdun, a factory area of Montreal with a significant anglophone population. Her father's angry presence dominated her family members' daily lives along with a sense of financial insecurity. Her uncle, a war veteran and indigent drunk, and her aunt, a domestic worker, both loved literature and were formative influences. Sand began suffering from "emotional and mental distress," however, when she confronted the middle-class milieu of the university as a scholarship student. She turned to drugs and alcohol to assuage her acute sense of alienation, and when expected to speak in public (as a scholarship student), she attempted suicide. Without finishing her degree, she moved to British Columbia, where she "came out" as a lesbian, worked part-time on a cleaning staff, and wrote and published only intermittently while in recovery.

"A Question of Identity" first appeared in 1987 in a small feminist magazine, *Fireweed,* and was reprinted in Zandy's (1990) *Calling Home: Working Class Women's Writing: An Anthology.* Sand has not written much for publication since this essay first appeared. It was written when she was in recovery and resembles the sort of piecing together of fragments and trauma with key figures and causes that might constitute part of the process of personal recovery as well as that of a political awakening. As literary testimony, however, the essay has the potential to transcend confession and to recover, explain, and reconstruct fragments of lived experience for the purpose of making individual identity more coherent and legitimate as the basis of social action.

Among the formative experiences that Sand related, besides that of learning from her father's sense of economic and personal powerlessness, are two important types of exclusion that ultimately converge in her life story: the sense of symbolic exclusion revealed through her troubled relation to language and the sense of lived exclusion from high culture revealed through anecdotes about cultural isolation. Like people colonized by external powers, generations of Sand's family had been exploited and silenced and unable to participate fully in the dominant culture either of their country of origin, Scotland, or their country of destination, Canada (or the francophone city where they settled). For example, she remembers her shell-shocked uncle citing Yeats to passing cars in a pained, drunken stupor and her aunt reading "great literature" late at night after her domestic work, a stolen act beyond her station:

> Did she want to write? Did the cultural authority which breathed its history and power into the very room in which she sat convince her of the impossibility of that notion? The gender and class of writing are not embodied in an off-duty cook scribbling in her room. What would she write about? What pronouncements on philosophy, history, society, God, or nature would a woman with sore feet have? Did she try to write and then judge her work to be mere footnotes to the real world of writing? Did she

> think of her nephew Steve as a poet? Did she connect his inebriated attempts at coherence to her own desire to write? (Sand, 1987, pp. 56-57)

Here Sand echoes and reframes within a sense of class difference Woolf's famous questions about women's limited access to the literary profession, adjusting the bourgeois woman's question of "a room of one's own" to the limited, borrowed spaces of a domestic worker's life. Her aunt's limited access to high culture and literary voice resulted from gender as well as class imperatives and is echoed later in the words of Sand's doctor when he defines her university studies as a "secretarial asset to any boss" (p. 60). The mirroring between these two generations of women stresses the contradiction between the subject/author of high culture and the object position of women as well as the enduring social script according to which generations of poor and working-class women must accept their place as doubly silenced subjects.

Sand's aunt and uncle, although partly thwarted in their access to high culture, were the only models for her cultural aspirations and her turn to literature and libraries as nourishment and escape. The improving, enlarging psychosocial aspect of culture is dramatized in the preceding quotation through the image of cultural authority "breathing" life into a room, an image in direct opposition to the constrained, squeezed spaces and symbols for workers' flats, cited earlier, which concretized material limits and those of a culture of poverty as well as the oppressive authority of the family patriarch. As art lovers, her aunt and uncle saw beyond the materially and emotionally limited life of labor that her father led. The desire to see beyond also figures largely in Sand's inner landscape. But the out-of-place nature of literature and the expansive spirit it engenders in these restricted working-class lives resulted in images of breakage, public humiliation, madness, or a particular type of defiance that we might refer to as "cultural smuggling."

The aunt's form of "smuggling" was to absorb the cultural capital of her employees' huge libraries voraciously in her off hours and to leave the country a retired domestic, homeless but with a "trunk of first editions, her most cherished possession" (Sand, 1987, p. 56). Her uncle's form of "smuggling" was to appropriate high culture from the Old Country (Wordsworth, Coleridge, Yeats, and Burns) to import it and graft it on everyday life in Canada, orally and in street scenes. However, although he seemed to master poetry, which "slipped off his tongue" while he was "lecturing away," he also was "shell-shocked and broken," and relatives referred to him as "poor Stevie" (p. 56). The contradiction of his association with beauty, mastery, and high art, on the one hand, and rank smells, stupor, and indigence, on the other, constitutes a form of transgression whose illegality is echoed in the oxymoron that Sand uses to describe his precarious balancing act as "inebriated grace" and in the irreverent synecdoche that explains that "poetry had become the language of his twenty-six ounce addiction" (p. 56).

There is a parallel to her uncle's "inebriated grace" in Sand's own daring self-disclosure and cultural smuggling. In opposition to her working-class father's internalized rage, limited choices, and resentful labor, the daughter externalized her anger and shame through public testimony. Her search for cultural coherence through class politics and working-class literature, and her choice to try to be a writer, admits her to a dance that is not "choreographed" puppet-like from above, like that of her family for generations back, but is performed on the thin sliding edge between the worlds of high culture and subculture, where she must balance with her own genre of "inebriated grace." The fissure between cultures climaxes in her experience at the university, where the exclusions from language and high culture come together. Her fear of public speaking, of being shamed publicly by the negative Self as it steps into the participant position, precipitated a suicide attempt: "At the moment I swallowed that bottle of pills I collided with the most negative messages of my working-class childhood: Who do you think you are? Who do you think you are getting all this education and trying to be one of them?" (Sand, 1987, p. 60). The question alludes to Munro's (1978b) semiautobiographical work by that title, *Who Do You Think You Are?*, and opens the narrative to the testimony of distance between a poor home and the university. As in Munro's account, Sand's testimony reveals the impact of class difference in cultural education on the writer's identity:

> I walked those Concordia corridors high on pills and was told by professors and peers that women waste their time getting degrees. I walked those corridors as my father's daughter, "that conventional Sunday-best type of working-class person who cannot bear to be seen even carrying a parcel or doing anything that might attract attention to himself" (J. R. Ackerley). . . . My ambition defied my gender role but I was the daughter of a class and a family which is echoed in Alice Munro's words: "Ambition was what they were alarmed by, for to be ambitious was to court failure and to risk making a fool of oneself. The worst thing . . . that could happen in this life was to have people laughing at you." (pp. 60-61)

Importantly, the method Sand chooses of finding a "home" in high culture and its institutions is by creating a sense of community, by assembling kindred working-class voices that render her isolation and feelings of inferiority comprehensible as a shared class and gender phenomenon. Assembling these voices in her head, she is able to counter the messages with which the academy silences her and to see a place inside of her silence for an oppositional culture and an alternate vision of reality.

But there is no neat, magical conversion from "poor me" to "defiant us," for Sand also identifies more readily with the cleaning staff at the university than she does with well-spoken academics and identifies more readily with the institution for drug addicts and madwomen than she does with the institution of higher learning. After mapping a family history, generational in scope, of the frustrated impulse to share fully in literary culture, Sand confesses intimately and painfully how her writing voice and core of identity are constructed from the history of silence and broken voices: "Speaking and writing do not come easily for me" (Sand, 1987, p. 59). She explains the ways in which she is divided from a bourgeois woman she befriends at the university: "Your father was a writer who made quite a name for himself. My father's stammer made it difficult for him to say his and he worked as a supplies clerk in a school board basement office" (p. 58). And another refrain is added to her story, distinguishing her own classed female identity from that of a female friend: "We are divided in terrible ways" (pp. 58-59).

Robinson and Vogel (1978, p. 30) suggest that members of the working class who attempt to absorb "high culture" are described by the semantics of acculturation as "improving" themselves. And they must do so at a high cost to their own identities by submitting to a process of acculturation as unnatural as "changing race." However, they also note that few working-class people submit to acculturation because the "irrelevancies" of high culture do not offer enough incentive to have them consent to having their identities co-opted in this way. In Sand's essay, we see her remaining on the fringe of university life, roaming the halls high on drugs, attending classes but not speaking, and later befriending lecturers and artistic types but cleaning toilets for a living. In a longer reading of Sand's essay, her extreme outsider position in the academy as a lesbian and working-class woman could be considered alongside more traditionally gendered plots of heterosexual working-class women who experience the university as a site where they can "marry up" through the academy to professors or men from higher classes as an alternate form of social mobility and acculturation (see, e.g., Laurence's [1974] *The Diviners* and Munro's [1978a] "The Beggar Queen" in her book *Who Do You Think You Are?*).

Of all the marginal positions that are dramatized as contours of Sand's inner landscape, the most highly dramatized is that of her symbolic relation to language as a colonized subject. In the primary position more ordinarily given to circumstances of birth, Sand's first sentence relates her slowness to speak: "I spoke not a word until my fourth year of life and then language came out garbled and hesitant" (Sand, 1987, p. 55). Later she admits identifying with institutionalized women: "Few of them speak. The ones who do usually shout or force the odd syllable from drug swollen tongues" (p. 59). At the university, the exclusions from high culture and from language converge. Significantly, Sand dramatizes her experience of education as stage fright: "To get up and speak before people, to make a public statement of any kind, sometimes even to state my name became unbearable, impossible, terrifying. I asked not one question, spoke not one classroom word in four years of university" (pp. 60-61). The two stages of silence and growth, 4 years of infancy and 4 of university education, converge to suggest that cultural and linguistic initiation is, for a working-class woman, also initiation into exclusion.

Bourdieu (1973) suggests that the university, despite its promise to offer a means to social mobility, actually is the place where the working class often is discreetly but ultimately excluded. Bourdieu argues that working-class youths are subtly excluded from the word games of examinations and classroom discussions because they enter university without the necessary "cultural capital" to decode the objects of high culture or to express themselves like people who have a claim to that culture. In stressing the role of social definitions and judgments of competence in cultural struggle, Bourdieu exposes the special power of language and academic discourse to convince members of the working class of their own cultural deficiency and exclude them anew. Despite the fact that Bourdieu's positivist research on this score has been challenged, the enduring value of his theory lies more in the connections he suggests among culturally reproduced inequality, cultural capital, working-class identity, and university methods of teaching and recruiting—connections that expose the logic of this form of institutional exclusion but have been "systematically neglected by recent sociology" (Jenkins, 1992, pp. 179-180).

Sand continues to express self-consciousness toward the subject position throughout her essay, culminating dramatically in the final sentence, which not only posits a collective and politicized "we" but also dramatizes how silenced subjects may finally demand the position of speaker and witness:

> Fear of poverty made us tiptoe around life's possibilities, around authority, and even around our anger at our own compliance. My father could not externalize what he understood so clearly. . . . But some of us are daring to dance along the edge of economic and social uncertainty to challenge self-oppression. We know who paid for those avenues of brick and to the ruling class we join with David Fennario [another anglophone working-class author from Verdun] in saying "We shall walk backwards and applaud no longer. We shall celebrate ourselves. We will create a forum for our thought. We will have it out with you." (Sand, 1987, p. 62)

The closing passage of the piece reveals a self-consciously divided identification between the "us" of her family and a new, more powerful "us" of a politically aware working-class community. This public avowal of divided identification places the "I" between the invisibility of the forgotten working-class figures in her family and the small but visible community of working-class intellectuals writing in Canada. This participant shift marks her identity conversion, whereby the fragmented and damaged "I" of her past meets others who have been silenced and excluded across the interdiscursivity of texts. Through quotation, again in the form of cultural smuggling but smuggling she now flaunts and legitimates, the "I" of her personal story transforms into the "we" of Fennario's (1984) text from *Blue Mondays.* (In a longer study, the absence of the majority francophone culture in Sand's essay would need to be probed to situate her own inscriptions of language and exclusion.) Together, the two authors' working-class voices redefine their position of invisibility and subordination as one of solidarity, historical insight, and cultural opposition.

The stylistic nuances such as the tropes of restricted space and movement, the fixed local setting of brick buildings and narrow halls of a factory neighborhood altered by historical knowledge, and the shifting referent to indicate shifting identification—"us" (family) to "us" (class), individual "I" to collective "we"—all reflect the enclosed and expanding parameters as Sand dances discursively through and around negative constructions of identity. The speaker dares to dance on the very notion of the margin, not to erase it but to call attention to the nature and importance of such boundaries to her sense of who she is and how she speaks. This dance on the margins begins when she posits herself as speaker, no matter how tentatively, and as a literary witness who joins the assembled collage of oppositional testimonies (Fennario, Munro, and Ackerley) that testify to the oppression and yet still celebrate class difference. Given the need to testify beyond the silencing of her class and her personal voice, she does not dance on the margin in a postmodernist celebration of fragmentation, deferred meaning, and verbal play; rather, she does so with the use of psychological and social realism, concrete metaphors, and a transparently testimonial voice.

Thus, from the fringes, Sand smuggles out "cultural capital" for elicit ends. She has learned how to assemble quotations and a muted literary heritage around and behind her own voice to invoke a renewed sense of identity based on difference and class solidarity. Quoting here and there from working-class authors, she allows us to glimpse this new identity and the possibility it holds out for her, not instead of but alongside the ever-present negative images. The prose of Sand's essay is simple but eloquent and is resonant with a longing for familiar silence and invisibility. Her "garbled language" obviously has been refined by education. But when we learn how culturally excluded she felt at the university, we receive this refined prose as smuggled goods. And with the smuggled cultural capital comes knowledge of the systemic causes of her poverty and shame. The brick buildings of Verdun no longer are confining in the same way; the landscape is filling out through the trick of seeing beyond stigma not only through literature but also through history. She writes,

> The messages are deciphering. I am walking through the geography of my childhood and my family's history is coming into focus. The narrow hallways of Verdun were built to contain and control its working class and their children. . . . We know who paid for those avenues of brick. (Sand, 1987, p. 62)

Campbell's Mode of Making Meaning "Stick"

Among working-class women's autobiographical writing in Canada, Sand's essay is an anomaly, for very few of these narratives use Marxist class discourse to reconstruct identity from the margins. There are other class-conscious women's autobiographical works, of course, such as those by Potrebenko (1988) and Sykes (1987) as well as Knight's (1974) *A Very Ordinary Life,* but there are relatively few. Contrary to what one might assume, among Canada's marginalized groups—the poor, Natives, blacks, Asians, minority ethnic groups, women, and so on—it is those marginalized by working-class or poor status who are least able to recuperate positive self-images as members of that class. On the other hand, negative discourses on poverty and class are often countered by positive identity strategies recuperated through other subcultures, especially race and ethnicity, for example, in works by Campbell (1973) and John (1989) through Métis culture, by Salverson (1939/1981) through Icelandic culture, by Brand (1991) and Tynes (1989) through black culture, by Roy (1984) through Franco-Canadian culture, and many others.

This trend of expressing positive identity through subcultures other than class is in keeping with Aronowitz's (1992) thesis, which examines the erosion of working-class identity in contemporary North American society given the delegitimation of Marxist discourse and the weakening of union power under deregulated capitalism and given, in addition, the global and local dispersal politics of capital and workers by corporate management. Aronowitz claims that for the past 15 years, North America in particular has seen a loss of dignity associated with working-class identity and a growing identification among other subcultures based on race, ethnicity, religion, gender, and so on. Workers, he claims, have become invisible in public representation, their oppositional "subject position" being occupied now by other emergent social groups. Although few self-representations by poor and working-class women in Canada employ a discourse about class, most address the experience of classed exclusion in the context of a strongly felt absence of community, which is addressed, if at all, by forms of group affiliation other than class or by close personal ties.

Waxman (1983), in his study of poverty as stigma, explains that the poor and working class from ethnically and racially stigmatized groups sometimes may convert negative status into positive status through a strong sense of group affiliation:

> Where the stigmatized group is an ethnic minority, the fact that it is a more or less homogeneous group makes it considerably more likely that that group will develop and retain its own unique status-honor and value system as a reaction to the stigma. When, however, the stigmatized group is an

> economic unit rather than an ethnic unit, unless the lower economic class can "unite" to the point where it is in the position to reject the existing economic and value system and replace it with another, it will have to seek other means for adjusting to the stigma. . . . With a heterogeneous lower class—that is, a lower class which does not share a common positive ethnic and/or religious heritage and identity or a common physical characteristic—there is little basis from which may be formed an alternative system of status-honor. (p. 94)

Consequently, among the heterogeneous poor, Waxman argues, the negative and self-defeating traits described as the culture of poverty are most likely to take hold precisely because of the absence of alternative status-honor systems. In the two texts chosen for discussion in this chapter, an alternative status-honor system arises from different sources. In Sand's (1987) essay, it arises from a Marxist discourse and working-class literature that redefine class and culture on the fringe as positive rather than as negative. In *Halfbreed,* Campbell (1973) appeals to an alternative status-honor system through the positive redefinition of the Métis racial group, through an elder's teachings, and through the speaker's political activism.

Campbell's struggle for positive identity through a reconstituted sense of racial identification is achieved mostly by internalizing her grandmother's teachings. The narrator depends on these teachings to comprehend poverty; racial discrimination; and a history of her people's colonization and suppression, social exclusion, and the resulting shame. The primary function of these teachings is to pass on racial pride and a knowledge of racial history. Campbell's own historicizing strategy is unfolded in the first chapters where, instead of her personal beginnings and earliest memories, she recounts the history of her people, four generations back, beginning during the mid-1800s. (Campbell was born in 1940.) She relates the conditions that led the Métis to move westward across Canada away from settlers and eventually to confrontations with the government in the form of armed rebellions in 1869 and 1884 under the Métis hero, Louis Riel, and his ally, Gabriel Dumont. She also tells of the aftereffect of those events on the identity of "halfbreeds." The Métis are distinguished from Natives and whites not only because of their mixed blood but also, materially and historically, because they failed to have their land claims honored like full-blooded Natives and they also failed, through poverty and disinterest in farming, to meet land improvement requirements for homesteading claims among whites. Hence they were exiled as squatters to the narrow strips of government-owned land beside roads and highways and were given the pejorative label "Road Allowance people" (Campbell, 1973, p. 13). From these historical traumas, Campbell slowly begins to construct the more personal details of her own story—but broadly, laying out the landscape of her family's past four generations back.

Her personal story relates some pleasant experiences, such as a happy home and feelings of close community ties, during her early childhood, but they soon become remote with the death of her mother and her father's subsequent lapse into despondency and alcoholism. Campbell recalls her struggle to support and care for younger brothers and sisters through extreme poverty, which included dropping out of public school, working long and hard at cleaning and other forms of child labor, scrounging for food, and hiding from the welfare agency. Numerous concrete scenes perform a testimonial function in the narrative, for example, feeding a newborn baby out of a beer bottle with a nipple; tying a baby brother to nearby trees so that her younger brothers and sisters could attend school, acting "ignorant, timid, and grateful" to welfare officials; and working like harnessed horses to uproot trees under a government make-work project. When Campbell tried to protest the biblical adage "blessed are the poor in spirit for they shall inherit the Kingdom of Heaven" because it did not apply to her people or to her personal experience of poverty, a teacher punished her by making her hold up the Bible while kneeling in the corner all afternoon. Campbell (1973) remembers defiantly, "I used to believe there was no worse sin in this country than to be poor" (p. 56). Here, the early Christian construction of the poor collides with the child's knowledge of her own 20th-century identity as an outcast of affluent society. She had to contest institutional constructions of poverty by the church because of what she knew to be true, and later she had to contest institutional constructions of the poor by welfare agencies because they threatened to break up her family. At age 15, Campbell married for the sole purpose of becoming legal guardian to her younger brothers and sisters. After the marriage failed and welfare authorities broke up the family anyway, she began a free fall into street life, prostitution, and drugs that finally ended with the private process of drug rehabilitation and spiritual healing and the public process of political activism.

The literal, unadorned style of *Halfbreed* makes two dominant metaphors for identity conversion stand out in one's mind long after reading. These are couched not in literary language but in the words of the author's grandmother and teacher, Cheechum. The first is a lesson about shame and self-blame. The author remembers returning home from school after being humiliated by the taunts of white children for her poor clothing and lunches of wild game. Insults are a frequent occurrence during her childhood. They are called "dirty halfbreeds," "Road Allowance people," and "squatters" by the whites, and they are called "poor relatives" and *Awp-pee-tow-koosons* (meaning "half-people") by full-race Indians. By history, they are called "madmen and criminals" who rebelled, following the popular but doomed hero, Riel, himself branded a madman by whites (Campbell, 1973, pp. 10-11, 13, 26). On this particular day, however, the author returned home more hurt and ashamed than ever by the insults from the white children and began striking out physically at her mother and father, calling them "no-good halfbreeds" and blaming them for the lack of good food and clothing (p. 47). At this point, Cheechum stepped in, led the author half a mile from the house, and told her a story about her people before beating her with a willow stick. The author remembers beatings as part of her education rather than as abuse. Here the beating functions ironically. In addition to being a brutal form of discipline and a reassertion of dominance over the child, the beating also purges racial dominance by externalizing the "stick" of ethnic and class shame and self-hate and putting it back into the hands of the Métis elder.

Cheechum said that when she was a girl, the Métis had had the chance to follow a great leader who came west and promised to show them the way to freedom, but because some people held back for clothes and horses and called their own people "no-good halfbreeds," they "lost their dream." "The white man saw that that was a more powerful weapon than anything else with which to beat the halfbreeds, and he used it and still does today. Already they are using it on you. They try to make you hate your own people" (Campbell, 1973, p. 47). In Cheechum's story, the white culture makes its meaning stick to the subject by eroding collectivity and implanting negative constructions of identity.

Berger (1981) comments in *Fragile Freedoms: Human Rights and Dissent in Canada* that the problem of 20th-century Métis are "not simply problems of poverty, but of a people trying to preserve their cultural identity" (p. 55). Whereas the Métis now are developing a political vocabulary that asserts identity, Berger observes, early generations lacked the language to proclaim their distinctive identity and their rights to land and services. The only political vocabulary they possessed was that of Riel's armed revolution, and this was not enough to combat the passage from hunting and trapping to an agricultural economy. Nor was it enough to combat the ingrained attitudes of whites such as that of Sir John A. MacDonald, the Canadian prime minister who executed Riel for insurrection: "If they are Indians . . . they go with the tribe; if they are halfbreeds, they are white" (quoted in Berger, 1981, p. 52). The 1981 Report of the Métis and Non-status Indian Constitutional Review Commission thus argued not simply for individual integration into Canadian life but for the collective integration of people with histories (pp. 55-56).

Campbell's political narrative asserts itself over the hegemonic implications of autobiography largely through its testimony of collective identity and history. She uses autobiography effectively to expand our knowledge not only of the Self but also of the people who had been erased by the label "halfbreed." She subverts the negative power of "halfbreed" as an insult by using revisionary history in an act of cultural and political intervention. The "I" of her story is clearly shaped more by her relation to history, her people, their material oppression, and her grandmother's spiritual teachings than it is by the textual politics of an "I" with its European cultural assumptions of a unified and individual Self.

Another of Cheechum's teaching images is carried through the text to transform the negative "I" of racial and class shame to one of inner stability and collective spirit. Cheechum chooses to teach the lesson through the image of a blanket, an apt symbol of colonization because it is an icon of trade with the whites and also a symbol of the material comfort they promised. Cheechum, who always refused charity and welfare, chose to live by trapping, and dressed in the traditional way, teaches the author a lesson about the incompatibility of the materialistic world of the colonizers and Métis's spiritual survival:

> "When the government gives you something, they take all that you have in return—your pride, your dignity, all the things that make you a living soul. When they are sure they have everything, they give you a blanket to cover your shame." . . . [Cheechum] used to say that all our people wore blankets, each in his own way. She said that other people wore them too, not just halfbreeds and Indians, and as I grew up I would see them and understand. Someday, though, people would throw them away and the whole world would change. I understood about the blanket now—I wore one too. I didn't

> know when I started to wear it, but it was there and I didn't know how to throw it away. (Campbell, 1973, p. 137)

In the context of her personal lived experience, the "blanket" that keeps Campbell from knowing herself and her people with any sense of pride is fast money, drugs, and alcohol. The trajectory of the Self in her story is a plot line that too many Native and Métis women have lived in Canada, leading rapidly away from past subsistence in a rural setting to dispossession of land, increased poverty, family illness, underpaid hard labor, the intervention of welfare agencies, dissolution of the family, domestic violence, migration to the city, homelessness, drug addiction, and prostitution. The author can cast off a blanket of denial about the destructiveness of this lifestyle only when she joins a collectivity and becomes an activist for her people and against drug addiction. This is not the exemplary, representative life of the upwardly mobile class subject or the assimilated racial Other; rather, it is the exemplary life of a political radical, and therein lies the secret of the appropriation of the "I" for political purposes. Campbell does not advocate armed revolution but fosters a dream of an inclusive society and racial pride as well as a historically rooted language of resistance. This is how she is able to throw off her "blanket" to look without despair at her identity in the context of the ugliness of colonization, class oppression, and racial decimation:

> The years of searching and loneliness and pain are over for me. Cheechum had said, "You'll find yourself, and you'll find brothers and sisters." I have brothers and sisters, all over the country. I no longer need my blanket to survive. (p. 157)

Conclusion

Both Campbell's image of the blanket of denial being thrown off and Sand's image of the silenced audience claiming the right of speech recall Franz Fanon's statement about colonized subjects throwing off obscurity and silence to define themselves and rewrite their own history:

> Decolonization never takes place unnoticed, for it influences and modifies [the colonized] fundamentally. It transforms spectators crushed with their

> inessentiality into privileged actors, with the grandiose glare of history's floodlights upon them. (Fanon, as quoted by Smith, 1991, p. 186)

Such dramatic symbols of empowerment through speaking out, however, are more useful as inspiring dramatizations than they are as theoretical models. They do not allow for the complicity of colonized subjects in their own colonization, for unresolved questions of identity, or for generic constraints that may impose themselves as discursive limitations. Just as the spectator does not become an actor merely by standing on the stage, the subject does not decolonize herself simply by occupying the public position of the autobiographical "I." As covered in the discussions of "A Question of Identity" and *Halfbreed,* the autobiographical "I" and even the collective inscription of "we" do not automatically displace or overpower negative constructions of identity, although they can convert their negative power into knowledge of systemic oppression and a will to resistance. Above all, a politicized view of negative constructions of identity shows whose interests they serve and allows the subject to free herself from the "meaning stick" of the master narratives. Thus revisionary historical knowledge, in particular, often will allow the subject to see beyond self-blame and despair and free her for more oppositional forms of self-expression and self-representation.

Not surprisingly, many writers begin to narrate poverty or working-class status in Canada by gesturing toward the silence that surrounds the issue of poverty and class in an affluent society, or they report, at some point in their life-writings or oral histories, the sensation of speaking through that silence. Also, a significant number relate the sensation of being named by insult and having to find a strategy—self-representation being one possible dimension of that strategy—to escape or come to terms with the shame of having one's identity fixed in that way. Many autobiographical subjects who identify themselves as poor women or as having been poor at one time in their lives also identify themselves as witnesses to buried truths and as voices seeking and needing a community of readers/witnesses to affirm their classed experiences and make them credible. Zandy (1990) describes the task of writing as cultural intervention in the following way:

> Like Lot's wife, the working-class writer must keep looking back. She has to be multi-voiced in witnessing for the silenced many, in negotiating with

the dominant culture, and in claiming her own identity as a woman with a particular ethnic and racial culture. (p. 12)

Notes

1. For a detailed discussion of Smith's theory with respect to narratives, see Rimstead (1994).

2. Recently, the term *testimonial literature* has been applied to autobiographical narratives about extreme violence, oppression, and silencing such as those by Latin American women, Holocaust survivors, incest victims, and war survivors. It is the *extreme* invisibility/inaudibility/incomprehensibility of the historical or political events that seems to invite the metaphor of testimony, and it is the context of silence and injustice that gives power to these versions to question assumptions about truth. Much testimonial literature is mediated or transcribed by a participant/observer. See Beverley's (1989) description of Latin American *testimonio* and Sommer's (1988) slightly different description.

References

Adams, I., Cameron, W., Hill, B., & Penz, P. (Eds.). (1971). *The real poverty report.* Edmonton, Alberta: M. G. Hurtig.

Aronowitz, S. (1992). *The politics of identity: Class, culture, social movements.* New York: Routledge & Kegan Paul.

Barrett, M. (1988). *Women's oppression today: The Marxist/feminist encounter* (Rev. ed.). London: Verso.

Berger, T. (1981). *Fragile freedoms: Human rights and dissent in Canada.* Toronto: Clarke, Irwin.

Beverley, J. (1989). The margin at the center: On *testimonio* (testimonial narrative). *Modern Fiction Studies, 35*(1), 11-28.

Bourdieu, P. (1973). Cultural reproduction and social reproduction. In R. Brown (Ed.), *Knowledge, education, and cultural change: Papers in the sociology of education* (pp. 71-112). London: Tavistock.

Brand, D. (Ed.). (1991). *No burden to carry: Narratives of black working women in Ontario, 1920's-1950's.* Toronto: Women's Press.

Bromley, R. (1988). *Lost narratives: Popular fictions, politics, and recent history.* London: Routledge & Kegan Paul.

Campbell, M. (1973). *Halfbreed.* Toronto: McClelland & Stewart.

Daly, M. (1989). *Women and poverty.* Dublin, Ireland: Attic.

Delphy, C. (1984). *Close to home: A materialist analysis of women's oppression.* Amherst: University of Massachusetts Press.

Denith, S., & Dodd, P. (1988). The uses of autobiography. *Literature and History, 14*(1), 5-22.

Fennario, D. (1984). *Blue Mondays.* Verdun, Quebec: Black Rock Creations.

Gelpi, B., & Hartsock, N. (Eds.). (1986). *Women and poverty.* Chicago: University of Chicago Press.

Goffman, E. (1963). *Stigma: Notes on the management of spoiled identity.* Englewood Cliffs, NJ: Prentice Hall.

Goldberg, G., & Kremen, E. (Eds.). (1990). *The feminization of poverty: Only in America?* New York: Greenwood.

Gunderson, M., Muszynski, L., & Keck, J. (1990). *Women and labour market poverty.* Ottawa: Canadian Advisory Council on the Status of Women.

Hansen, K., & Philipson, I. (Eds.). (1990). *Women, class, and the feminist imagination: A socialist-feminist reader.* Philadelphia: Temple University Press.

Harrington, M. (1962). *The other America: Poverty in the United States.* New York: Macmillan.

Harvey, D., & Reed, M. (1992). Paradigms of poverty: A critical assessment of contemporary perspectives. *International Journal of Politics, Culture, and Society, 6,* 269-297.

Jenkins, R. (1992). *Pierre Bourdieu.* London: Routledge.

John, M. (1989). *Stoney Creek woman: The story of Mary John* (Transcribed by B. Moran). Vancouver, British Columbia: Tillacum.

Kaplan, C. (1990). Pandora's box: Subjectivity, class and sexuality in socialist-feminist criticism. In T. Lovell (Ed.), *British feminist thought: A reader* (pp. 345-366). Oxford, England: Blackwell.

Knight, P. (1974). *A very ordinary life.* As told to R. Knight. Vancouver, British Columbia: New Star Books.

Laurence, M. (1974). *The diviners.* Toronto: McClelland & Stewart.

Lewis, O. (1961). *The children of Sanchez: Autobiography of a Mexican family.* New York: Random House.

Munro, A. (1978a). The beggar queen. *In who do you think you are?* Toronto: Macmillian.

Munro, A. (1978b). *Who do you think you are?* Toronto: Macmillan.

Pearce, D. (1978). The feminization of poverty: Women, work, and welfare. *Urban and Social Review, 11*(1-2), 28-36.

Porter, J. (1965). *The vertical mosaic: An analysis of social class and power in Canada.* Toronto: University of Toronto Press.

Potrebenko, H. (1988). My mother, the troublemaker. *Fireweed, 26,* 54-65.

Rimstead, R. (1994). Visits and homecomings: Notes toward discovering the psychosocial places of poverty. *Textual Studies in Canada, 5,* 46-63.

Robinson, L., & Vogel, L. (1978). Modernism and history. In L. Robinson (Ed.), *Sex, class, and culture* (pp. 22-46). Bloomington: Indiana University Press.

Roy, G. (1984). *La détresse et l'enchantement.* Montreal: Boréal Express.

Salverson, L. (1981). *Confessions of an immigrant's daughter.* Toronto: University of Toronto Press. (Originally published in 1939)

Sand, C.-T. (1987). A question of identity. *Fireweed, 25,* 55-62.

Sidel, R. (1986). *Women and children last: The plight of poor women in affluent America.* New York: Penguin.

Smith, R. (1989-1990). Order and disorder: The naturalization of poverty. *Cultural Critique, 14,* 209-229.

Smith, S. (1991). The autobiographical manifesto: Identities, temporalities, politics. In S. Neuman (Ed.), *Autobiography and questions of gender* (pp. 186-212). London: Frank Cass.

Smith, S., & Watson, J. (Eds.). (1992). *De-colonizing the subject: The politics of gender in women's autobiography.* Minneapolis: University of Minnesota Press.

Sommer, D. (1988). Not just a personal story: Women's *testimonios* and the plural Self. In B. Bodzki & C. Schenck (Eds.), *Life lines: Theorizing women's autobiography* (pp. 107-130). Ithaca, NY: Cornell University Press.

Steedman, C. (1986). *Landscape for a good woman: A story of two lives.* London: Virago.

Sykes, J. (1987). Confessions of a working-class crone. *Fireweed, 25,* 82-85.

Tynes, M. (1989). In service. *Fireweed, 26,* 8-11.

Vogel, L. (1983). *Marxism and the oppression of women: Toward a unitary theory.* New Brunswick, NJ: Rutgers University Press.

Waxman, C. (1983). *The stigma of poverty: A critique of poverty theories and policies* (2nd ed.). Elmsford, NY: Pergamon.

Zandy, J. (Ed.). (1990). *Calling home: Working class women's writing: An anthology.* New Brunswick, NJ: Rutgers University Press.

Name Index

Subject Index

About the Editor

Stephen Harold Riggins (Ph.D., University of Toronto) is Associate Professor of Sociology at Memorial University of Newfoundland, St. John's. His research interests concern the sociology of culture and mass media, Midwestern social history, and the study of material artifacts. He is the editor of *Ethnic Minority Media*, *Beyond Goffman*, *The socialness of Things* and has published articles in *Current Perspectives in Social Theory*, *Semiotica*, *Semiotic Inquiry*, *Semiotic Review of Books*, *Midwestern Folklore*, and the *Indiana Magazine of History*. He has worked as a reporter for Canadian native newspapers and edited a special issue of *Anthropologica* on native journalism in North America.

About the Contributors

Teresa Carbó is a senior researcher at the Centro de Investigaciones y Estudios Superiores en Antropologia Social in Mexico City. She is the author of *Mexican Parliamentary Discourse Between 1920 and 1950*, *Political Discourse: Reading and Analysis*, and *Educating from the Chamber of Deputies*.

William E. Conklin, Professor of Law at the University of Windsor, Canada, has co-edited four volumes in the field of legal theory and authored *Images of a Constitution* and *In Defence of Fundamental Rights*.

George J. Sefa Dei is Associate Professor in the Department of Sociology in Education, Ontario Institute for Studies in Education, University of Toronto. His teaching and research interests are in the areas of anti-racism education, development education, and international development. He is the author of *Anti-Racism Education: Theory and practice*.

Philomena Essed, Associate Professor at the Institute for Development Research, University of Amsterdam, has published widely in journals and is the author of several books, including *Everyday Racism*, *Understanding Everyday Racism*, and *Diversity: Gender, Color and Culture*.

Jane Helleiner is trained as a social anthropologist and is presently working in a multidisciplinary Department of Child Studies at Brock University. She has conducted anthropological field work in Ireland and has published a number of articles on the Irish Travelling People.

Michael Hoechsmann is a doctoral student in the Department of Curriculum at the Ontario Institute for Studies in Education, University of Toronto. He has written and lectured extensively on the Benetton Corporation, Generation X, and the broader topic of youth and consumption.

Karim H. Karim holds a Ph.D. in communication from McGill University in Montreal. He is Senior Researcher at the International Comparative Research Group of the Department of Canadian Heritage in

Ottawa. His work includes the analysis of cultural policy, multiculturalism, race relations, and the global information society.

Roxanne Rimstead teaches literature, cultural studies, and Canadian studies in the Department of English at McGill University. She has published articles about working-class intellectuals, poverty narratives, feminist theory, oral history and autobiography, and Canadian literature.

Bohdan Szuchewycz is Associate Professor and Director of the Communications Studies Program at Brock University, St. Catharines, Ontario. His research concentrates on the ethnography of communication, particularly with respect to issues of language, power, and ideology in the spheres of religion, racism, and the media.

Teun A. van Dijk is Professor of Discourse Studies at the University of Amsterdam. Since the 1980s his work has focused on the study of the structures, production and comprehension of news reports in the press; and the analysis of the expression of ethnic prejudices. His major books in English include *Communicating Racism*, *Racism and the Press*, *News Analysis*, *News as Discourse*, and *Elite Discourse and Racism*.

Ruth Wodak, Professor of Linguistics at the University of Vienna, has done extensive research on anti-semitism and is the editor of *Language, Power, and Ideology* as well as the author of *Disorders of Discourse*.